Fish Raincoats

FISH RAINCOATS

A Woman Lawyer's Life

Barbara Babcock

QUID PRO BOOKS

New Orleans, Louisiana

Published in 2016 by Quid Pro Books. Part of the series *Journeys and Memoirs*.

ISBN 978-1-61027-359-6 (pbk.)
ISBN 978-1-61027-357-2 (hbk.)
ISBN 978-1-61027-361-9 (eBook)

QUID PRO BOOKS
Quid Pro, LLC
5860 Citrus Blvd., Suite D-101
New Orleans, Louisiana 70123
www.quidprobooks.com

Publisher's Cataloging in Publication

Babcock, Barbara.
    Fish raincoats : a woman lawyer's life / Barbara Babcock.
        p. cm. — (Journeys and memoirs)
1. Babcock, Barbara Allen. 2. Lawyers—United States—Biography. 3. Women lawyers—United States—Biography. 4. Law professors—United States—Biography. 5. Women's movements—United States. I. Title. II. Series.
KF373.B32A3 2016
Library of Congress Control No.: 2016948126

Front cover image depicting the author is adapted from Howard Schatz, *Gifted Woman*, p. 72 (Pacific Photographic Press, 1992), used with permission. Author photograph on back cover inset, 2010, is by Jeanne de Polo, used with permission.

Chapter 9 is adapted from Barbara Allen Babcock, "Falling into Feminism: A Personal History," *Stanford Journal of Civil Rights and Civil Liberties*, vol. 11, p. 269 (2015), used with permission.

To Dinah Grey Luomanen –
My San Francisco girl I've loved from her first hours on earth,
who brings daily joy and "forward-looking thoughts."

CONTENTS

Preface: Things Past i

Acknowledgments v

1. The Lawyer's Daughter 1

2. An Ivy League Education: Penn and Yale (1956-1963) . . . 13

3. Woman and Man at Yale (1960-1963) 31

4. Into the Real World: Clerkship and Early
   Practice (1963-1966) 39

5. Mob Memories (1964-1966) 53

6. Precious Freedom: Favorite Cases (1966-1968) 65

7. Taking Charge: The D.C. Public Defender
   Service (1968-1972) 77

8. Defending the Guilty 91

9. Falling into Feminism 107

10. Becoming a Californian (1972-1976) 127

11. "General Babcock" (1977-1979) 141

12. Love and Friendship in Scholarland (1980-present) 165

13. Teaching and Testifying (1980-present) 179

14. Writing a Life: Recovering and Marketing
    Clara Foltz 199

Afterword: About Remembering 221

PREFACE: THINGS PAST

Growing up in the 1950s, I assumed that I would marry, have children, and be a homemaker like my mother and all the other women I knew. At the same time I also formed the idea that I would be a lawyer like my father. From an early age, I loved the stories he told about his work, which always seemed to start: "A lady came into the office today and. . ." followed by an account of the rescue of a client from dire straits by means of a lawyer's special powers. I soon came to believe that I could have such powers, and could also use them to rescue people who were in trouble.

Before anyone spoke of "having it all," I planned on doing just that. I had no conception of the obstacles and even by the time I entered law school in 1960, had not yet heard of sex discrimination. By the end of the decade, however, I knew it firsthand and had committed myself to the movement for gender equality. At the same time, I decided that I wanted to use my lawyerly skills on behalf of the criminally accused.

By the time I was thirty, I had tried dozens of cases to verdict before juries, and had become the first director of the Public Defender Service for the District of Columbia. A few years later, while still practicing criminal defense, I taught some of the first courses offered in the brand new field of "Women and the Law." The women's movement carried me to two more firsts: first woman on the Stanford Law Faculty in 1972, and in 1977, one of the first women to be an Assistant Attorney General of the United States.

As I passed through the various stages of my career, interviewers often asked me some version of the same question: *How does it feel to get your job because you are a woman?* To which I developed a stock answer: *It feels a lot better than not getting it because I am a woman.*

Now, no one would be likely to ask such a question. Women have come far and fast in the legal profession, with gathering momentum in recent years. During my life, I have seen the first woman Supreme Court Justice;

at least as improbably, the first woman Dean of the Harvard Law School; and many more firsts.

Though being first draws special scrutiny and can be lonely, it is in itself a singular kind of success: there is only one of you, which leaves little room for negative comparisons. In these pages, I will recall some events from my "first-woman" career: the movements I joined, the cases I tried, the classes I taught, the pieces I wrote, the agencies I led, and the people I loved. The main settings are Washington, D.C., my native city where I started as a lawyer, and northern California, where I have witnessed both technological and social revolutions.

Most notable to me has been women's progress from a discounted and miniscule minority in the legal profession to something close to equality, at least in access to education and employment. The contrast with my own experience fifty years ago is striking. I went through law school without having a woman teacher, or hearing a single class touching on women's prospects or position. We were fewer than four percent of the nation's law students, and no one took much interest in us. Famous judges of incandescent liberal credentials declared themselves uneasy about employing female law clerks (they liked to work in their shirtsleeves; to tell salty jokes; to labor late at night). Law firms were doubtful about our staying power and intellectual drive.

This all changed so quickly that by my retirement in 2004, I taught on a faculty full of women stars, to a student body that was nearly fifty percent female. Women's issues now pervade the curriculum, and gender discrimination is everywhere treated as requiring legal attention. There may be a few judges who still do not feel comfortable with women clerks, but most want the best help they can get without regard to gender, and of course now many judges at every level are themselves female. In short, overt sex discrimination of the old-fashioned kind has virtually disappeared.

Ironically, though women lawyers have progressed further in the past few decades than in all earlier years combined, the profession in which we have finally gained equal opportunity seems to be falling apart. Needless aggression and soulless unconcern about societal consequences—such is the indictment from the outside. Internally, the complaint is that our learned profession has become a bottom-line business. The legal workplace is built on the ten-hour day, the six-day week, extreme hierarchy, constant testing, and all-out competition. Everyone from the freshest associate to the graying partner works too hard, leaving no time for family and communal life, for leisure, or for work devoted to the public good.

Many women do not want to live like that and are abandoning the practice of law in disproportionate numbers. Many men would also prefer a life that allowed for familial engagement and public service over the course of a career. The movement to make that possible is, I believe, underway, though so far mainly in the efforts and accomplishments of individuals. But their models, and the sheer numbers of women lawyers with their male allies could change everything, and it could happen fast.

In the spirit of my favorite slogan, I believe that the personal is indeed political and hope that the record of my experiences will contribute to the next wave of the women's movement. To these I also bring the life of Clara Foltz, the first female lawyer in the West,[*] who was convinced that women had special gifts for the profession and who conceived the idea of public defense.

I have lived in interesting times, had a part in one of the great social movements that shaped those times, and engaged deeply in learning, practicing, and teaching law.

Here are my stories.

BARBARA BABCOCK

Stanford, California
June 2016

---

[*] Babcock, *Woman Lawyer: The Trials of Clara Foltz* (Stanford University Press, 2011).

ACKNOWLEDGMENTS

Any acknowledgments must start with Tom Grey, beloved partner, brilliant editor.

There is not space enough to name all the relatives, colleagues, and former students, the ones I call "my people," who have been my aid and inspiration over many years. You know who you are and I trust you will overlook my failure to tell the stories that include you or to list you here.

I do want to thank specifically the students at Georgetown University who persuaded me to teach "Women and the Law" in 1970. I wish I could thank you personally for launching me into academia.

Several people made helpful comments on the whole manuscript: thanks to Florence Keller, Roanne Mann, Toni Massaro, Mary Erickson, and Patricia Tatspaugh. For the public defender days, Neal Kravitz, Bill Schaffer, Bill Taylor, Robert Weinberg, and Mat Zwerling. For the Justice Department chapter, Tom Martin and Janice Cooper.

To a little group of feminist legal biographers that we formed for mutual support, I'm indebted for their help and enthusiasm: Jane DeHart, Pnina Lahav, Tomiko Brown-Nagin, Constance Backhouse, Mae Quinn, and Marlene Trestman.

Much of this book, like my biography of Clara Foltz, was written at a beautiful house on the sea in Monterey Dunes. Thanks to Tom and Sue Nolan for their generosity over many years in sharing their lovely retreat.

Finally, my appreciation to Alan Childress, publisher of Quid Pro Books, and the press's senior editor Lee Scheingold, whose interest, efficiency, and technical assistance have made the concluding months of this project a pleasure for me.

B.B.

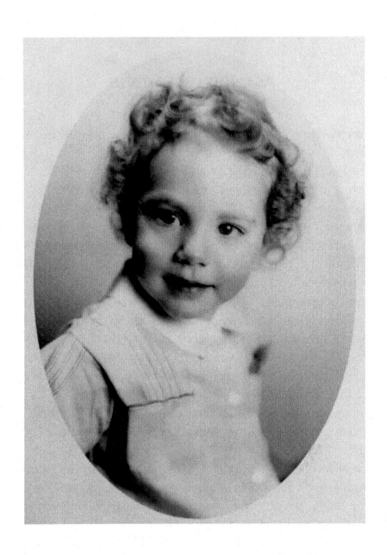

Barbara Allen Babcock, age 3

Fish Raincoats

Gallatin Street house, Hyattsville, Maryland

1

THE LAWYER'S DAUGHTER

If my life were a museum, one wing would house a collection of stories I have repeated so often that the retellings virtually supplant the memories themselves. Most are in the southern style of my Arkansas father, which means many small details lend verisimilitude and they are humorous even when the subject is dark. "Nobody could make that up," the listener is meant to think, "so it must be true."

Some of my favorites come from my years as a jury lawyer, others from the feminist front-lines in the second wave of the women's movement. I turn first to stories from girlhood, starting with one on the power of reading.

The setting is the "little" school, referring to the size of the children who went there, a block from our house on Gallatin Street in Hyattsville, Maryland. Built in 1904 and long since demolished, the school building lives in memory: stately brick exterior, dark wooden floors, seesaws and swings on the cement playground. I thought it was wonderful and did not notice the regimentation or the rote nature of our learning. It did not matter that we sat for hours in rows of desks that were nailed to the floor and that we had to raise our hands for permission to speak or to leave the room. What mattered to me is that at the little school I officially became an avid reader.

One day in second grade, I was so engrossed in a book that I forgot where I was until the teacher put her hand on my shoulder. Later she told the whole class: "Barbara Babcock was so interested in reading that she did not even hear the recess bell." It was the proudest moment of my life to

1

that point. For several days afterward, I tried to duplicate that absorption, but soon I was rushing out to recess with everyone else.

In a larger sense, however, that thrilling moment stayed with me. Reading has shaped my character, perhaps more than anything else. Mother read to my brother David and me: A. A. Milne and fairy tales and Hurlbut's *Story of the Bible*. The books I read and reread on my own were a mixed lot: *Call of the Wild, Robin Hood, Little Women, Dick the Bank Boy* and other Horatio Alger-style stories, *Tom Sawyer, Huckleberry Finn,* Alan Paton's *Too Late the Phalarope,* Hemingway, C.S. Forester's *Horatio Hornblower* novels. As a precocious ten-year-old, I read *Gone with the Wind,* whose first sentence riveted me: "Scarlett O'Hara was not beautiful, but men seldom realized it when caught by her charm. . . ."

The public library was a few blocks away, and I walked there on my own at least once a week, pulling a red wagon to carry returns and new acquisitions. No one supervised my choices or suggested that any book was inappropriate for my age. My plan was to read all the books in the library, but I didn't even make it through the A's. I read a lot though, and since the day I first got lost in a book, I have never been bored.

Another formative event from my early years happened in the fourth grade. Though originally the stuff of nightmares, I've tamed the story by repeated telling: to classes, family gatherings, and therapists helping me probe for the sources of fears and anxieties. It began with my teacher selecting me to represent our school in a quiz contest because, she told me, I had the highest IQ in the class. So that's what I said when people asked why I had been chosen.

In my joy, I forgot that my store of general knowledge was almost nonexistent. Nor did it occur to me to prepare by boning up on geography and history. I figured that being smartest would get me through. A terrible lesson was in store.

The quiz show, broadcast on local radio, pitted two elementary schools against each other every Saturday morning, with one contestant from each of grades four through six. An audience of parents and students filled the auditorium. On a big stage, the six contestants and six alternates were seated in rows. Behind me was Billy Davis, my alternate, who had the second-highest IQ in the class. The prizes for the winning school—a movie projector, an encyclopedia set, and other goodies—were laid out on a table between the teams.

I was the first called to the microphone, which seemed a long way from my chair. The question: "Where is the Sahara Desert?" I had no idea. The nice moderator gave me a hint: "It begins with an A." Unluckily, I guessed "Asia." Bong.

I returned to my seat, and Billy Davis leaned over and said, "I knew that." As I heard the other kids give smooth answers to what seemed to me hard questions, my heart pounded. And it sank at my second question: "Who was the great French scientist who invented a process to purify milk?" Again I did not have the faintest notion, and again the moderator was ready with a hint: "Think what's on the milk carton." I scrunched up my eyes and formed a visual image from which "homogenized" rather than "pasteurized" jumped out at me. "Homogene?" I ventured, pronouncing it "homogenay."

This time, my answer got a big laugh from the crowd. Again I went back to my chair in defeat; again Billy Davis said, "I knew that." Now we were losing. I went up for the last question: "What did the Indians use fish for, other than for food?" I thought hard and came up with "Raincoats." The answer, as many others including Billy Davis knew, was fertilizer.

That was it; I had failed spectacularly. Walking home, my father patted me on the back, roaring with laughter: "Raincoats! Ha ha ha ha! Homogenay! Ha ha ha!" He didn't realize how humiliated I felt. On Monday, the teacher called me out into the hall and said, "It wouldn't be so bad that we lost the encyclopedia and the movie projector, but you were very wrong to tell people you were the smartest person in the class, especially the way it turned out."

Shame overcame me, and I felt that I could never return to school. For the next several days, I pretended to set off in the morning as usual but slipped around to our back yard, climbed the magnolia tree, and read behind its big leaves until it was time to come home. Eventually of course, I did go back, though I don't remember how. For me, the story ends in the magnolia tree.

I first started telling the fish-raincoats story when I came to teach at Stanford. Somehow I transformed it from a private example of embarrassing hubris into an amusing tale of childish exuberance and miscalculation. A few years ago my colleague Pam Karlan—who, like all my friends, had heard the story several times—provided me with a postscript.

One day after arguing a case before the United States Supreme Court, Pam went over to the Smithsonian's Native American Art Museum and found on display "a circa 1910 Yu'pik coat called a Qasperrluk—officially translated as 'fish skin raincoat.'" Pam fired off an e-mail to me:

> So, Barbara, nearly sixty years after your school was wrongfully denied its movie projector, *you have been vindicated!* You were right: Indians *did* use fish for raincoats! That annoying little Billy was wrong! Once I've recovered from post-argument exhaustion, I shall be hard on the trail of figuring out the contribution of Louis L'Homme a Genêt to modern chemistry. This should give you a great new ending to the story.

At the heart of my childhood memories is our house on Gallatin, "a shady, tree-lined street." Though I know this particular cliché should be avoided in memoirs, it best describes our block in Hyattsville. We moved there in 1946 when I was eight and my brother David was almost seven; Starr was born the next year. In my Yale snob days I called my hometown "Hiatusville," but I have many vivid and happy memories of the place.

Our house was a great old Victorian which my father had bought on the GI bill after he returned from World War II service in the Navy. Built in 1872 by a wealthy merchant, it was known as "Senator Brookhart's house," after the Iowa politician who had lived there during his twelve years in the U.S. Senate in the early twentieth century. But by the time we moved in, rats had overtaken the basement and attic, and the previous owner had raised pigeons on the back porch.

I remember the day we saw the house for the first time. David and I were ecstatic because we would each have our own room, and a whole acre of yard for play. Apple and cherry trees were in bloom, and there was a vineyard, a snowball tree, and a spacious front porch. I could not understand then why Mother did not seem happy, but I realize now that when she saw how dilapidated it was, she doubted we would ever be able to fix things up. She was right, Dad having nothing of the handyman about him, but she had her own way of disguising defects: paint everything gold and keep the lights low.

To me, the house was magical with its two staircases, high ceilings, a beautiful fireplace of local stone in the large living room, and smaller fireplaces in almost all the other rooms. I loved the nooks, the real doors and their moldings, my special reading stair next to a window, and a secret passageway I found between the basement and the back of the living room. We joked that the size of the house, where everyone could go somewhere and shut the door, enabled our survival as a family.

I soon made a best friend, Patsy Tatspaugh, who lived around the corner. We were inseparable from the time we met in second grade until our graduation from Northwestern High. We walked or rode to and from school together, had classes and activities in common, came back and stood on the corner halfway between our houses to chew over the day, and chatted on the phone after supper. Neither of us can now remember what we talked about for so many hours, nor could we then have imagined the lives ahead of us. Today Patsy lives in London and is a Shakespeare scholar, theater buff, and author, and I am a retired law professor writing my memoirs on a hillside in California.

My parents, who lived on Gallatin Street until my father's death in 1982, were from Arkansas: Doris Moses from Hope and Henry Babcock from Batesville. They had met at Arkansas College, a small Presbyterian school in Dad's hometown in the Ozark foothills. I used to pore over their college yearbook from 1929, the year she was a freshman and he a senior. It thrilled me to see her soulful photo and that she had been elected "Most Attractive" in the school. She was the only "Most Attractive," which made it special since four other girls were designated "Most Beautiful." Dad looked sweet and intellectual, and his bio entry referred to a budding romance with Doris Moses.

They often spoke of the happiness of their year in college together. I'm not sure what Dad had envisioned doing after graduation, but the Great Depression intervened and changed everything. Like many of his friends from small Arkansas towns, Henry Babcock moved to Washington, D.C., where there were still jobs.

Mother was the first in her family to attend college. Her father was a farmer of modest formal education who had moved into town and opened a feed store. Floyd Moses was proud of his smart daughter and happy to send her to college. But after her second year, he could no longer afford the tuition because he had lost his store in the Depression. (Family lore has it that he could have saved himself by bankruptcy but chose to honorably pay off his creditors.)

Doris returned to Hope, taught in a one-room country school, and wrote love letters to Henry. After a few years, she managed to join him in Washington. On December 2, 1935, she telegraphed her parents: "I have always loved Henry, and so we were married tonight. Love me and love him too."

They lived and worked in Washington for three years—Mother at a government clerical job and Dad in the Masonic Temple Public Library. He went to law school at night at George Washington University, paying his tuition with his winnings from bridge and poker. I think these were happy years for my parents, though it must have been a financial strain once I was born in 1938 and David in 1940. They moved to the Virginia suburbs, and in 1943 Dad joined the Navy—an impulse inspired I always assumed by some mix of patriotism and alcohol. Perhaps, however, he was about to be drafted and wanted to avoid the Army, which was suffering the most casualties in the war.

David and I were sent to Arkansas to live with relatives while Mother continued working in Washington. I do not remember much about my time in Arkansas, from the ages of five to eight, though I have read that those are the years when accents are formed, and my speech retains a Southern inflection. David went to live with Mother's parents in Hope, and I went to Dad's family in Batesville. But it soon turned out that David and I cried constantly for each other until I ended up on the farm with him in Hope.

My recollections of farm life are few but bright: feeding the pigs, for instance, calling, "Soo-eee, soo-eee, soo-eee," then pouring out the slop and watching them jump into the trough feet first. I thought it was funny to call them, when they came running at the sight of anyone carrying a bucket. I also remember playing hide-and-seek in the corn rows, risking ticks and chiggers. And at least once I saw Grandmother chase down a chicken and wring its neck.

At the end of the day, Pop, our grandfather, would invite David to help him bring the cows home." He never asked *me*; I should have jumped up and said, "Me, me! I'd like to go get the cows." I did want to join them, even though it was a dusty job and seemed a little dangerous because the cows were so big.

We were in Hope when Pop died. I was playing in the yard with our cousins and heard Grandmother's cry. Someone came out to the swings and said, "Your grandfather is dead. Stop playing." I thought that meant stopping forever and wondered what we would do instead.

When Dad came back from the Navy, late in 1946, the family re-grouped, we moved to the big house in Hyattsville, and the part of my childhood that I remember well began. As with many people in her generation, Mother's perspective on money had been fixed by the Great

Depression, which had instilled in her a deep wariness about extravagance of any kind. She mortified my brothers by bringing home clothes for them from church charity bins. She and I made a sport out of shopping for sales, sometimes returning week after week in hope of further markdowns (taking the chance of missing out on the sought-after item). Our game had one unbreakable rule: never pay retail.

Our financial situation fluctuated, a flush period almost always followed by a crash. The crashes came because of the aspect of my childhood that supplies my darkest memories, Dad's alcoholic binges. These could last for months and often landed him in the hospital. More than once, the doctor said he would die by morning, and once I saw him in the terrors of delirium tremens. Through such traumas, we Babcocks kept up a respectable front. I never told anyone—not my best friend Patsy or my high school boyfriend or any counselor or teacher—what my grandmother told me when I was nine.

I had been reading a library book called *The Problem Child at Home*, which featured a number of accounts where the child's problem was an alcoholic father. (Why I selected this book, inappropriate as it was for my age, is a mystery.) Something in the descriptions of the problem families rang a bell, and I asked Grandmother Moses, who lived part of the year with us, about it. Not one to mince words, she said, "Don't you know, honey, your Daddy is a drunk?" In my innocence, I was confident that I had only to ask him to stop drinking, that he would do anything for me. But he didn't, and, I learned much later, he couldn't.

Also in my ninth year, I wrote a short story entitled "Betsy and the Big House." Betsy was an orphan who had inherited a fortune administered by a kindly guardian. She purchased a great old Victorian house with a secret passage and two stairways and turned it into a model home for underprivileged orphans. She lived happily ever after.

In the story, Betsy looked a lot like me, and of course the house she lived in was mine. The big differences between us were that she had unlimited financial resources and she was free from parents with their messy adult issues, whereas I had just learned of my father's alcoholism and that I could not combat it. Unlike Betsy's, my childhood was often sad and at times even hard. But nobody, including me, noticed the dark subtext of my writing. Dad proudly and obliviously sent the story off to his mother in Batesville, where it was printed in the local paper.

For years I had mixed feelings about my father: anger at the drunkenness that had shadowed my childhood and ruined my mother's life; appreciation of the brilliant mind, the humor, and the lovable personality he displayed when he was sober. But the negative feelings came more and more to the fore. I seemed to remember only the times he had failed me. In later years, when interviewers asked me why a girl would want to be a lawyer, I babbled on about my concern for the underdog instead of saying, "My father is a lawyer, and his example inspires me."

I don't recall just when I started saying "a lawyer" in answer to the question, "What do you want to be when you grow up?" But when I was little, it was a sure attention-getter. I was not certain what a lawyer did, but I vaguely imagined publicity and acclaim for saving the friendless and the falsely accused. One of Dad's favorite sayings was that a lawyer's job was to "comfort the afflicted and afflict the comfortable."

I can see him now, telling his lawyer-as- hero stories, cocking his head, his eyes glistening with amusement at some exhibition of human folly. At the end, he would laugh first and loudest, his roars subsiding to chuckles, then a low "dee-dee-dee." Unlike my brothers, who held this routine against him, I found it endearing; now their children accuse them of laughing too long and hard at their own jokes.

Besides my father's profession, my mother's religion also influenced who I became. When the family moved to Hyattsville, Mother, though she was raised as an uncompromising "hard-shell Baptist," became a more relaxed Presbyterian. The church was around the corner on Farragut Street and had a saintly minister, D. Hobart Evans, whose well-crafted sermons did not mention cold Presbyterian doctrines like predestination. "In my father's house are many mansions" (John 14:2) was a favorite text of his.

Mother was a pillar of the church, teaching Sunday school, serving as president of the Woman's Association, and even holding governing offices usually reserved for men at that time. She cooked and cleaned for church suppers, participated in bazaars and bake sales to support far-flung missionaries, visited the old and lonely, and took food to the poor. The church was the center of her social life. When she died, a friend of hers wrote to me about the "special group in that little stone church. The group worked hard but we had so much fun and laughter that it wasn't work. . . . I have never known anyone with a more profound faith than your mother had."

I taught Sunday school and Vacation Bible School, was president of the youth group, and never missed a church service unless I was sick. My desire to do good and to serve others grew partly out of the teachings of Jesus. I longed for a born-again experience like my mother's, in which God had spoken to her personally. I never had one, though not for lack of trying. Faith was generally effortless for me. I did not puzzle over why an omnipotent God allowed evil and addiction to exist and ignored my mother's prayers to save my father. On the other hand, I did not accept her explanation that He always answered prayers, but sometimes the answer was "No."

Dad never went to church, not even on Christmas and Easter. With a twinkle in his eye, he claimed he was a Methodist so could not possibly join in Presbyterian rituals. I faulted him for not faking it for an hour on Sunday to make Mother happy. Years later I softened my judgment when I found myself unwilling to sacrifice my own Sunday mornings to accompany her to church.

Without religious faith, my father possessed many of the virtues associated with it. He was kind and tolerant, slow to anger, fair and honest in his dealings, and he often gave free legal services to the needy. Calling himself a country lawyer, he looked the part, with his suspenders and rumpled suit off the "Big and Tall" rack, and he sounded it with his slow Arkansas accent. Many city lawyers made the mistake of assuming that a man calling himself "country" was less than shrewd or legally sophisticated.

I assume he shared the prejudices of his Arkansas upbringing, but I never heard him use a racial epithet, and he had a number of black clients (whom he called "colored"). Unlike many others in the local legal profession, he was also comparatively free from anti-Semitism. Once I was speaking at a national meeting of women judges, and met a prominent appeals court judge from Maryland, who told me my father had been responsible for her admission to the Bar Association, which had previously banned women and Jews. She said it had been a hard fight; I was especially touched because it was not a story he ever told me himself.

Although I did not realize it, my early and enthusiastic pursuit of public speaking opportunities was preparation for the legal career I was planning. I still recall that my report on the assassination of Lincoln brought my sixth-grade class to tears, including the boys, the teacher, and me. From the first, I had a gift for public speaking, which I developed by careful preparation. "Do not speak from the heart," I advised. "Speak from notes." And I always did—and still do.

At Northwestern High, I excelled in Speech class but discovered in Drama that despite my strong voice and excellent memory, I could not take on another identity. Not being a good actor was a disappointment I found easier to diagnose than to accept, so I continued to try out for the leads in plays long after it was clear I lacked dramatic talent.

The scrapbook of my senior year in high school includes stories, themes, and term papers. The neatness of the penmanship (a long-lost art for me) and the frequency of spelling and punctuation errors are equally noticeable; the lack of imagination and invention in the writing also strikes me. Yet at the time, knowing nothing of the world beyond our suburban streets, I saw myself as a brilliantly successful fish in a pretty big pond.

My scrapbook shows that my friends and fellow students were all middle class and white. The 1954 decision *Brown v. Board of Education* finding school segregation unconstitutional had produced no visible results by the time I graduated two years later. But I do remember when *Brown* came down, because the biggest headline I ever had seen was emblazoned on the front page of the Washington Post: *School Segregation Banned in Nation.*

Only in looking back am I aware of the absence of black, brown, or Asian children; of foreign accents; or of anyone who was really rich or really poor. Perhaps the most arresting items in the scrapbook are clippings reporting Northwestern High's state basketball championship in 1956. Not until long afterward did I wonder that a team of short white boys had done so well. Of course, there must have been a separate black league and championship, where they probably played quite a different game.

My scrapbooks have other mementos: dance cards from proms; ticket stubs for plays at the National Theater; a program from a reading by Robert Frost on which I wrote, "I have seen a giant among men." There is a picture of Joe Irwin, my boyfriend in grades nine through eleven. Missing are the many letters, cards, and notes he wrote me, which I burned in a dramatic conflagration when we broke up. I still remember hearing his step on the porch as he left a love note in the mailbox after every one of our dates.

We went bowling (duckpins) and to the movies, to basketball games (it was exciting to watch the boys running around in those short shorts), and to football games and dances. Afterward we had hamburgers and shakes at the Hot Shoppe. In the summer we drove to the beach at Chesapeake Bay. We did not drink, smoke, gamble, or have sex (by any definition). Joe was the first boy I ever kissed; we enthusiastically worked at that. I dated him exclusively. Oblivious to the fact that no one else was asking me out, Mother objected to my "going steady." Never one for (unstructured) confrontation, I would slip Joe's ring on after I left the house.

In our high school of fifteen hundred in three grades, one person became famous: Jim Henson, creator of the Muppets. He was a friend of Joe Irwin's, so I knew him some, though not well. A friend of mine dated him for a while in the tenth grade, but she was discouraged by her mother who said not to get involved with someone who spent his time "playing with puppets." I remember that he built the sets for plays and painted a mural of a woodland scene on the walls of his parents' prosaic tract house.

Looking back on my youth in Hyattsville through scrapbooks and the yearbook that Patsy and I edited, I see that I led a double life. At school I was happy and successful (an officer in all three honor societies, the class, and other organizations) and a top student. But at home things were often out of control. Even when Dad was sober, Mother and I were always on the lookout for signs of the next binge, which would start with his being late for dinner or not coming home at all. I thought of his periods of sobriety as our real life and the rest as a bad dream that might not recur if we were lucky and good.

A hit song in 1955 was "The Great Pretender" by the Platters, and as I danced with Joe, the words had a secret meaning for me:

> Oh-oh, yes I'm the great pretender
> Pretending that I'm doing well
> My need is such I pretend too much
> I'm lonely but no one can tell.

Going away to college was to be my escape. I had no idea where to go, but I was clear on one thing: I would not live at home and attend the University of Maryland as most Hyattsville kids who went to college did. I sent off applications to a random assortment of colleges that I had heard of one way or another and was admitted and received scholarships everywhere I applied. The University of Pennsylvania offered the best aid package. It turned out to be the ideal place for me.

Penn Debate Team, 1957, after winning a tournament;
Barbara's partner Edward Cohen to her right

2

AN IVY LEAGUE EDUCATION: PENN AND YALE
(1956-1963)

Before I left for Penn, my mother's friends gave me a shower—perhaps thinking they might not have a chance any time soon to reciprocate for the wedding and baby celebrations she had held for their daughters. Though a college shower was a little odd, I liked the idea. Our family had never made much of birthdays and a party centered on gifts for me sounded good.

Mother urged me to choose a silver pattern so people would have something to give me for graduation and for future big occasions. I think she wanted to make sure that no matter what happened on the marriage front, I would not go through life as she had: without a set of silver. Kirk Repousse sterling, an old-fashioned rococo pattern, was her taste (and therefore mine). I have accumulated quite a few pieces over the years.

With linens and luggage from the shower and a silver pattern for life, I moved to Philadelphia in the fall of 1956. This was my first deliberate step toward the legal career I envisioned. I expected to find a good man along the way and did not worry about combining marriage and children with law practice. In fact, I didn't think about it at all; I simply assumed that life would unfold in my favor. Though I've never divined the source of this preternatural self-confidence and optimism, they sustain me still.

While already thinking about law school, I planned also to re-live my parents' stories of college as a golden, carefree period. My Penn scholarship included tuition, books, room and board, and for spending money, I waited on tables in the dining halls and did shifts on the switchboard of the girls' dorm where I lived. Dad's irregular income was no longer a daily concern.

In my quest for easy ways to make money without spending too much time, I signed up to be a subject in an experiment; it paid a handsome twenty-five dollars for a couple of hours. I reported to an office in the psychology department, where I was given a test. I'm not sure of the format, whether multiple choice or fill-in the blanks, but whatever the questions were, I could not answer any of them.

I rang for the test administrator and told him that I could not do the test. Showing concern, he asked me to keep trying. "Look, I said, this is math, and I'm no good at math." "No," he responded, "it's not math, it's a basic intelligence test, predictive of how you will do in your grades at college. It looks like you may have to reconsider coming to Penn." To his consternation, I was unfazed, and continued to insist that it must be built on mathematical concepts because otherwise I could do it.

It turned out that the test was designed to measure stress, and if I had responded as most did, the testers would have me fill out a second questionnaire about the experience of failing. I doubt that an experiment like that would be allowed by a human subjects committee today. But it did me no psychological harm because I believed so deeply that I could do anything but math. Since then, I've found quite a few other things I'm not good at doing—most regrettably, foreign languages.

In the fifties, the University of Pennsylvania had a College for Women, a separate undergraduate program like the School of Engineering or the Wharton School of Business. The Dean explained on the first day that our education would be specially designed for the needs of twentieth-century wives and mothers. No mention was made of potential careers or even of single women. I do not recall being irritated about this assumed inexorable female fate, though the fact that I remember the speech fifty-plus years later may indicate that it had rankled more than I realized then.

Courses in the College for Women (CW) did not focus on female experience or history but simply offered the option of studying in a single-sex setting. We coeds (the usual term for women) could take our classes in CW or anywhere else in the university; the same was true for the men, though very few enrolled in CW offerings. Neither did I, perhaps sensing that I should establish a record of successful competition with men for my law school application.

Many school activities were mandatorily sex-segregated, most notably the staff of *The Daily Pennsylvanian*. We women had our own weekly newspaper with a much smaller circulation. A number of clubs had women's and men's branches, several all-female honor societies mirrored their male counterparts, and at graduation there were separate awards ceremonies. Women's sports were a minor program, though the yearbook claimed defensively that they were "quite significant" to their few participants.

That same yearbook revealed that in 1960, the year I graduated, Penn's student body was virtually all white. Very rarely, there was a black player on an athletic team, and one African American man is pictured in my graduating class. As far as I know and as I experienced it, Penn had no Hispanics and few who met any other definition of diversity. The only clear-cut division was between Jew and Gentile, with membership in fraternities and sororities and some other clubs kept rigorously distinct by custom, bylaws, or both.

At freshman orientation, I met Rosemary (Bunny) Yaecker, who would become my second "best friend for life" (after Patsy). The first thing I noticed about her, with some envy, was her great looks. Willowy with long blonde hair, green eyes, a wonderful smile, and exuding energy and health, Bunny's appearance initially drew people to her; her warm personality made them love her.

Bunny was the oldest of five; her father, like mine, was an alcoholic. My glimpse into her family life made me realize that I was lucky to have a loving gentle parent despite his failings. When Bunny was chosen for Phi Beta Kappa, her father was dismissive and sarcastic. By contrast, when I made it, Dad wrote that he had always hoped for this for me (though he had not mentioned it before). "What's left of my chest is really sticking out today," he said.

When Bunny (now Rosie) and I recently talked about women's place at Penn in our day, she said that though we were in the minority and often felt like second-class citizens, "I was glad that there were three men at Penn for every one woman. It gave me more to work with in finding a husband, and I had no plan to have a career at all. All I wanted was to have lots of children and raise them far better than my parents had raised us." She added that she worked at getting good grades because they would enable her to go to graduate school if necessary to find a mate.

As a Philadelphia commuter, Bunny was not entitled to live in a dorm, so we roomed together in the Kappa Alpha Theta sorority house. I'm quite sure I would not have been invited to join this exclusive group without my connection to Bunny. She was the epitome of the pretty, outgoing type of girl for which the sorority was known. In our junior year, she was chosen Miss University of Pennsylvania only a few months before being elected to Phi Beta Kappa. She was probably the first to hold these honors simultaneously—belying the widely held belief at the time that girls could be beautiful or brilliant, but not at the same time.

Bunny's attractions also made a big impression on the young men in Hyattsville one summer when she lived with us and worked in D.C. My brother Starr and his teen-age friends would lie in wait for an hour in a stand of bamboo, hoping that she would come outside to hang her underwear on the clothesline. Gleefully Dad reported seeing a boy walk smack into a telephone pole while staring at her from across the street.

Both of us majored in American Civilization, then an exciting new course of study; only Yale had offered an earlier version. I was drawn to its eclectic feel—a combination of history (my favorite subject), sociology, art; and all without a foreign language requirement. The major also seemed like a good preparation for law study.

Bunny and I were top students, disciplined and determined, with considerable capacities for organizing and memorizing. Our study habits were similar; both of us were early risers and did not need to pull all-nighters for last-minute paper writing and cramming for exams. I remember the pleasure of walking to class together from the Theta house along Walnut through the campus, feeling glad to be alive.

I don't recall details of many of my courses or much about my professors—though I know I took to art history, disliked economics, found symbolic logic way too much like the math I was trying to avoid, and enjoyed geology (and received a note from the professor saying I had written the best exam he had seen in thirty years of teaching). In a Greek history seminar, I shed real tears over Thucydides, and my Judaism professor was impressed by the amount of Old Testament history I knew (thanks to the Hyattsville Presbyterian Church).

Though I learned something about a lot of subjects in my courses, my true education was taking place elsewhere. Almost upon arrival at Penn, I joined the Debate Council. I had always wanted to debate, but we didn't have a team at Northwestern High. I took to it instantly and soon fell in love with my partner, Edward Cohen.

Intercollegiate debate was organized with weekend tournaments throughout the year at various colleges. I have clippings, for instance, reporting debate contests at Dartmouth, Harvard, Maryland and many other East coast campuses. A single question was chosen to be debated nationwide for a whole academic year. In the spring, there was a national championship at West Point. I remember that Eddie and I debated an end to nuclear weapons testing, and empowering Congress to reverse decisions of the Supreme Court.

A debate took an hour, with each team of two making two ten-minute arguments and two five-minute rebuttals. At a tournament, we would do this three to five times a day for two days, changing sides of the question in each round. It was physically and mentally grueling. I remember especially one time when we arrived in Scranton in a blizzard for the state finals only to find the event cancelled because no other teams had made it, so we hopped on a bus to a Brooklyn tournament where we placed second and I won best speaker. Every debate photo of me features dark circles under my eyes, but many of them also show the trophies we won—some rather large. These were my first trophies and I liked the idea of achievement made so tangible.

Debate turned out to be the perfect preparation for law school, but the most important part of the experience was getting to know Eddie Cohen. Growing up in Hyattsville, I had never met a brilliant Jewish intellectual (indeed, no Jews and few intellectuals of any kind). A Christian sorority girl was equally exotic to him. On our first date, we went out to dinner (*not* at a Hot Shoppe, in itself a thrilling development), and afterward he showed me his alma mater, Central High School in Philadelphia. We spent several hours on its campus while he told me his life story and outlined his ambitions.

Central was then an all-boys institution, one of the oldest and best public high schools in the country. Eddie had taken many Advanced Placement courses and had come to Penn with two years of college credit. He planned to get his Ph.D. in Classics, but then, he said, he would become a lawyer and a multi-millionaire by the age of thirty. I had never heard such a story, and Eddie had never had such a listener.

To my friend Patsy, who was then at the University of Maryland, I wrote ecstatically about Eddie: "He's truly the most entertaining person

I've ever known ... really and truly brilliant. I know he won't turn out to be merely intelligent with aptitudes ... he has such a gorgeous, perfect mind.... He tells me things....Wish I could find someone just like him, except Christian. ... I think I will marry an ugly brilliant man. I just hope I can find a big one." (letter to Patricia Tatspaugh, May 30, 1958)

As debaters, Eddie and I were well suited to each other—his voice had an urban edge and I spoke with a slight Southern accent. He was incisive and I was persuasive; he had mastery and I had charm. Though no explicit points were awarded for charm, I almost always placed higher in the individual speaker rankings, which didn't seem to bother him. I fell easily into a two-track life—debating with Eddie and everything else, including football games, fraternity and sorority mixers, church on Sunday, and officership in several campus organizations.

Only occasionally did the disparity between the parts strike me. Once when Eddie and I returned from a tournament on a Sunday night, huge trophies in hand, we walked through the front rooms of the sorority house where some Thetas were entertaining their boyfriends. Suddenly Eddie's Philadelphia accent, his thick glasses and unathletic build, his badly tailored suit all stood out. I was ashamed of my embarrassment and angry at the others for what I saw as their disdain. Perhaps I imagined their reactions but there is no chance that I misread the responses of our families to our partnership.

Now I can't see why we even introduced each other to the Babcocks and the Cohens. It's not as if we had any long-range plans that needed their approval. Maybe our mothers instigated the meetings out of curiosity or suspicion. Eddie had told me that his father was an unemployed paper hanger; I thought he was kidding until I saw his family's small rooms plastered with huge floral patterns.

I remember, too, that Mrs. Cohen gave me the cold stare of a Jewish mother alert for a predator. That was the first but not the last time I saw that look on the face of a friend's mother. Eddie explained that she believed that every shiksa (Gentile girl) wants to marry a Jewish man because he will work hard and die young, leaving her a rich widow. I had never heard anything so preposterous and later concluded that her more likely concern was that for Jews a mother's religion determined that of the children.

Once when we were at a nearby debate tournament, Eddie and I went to dinner in Hyattsville. Afterward Mother's only comment was that he talked with his mouth full and gestured with a heavily laden fork. Eddie's table manners were an issue for me, too. But I thought it churlish to complain when his conversation was so learned and interesting. Finally, when I couldn't stand it any longer, I carefully raised the subject. I will never forget his reaction: "Oh, thank you. That's the kind of thing I need to know. Why didn't you tell me before?"

After finishing Penn in two years thanks to his Advanced Placement courses, Eddie moved on to Princeton for the doctorate in classics that was part of his life plan. With the loan of a friend's train pass, however, I managed to see him often. Even today, travelling from the 30th Street Station in Philadelphia to Princeton Junction stirs romantic memories. Looking back, I can't see how I managed to maintain top grades in hard courses, win at debate with a new partner (though winning slightly less regularly than before), carry on the life of an active coed, and spend days at a time with Eddie in Princeton.

At the beginning of my senior year, I wrote to Patsy. "Went to hear the Dean of Admissions, Yale Law School, give a talk—came back absolutely gung-ho Yale—seems like the _only_ place to go—they teach sociological law which actually is just logical—but they take approximately one out of five and only the best apply. It was the birth of a dream and we'll see." (letter to Patricia Tatspaugh, Oct. 3, 1959)

After filling out the Yale application, I sought a personal meeting with the Dean of Admissions. His assistant explained that they did not hold interviews. But on a debate trip to New York, I "stopped by" New Haven to see if he had a minute. I ended up with a wonderful interview, which probably bolstered my application.

Where did I get the idea that the eminently sensible rule against individual interviews should not apply to me? Even though these were prefeminist days, I may have dimly intuited that as a woman I needed an extra push, and thought an interview might supply it. For as long as I can remember, and despite some evidence to the contrary, I have believed that people will really like me and want to help once we have met.

In June 1960, I delivered the College for Women valedictory to a large audience in an impressive setting. No copy of the text survives though I do have notes and passages from it. Drawing on my American Studies major, I said: "This is the age of confusion: loss of values, uncertainty, moral decline, apathy, other-direction, the organization man, intellectual ennui— what have you. And we might add this is the age of analysis of the Age. We are the people of this much titled Age. We are the confused, other-directed apathetic victims of possible annihilation. Those people whose values were undermined by Freud, physics and evolution were our parents, and those people who haven't found any new insights to replace the old ones—we are those people." I concluded that our predicament had great dignity, however, if we would face it fully and devote ourselves to building new values on the foundation of the old ones. Or something like that.

My first year of law school awaited me in the fall. Bunny also was headed to New Haven, where she planned to get her Ph.D. in American Civilization. The thought of continuing to room together at Yale increased my anticipation. But over the summer, Bunny's enthusiasm began to fade: she had fallen in love with Robert Tancredi, a medical student at Penn.

Bob had emerged as the front runner among Bunny's admirers in our senior year. Tall and darkly handsome, he was a son of Italian immigrants, a gifted musician and the first in his family to go to college. Bob wanted Bunny's company in Philadelphia and did not see the point of her getting a Ph.D. She came to Yale anyway, but I could feel her slipping away as she spent hours writing to him from our scruffy little dorm room.

The day before Thanksgiving break, I returned to a certain emptiness in the room and realized that all her things were gone except her class ring from Penn, sitting on the middle of her desk. It was a signet worn on the little finger. We had both wanted one, but I had decided it was too expensive. She left a note asking me to wear it for her at Yale.

I was sad to lose Bunny's company and thought she was making a mistake and that Bob was acting badly. But the following June when I saw how happy she was at her wedding, I realized that her life was proceeding according to plan. Her son David was born during Bob's last year of medical school, and they went on to have two more boys and two girls. Ultimately the family settled in Rochester, Minnesota, where Bob was a cardiologist at the Mayo Clinic.

In the early sixties my life, like Bunny's, followed the course I had set for it. Indeed from my first moment at Yale Law School, I knew I was in the right place for me. I have told the story of my arrival to generations of Stanford law students at orientation. Henry Babcock was the star:

> My father drove me up to New Haven to help me get settled
> and to see Yale. Nothing in his experience had prepared him for
> the aura of privilege and learning that seemed to emanate from

the very stones and soaring spires. He had attended night law school, had passed the Bar after a couple of years of study, and had hung out his shingle in Hyattsville. His offices were up a narrow flight of linoleum-covered stairs above a busy boulevard. On his desk facing outward was a reminder to clients (credited to Lincoln): 'A lawyer's time and advice are his stock in trade.'

As we walked around the Yale campus and explored the law school, which had been modeled on an Oxford college, he said with wonder and pride: 'Honey, you have made it. You never have to do another damn thing, and you will still be a success.' I found these words very comforting, and I say to you the same. You have made it. All of you are capable of doing the work (we are experts at determining that), and you will have a Stanford degree and connections that will serve you all your professional lives. Now, I don't mean, and neither did my dad, that you should stop striving but that you should declare victory and proceed without insecurity and fear of failure.

Over the years many former students have told me that it had meant a lot to hear this message on the first day of law school. I felt that I was honoring my father when giving it, though I never told him about it. I wish I had.

Fifty-three years later, I clearly remember my first law school class at Yale. It was Civil Procedure, which I myself was to teach for three decades. I liked it, as well as Torts, Contracts, and Criminal Law. These subjects, along with Constitutional Law and Property (both of less interest to me), have been the heart of the first-year curriculum at American law schools for at least a hundred years. And the courses have been taught in much the same way—by a single professor who decides on the text, conducts every class, and grades each exam.

I prepared for the classes purposefully, reading not only the main and secondary cases but related articles and notes. My debate training served me well in spotting, categorizing, and prioritizing issues and arguments, and I longed to be called on in class to show what I could do. One day in Contracts, it happened. Like the fish raincoats of my childhood, this is one of my ur-texts, minus the humiliation. Grant Gilmore was the professor. Though he was not handsome or dashing, I felt something like lust for him because of the brilliance and subtlety of his questions.

As usual, I had thought deeply about the cases, which had to do with measuring damages when a contract is breached. For the entire hour, I was the target of the true Socratic Method. Gilmore's queries drew from me all the knowledge I had stored; at times I couldn't believe the answers were coming out in my voice.

Afterward my classmates gathered around and congratulated me on the performance. I rushed down to the pay phone in the basement to call my father: "Dad, Grant Gilmore just called on me for the whole class." And he said, "That's nice, honey." I said, "But Dad, don't you understand? This means I've made it. I'm going to be great." And he said, "That's good, honey." I realized then that nobody outside the insular Yale world would ever fully comprehend the triumph. Though I've won impressive awards and difficult verdicts over the years, that hour in Gilmore's class remains one of the proudest of my life.

The other moment when I knew I was in the right place occurred when I won the Harlan Fiske Stone Prize for best oral presentation in a moot court contest that the whole first year class was required to enter. Since I was the only champion debater in the first year, winning was like taking candy from a baby. In an early round, my opponent was Jack Danforth, the future United States senator from Missouri. He had a wonderful deep voice but no idea how to organize an argument. Years after our contest, I attended the swearing-in of an FBI director from Missouri and saw Jack's wife. We had not met since law school but we laughed together about how I had demolished him.

In the last round of the moot court contest before a packed auditorium, one of my opponents was Eleanor Holmes. It was the first time in Yale's history that one woman, say nothing of two, had been in the finals. Eleanor may also have been the first African American to make it to this point, but the buzz was more about our gender rather than her race. By the luck of the draw, I was assigned to argue the government's position, which I thought was the wrong side of the question. The case concerned the powers of the House Un-American Activities Committee to subpoena suspected Communists and hold them in contempt for refusing to answer questions about their friends and associates.

When I was announced as the individual victor, I used my acceptance speech to make a passionate appeal to the audience to ignore my winning arguments. Apparently I was convinced that the power of my oratory might lead the unwary into permanent error. Several professors and some fellow students thought it was unprofessional of me to have stepped out of the role of lawyer. But I thought the event's didactic purpose justified my becoming an advocate for my true views. Of course, if the government had been my client in the real world, I would not have done it.

In my three years at Yale I made many close friends, many of them men. Though I certainly did not come to law school with the explicit purpose to land a husband (and indeed have never known any woman who did), I hoped to find there the kind of social popularity that had so far eluded me. I was not aiming for Bunny's near-universal appeal, nor did I wish to administer a host of admirers as she did. But I did harbor fantasies of being pursued by tall, intelligent, handsome lawyers.

My mother, very attractive to men herself, had seen me through my acne-scarred, rail-thin, buck-toothed adolescence with the promise that "every doggie has his day." By this, she meant not only that my looks would improve but also that I would find men who would appreciate "an ambitious career girl" (her description of me). Mother thought, wrongly, that my day would come in college, but except for Eddie Cohen, most of the boys at Penn were just like those in high school, only older. Though Eddie was still in the picture, I felt our worlds growing apart when he made it clear that he considered law school to be a rather low order of intellectual enterprise, especially compared to study of the classics.

At the very first law school social event the night before classes started, I met two men who would become my lifelong comrades—closer than friends or associates though not the lovers of my imagination. One was John Ely; the other was Eli Evans. They could hardly have been more different in background and outlook, and neither cared much for the other. Here is a story I told about my relationship with John at his memorial service in April 2004.

> In our first year, John and I had most classes together: Torts with Clyde Summers, Contracts with Grant Gilmore, and Civil Procedure with Fleming James Jr. Either by alphabet or by choice, we sat next to each other. I remember being impressed by John's judicious note-taking and by his beautiful handwriting.
>
> I also remember how cold the classrooms were and the pale winter light through the high windows and the long tables that were too narrow to spread out the large law books and the harsh scraping noises even the least movement made in the room. If it sounds a little Dickensian, it was—or at least that is the way I remember it.

Now, in those days, we dressed up for class—the boys wore khakis with a sport coat and sometimes even a tie. And the girls wore stockings and heels and skirts. We left our heavy outer gear in our lockers and came to class—where, especially in the early mornings, I was always cold.

About ten minutes into the class, I would poke John lightly and say, 'Could I borrow your jacket?' He would roll his eyes, shake his head—and grumble: 'You knew it was going to be cold. It's cold every day. Why don't you bring a coat? I wore this jacket to be warm'—

He always did go on and on—grumbling and rebuking. And—he always took off his jacket and draped it around my shoulders.

When in 1982 he was appointed our Dean at Stanford, I was quoted in the paper as saying it was a splendid choice because he was such a "righteous" man. Now, John loved the *mot juste* —and he was delighted with my adjective. 'Some people might think you were suggesting 'self-righteous,'" he wrote. "But I know what you meant—like I've got some righteous dope in the freezer."

So I knew John Hart Ely as a young man, before he was a distinguished law professor whose work is and will be read by law students and cited by lawyers as long as our Constitution endures. What was he like as a young man? Not as an intellect, but as a character. Well, he was shy, which was often mistaken for arrogance (though he was a little arrogant also). He was off-beat, witty, and deeply humorous in his view of life. He was quirky, cantankerous, and hypochondriacal. He was sexy and flirtatious and loved women—and wonderful women loved him back.

In other words, the young John Ely was a lot like the John Ely of later youth and middle age, the one everyone here knew— And I think if we could have known him as an old man, he would have been the same.

My other friend from the start at Yale was Eli Evans of North Carolina—that state that inspires unusual devotion from its natives. His father was the mayor of Durham where Eli grew up; he graduated from the University of North Carolina and spent four years as a Navy lieutenant before law school. I think he felt like an outsider at Yale, at least at first, because of its heavy ration of Ivy League graduates and the many, like

John Ely, who were super-confident about their aptitude for legal argumentation.

Eli and I spent a lot of time together during our three years in New Haven. We talked for hours, mostly trading tales about our lives in the Southern storytelling tradition we shared. One of his best was about Navy duty in Japan. Eli and another lieutenant had studied the Japanese language together and on leave explored life beyond the portside bars, though his friend was more interested in the geishas and Eli in the gardens. He never mentioned the man's name and said he had lost track of him. So it was a surprise to all three of us when, a few years later, it turned out that my future husband, Addison Bowman, had been Eli's fabled friend.

Ten years after graduating from Yale, Eli published *The Provincials*, a book about growing up Jewish in the South. It has become a classic, always in print, widely read, and used in college courses. Eli went on to write other books, including a biography of Judah Benjamin, the Jewish vice-president of the Confederacy, and to have a notable career in philanthropy, ultimately becoming president of the Revson Foundation.

In law school, Eli and I started what became a ritual: his treating me to glorious meals in the best restaurants. He introduced me to sushi and sukiyaki, both previously unknown to this Hyattsville girl. Once in our first year, his parents visited and took us out to dinner. I liked them very much but did not feel that his mother reciprocated the sentiment. She reminded me of Eddie's mom back in Philadelphia. There seemed no way to tell her that though her son and I were best friends, she need not worry that our relationship would morph into romance—and perhaps it was not entirely true anyway.

I felt a bond with all the women at Yale, but I had a special friendship with Clotilde Benitez, an unusual and original character. Only seventeen when she entered the law school, having been taught mostly by private tutors in Puerto Rico (where her father was president of the university), Cloti was highly intelligent, fluent in several languages, and loved literature and music. She was also fun loving and funny. But the move from her island home (she had never lived anywhere else) to the predominantly male, hard-driving atmosphere of Yale Law School was a rough transition. It was also very cold in New Haven that first year. Walking to school one morning, Cloti chortled in her heavily accented but flawless English, "Thees ees an o-ffeeshal blizzard!"

For Cloti, the first semester of law school was a grand celebration, full of attractions and possibilities. Her father, also a Yale Law grad, had many friends on the faculty who had promised to watch out for her. Dean Rostow once invited her to house-sit while he was away, and I kept her company. While there, we threw several dinner parties cooked and served by the Dean's staff, and I encountered my first artichoke. Cloti also introduced me to Le De perfume by Givenchy, which her Puerto Rican boyfriend had sent to her and which she passed on to me. I still think no fragrance can compare.

While she enjoyed herself socially and found the classes entertaining and exciting, Cloti began to see what was also apparent to me: that she was utterly unprepared to study law. She became increasingly panicked, especially as the date drew near for first-semester grades to be distributed. In those pre-computer days, grades were posted on the registrar's door as they were received, not with anonymity but nakedly, by *name* and class.

A Benitez family friend on the faculty (maybe Fred Rodell) asked me to tell Cloti about her grades in advance, to save her learning of it in the barbaric public way. Earlier in the evening, she and Eli and I had seen *Hiroshima Mon Amour,* so that nuclear destruction and academic disappointment were forever linked in my memories. Ultimately, Cloti made it through law school and had a fine career as a lobbyist and consultant.

Though we remained close, I no longer saw Cloti regularly after I moved from the dorm into an apartment with Eleanor Holmes and John Ely's girlfriend, Judith Stein, who was studying for her Ph.D. in history. Our classmate, Neil Herring, was married to a local woman and was caretaker of a small apartment building for his father-in-law. He and his wife and baby lived on the first floor; Eleanor, Judy, and I on the second. We paid thirty dollars apiece each month—a bargain even in those days.

We divided the chores of apartment living by the week, with one buying food and cooking, one washing dishes, and the other vacuuming and cleaning. Eleanor and Judy already could cook; I bought *Joy of Cooking* (*the* cookbook of the moment) and learned the basics. When it was Eleanor's turn to cook, we had chicken every night. If we complained, she pronounced in a magisterial tone: "There are three basic foods: these are chicken, onions, and rice (or maybe it was mushrooms). People should eat them every day." She also claimed vast varieties in taste achieved through seasonings and modes of cooking the chicken.

I am flooded with fond memories of the three of us sitting around the table by the living room window—exchanging the news of the day and vigorously cross-examining Judy, who was less inclined than Eleanor and I were to divulge details of good gossip. Eleanor and Judy sometimes held heated political arguments, though the difference in their positions escapes me now, as it mostly did then. It was probably my first experience with the schisms of the left and certainly the first time I had heard new terms scornfully delivered, like "bougie," short for bourgeois, and "Trot," referring to a follower of Trotsky.

I also learned from living with El and Judy about the uses of swear words—the f and m-f bombs, which I had never heard spoken, were commonplaces for them as adjectives, nouns, gerunds, and adverbs. So were "shit" and imaginative variations such as "lower than whale shit." I was fascinated by the emphasis previously forbidden words brought to the discourse, and I enthusiastically echoed them.

What continued to shock me for a longer time was the taking of the Lord's name in vain, which I heard with the frisson stirred by breaking one of the Ten Commandments. Another frequent phrase of Eleanor's that disconcerted me was "shut up," sometimes said jokingly and sometimes not. Mother had taught us that those words were the worst possible insult. To this day, I never say it, though my brother David and I once named a cat "Shut Up Stupid" in order to be able to utter the affront.

I count friendship with Eleanor as one of the benefits of an Ivy League education. Though we were born only a year apart in the Garfield Hospital in Washington, D.C., we would never have met on our home ground. From maternity wards to cemeteries, D.C. was heavily segregated when we were growing up. A Caucasian could spend a day shopping, theater-going, and dining without seeing any African Americans except as service providers. What was true in D.C. was even more so in suburban Maryland. I mentioned earlier that in my huge public high school, there was no racial diversity. The same was true for Dunbar, the all-black public school for gifted students that Eleanor had attended.

As Eleanor has risen to national prominence as a civil rights leader and the unchallengeable Congressional Delegate for the District of Columbia, I'm sometimes called on to speak at affairs honoring her, where I sense that people want to hear more than an account of her achievements. They want to know what it was like living with her. One story captures her intrepid spirit in the early sixties. Our apartment was about ten blocks from the campus—too far to use as a base during the day. Usually we walked to school in the morning and returned home for supper after a day of classes, meetings, and study. I envied the men who had rooms right in the law school, some with suites and fireplaces. Women were not eligible to live in those quarters.

At the end of one cold winter day, it was already dark as El and I walked home together. Soon after we left campus, the streets grew quite sketchy. As we neared home, we saw a man lying unconscious on the curb. After trying to rouse him, we ran to our apartment (no cell phones then) and called for an ambulance. By the time we got back, it had arrived, and the man was coming to life. He was very drunk, and the paramedics were very angry.

"You should have called the police, not us," they complained and demanded that we give them fifty dollars for showing up. I was fishing in my bag for a check when Eleanor unloaded on them in her most cutting style: "What do you mean? This is your job. You must be crazy. We're not paying you a dime." And we marched off. I was filled with admiration and learned in that moment about resisting authority wrongly exercised.

Another thing I learned from Eleanor was how to do the twist, the dance craze at the time. She was really good at it, always the queen of the dance floor. Judy and I were determined to master the moves for the party to celebrate her passing her Ph.D. oral exams. As Chubby Checker blasted, we worked to swing to the off beat rather than doing the gyrations that came more naturally. But we just couldn't seem to get it 'til we hit on the idea of disrobing to better observe and emulate Eleanor's syncopated moves. By this method, we became pretty good at the twist, though never in a class with the queen.

The three of us often invited friends for dinner. Bob Johnson, who was a year behind us in law school, comes especially to mind. Bob had gone to a rival high school to mine in suburban Maryland, then to Amherst, and had spent a year in Denmark studying economics on a Fulbright. We were very close, and there were times over the years—I think for both of us— when each of us would have said we were in love, but those times seldom coincided. He went on to a successful legal career in Memphis, practicing with one of our classmates.

We also asked some of our law professors to dinner, though only Telford Taylor's visits linger in my mind. He was an eminent lawyer, had been a prosecutor at the Nuremburg trials, was a star Supreme Court advocate, and was handsome and debonair. After one dinner, he sent us anemones—a flower I still treasure and another Yale first for me, like the artichoke at Dean Rostow's and sushi with Eli.

I found most areas of the law interesting and tried to exercise care in choosing classes lest I become sidetracked by something that would not be useful in my future career. I was set on criminal defense (my dad's "comforting the afflicted"), though there were not a lot of courses or offerings related to that. In the further future, I also planned to teach at an elite law school, possibly Yale. Though criminal defense was not a usual ambition at the time, the thought of becoming a law professor *was* quite common at Yale; somehow it was in the air as the highest legal calling, arguably even better than a judgeship because of the autonomy a teaching post confers.

In my legal education, it was not so much the professors who instructed me as my fellow students and my own study and writing. We talked about the law and tried to think original thoughts about reforming it. I believed that the class of 1963 could change the world and that it was our duty to do so. That was Yale Law School's implicit message to those whom it admitted, along with the certain knowledge that we would succeed in whatever we chose to do. I had never before enjoyed such a sense of privilege or the immense pride of simply being among the chosen.

Recently I returned to Yale for our fiftieth class reunion. Walking the familiar streets and corridors brought to mind having seen the return of the geezers when I was a student. How ancient they seemed, and a little pitiful, as they hobbled about—seeking, I assumed, to relive the youth they could barely conjure up. And now I was one of them.

But now I felt only great admiration for the distinguished-looking old men and women with their illustrious and interesting careers—my classmates from 1963. Of course, those who are fairly happy in life are the ones who return to reunions, so the picture was perhaps a little skewed. Still, I was struck by how well we had done, how useful we had been. I was proud of our collective selves.

I gave a three-minute talk at the dinner, telling of my first day in law school when my father had looked around at the splendor of Yale and said, "Honey, you have made it. You never have to do another damn thing, and you will still be a success." And I read to the audience my diary entry from September 1960: "First class in law school was reassuring. It was extremely interesting, not over my head, and no one called upon seemed very smart." That got a big laugh.

3

WOMAN AND MAN AT YALE (1960-1963)

We women who entered law school in 1960 turned out later to have been the vanguard of a renewed women's movement—"the second wave." Yet I don't remember that we called ourselves feminists or felt in need of liberation. Sexism did not yet have a name, and my own consciousness was barely dawning. Mostly I just marched on toward my goals, oblivious to the surrounding culture. When I thought about it at all, being female was merely another hurdle to surmount, like not being as smart or as attractive as I wished. And occasionally it was even advantageous to be an outsider "other" and an underdog.

Though not antagonistic to women, neither was Yale welcoming, especially not to our class which had double the number ever previously admitted (thirteen of a total 170). We never learned whether admitting so many women represented a change in policy, better applicants, or pure chance, but it triggered an amount of alarm among our male classmates that seems comical today. Some of them charged that we were taking places from men who needed law degrees to support women like us. Some accused us of supplanting future world leaders—implying that it would be OK if we attended an obscure night school and, of course, that we would not be among those future world leaders.

At any rate, the furor died down when the next two classes dropped back to the usual numbers: five and seven women, respectively. It would be almost a decade before there was a permanent surge in women's admission. Although sex discrimination was all around us in law school, it was not yet a recognized legal concept, and I failed to recognize it in my own experience.

For one thing, most of the men were well-mannered so that there was not open unpleasantness. Romances, however, were rare. I heard that some of the men thought that women who studied law must be "frigid," a dreaded label in the fifties and sixties. Happily, it is commonplace now for couples to pair off in law school. I sometimes say the intermarriage of lawyers promotes reasonable argument and due process in relationships— I joke, but I'm serious, too. For myself, I can't imagine being married to a non-lawyer.

Though there was very little surface meanness, I did observe that daily life was different for women because there were so few of us. We could not, for instance, "foxhole" as the men could, sitting immobile in a large class when professors called their names. And even in these pre-consciousness days, I felt that I carried the reputation of all women on my shoulders. I never raised my hand, because a stupid question would be held against women and I was never positive my question was good. None of my female classmates ever volunteered either.

Casual prejudice was commonplace. A classmate once said that though he hoped I was different, women were generally not suited to the law. His proof: despite our hundred years in the profession, we had yet to produce a single famous female advocate, distinguished judge, or brilliant scholar. "But men are writing the history!" I thought but did not say. Years later, I would devote many seasons to recovering the story of Clara Foltz, a very great nineteenth-century lawyer, never recognized or celebrated before because of gender discrimination.

Any woman who went to law school in the fifties and sixties has stories about pervasive and routine bias. Another of my personal examples came while interviewing for a summer job at New York corporate law firms with high-sounding names (my favorites were Cadwalader, Wickersham & Taft and Lamb & LeBoeuf—both straight out of a Trollope novel). Though I still planned to do criminal defense, I wanted a taste of the most august level of practice. Being at Yale afforded me introductions to the firms, who came to the school and invited a few applicants to their glamorous metropolitan offices for a second interview. Not one firm called me back, however, though I ranked high in the class and was on the law journal.

Instead of the sour smell of discrimination, I sensed only that I lacked something they wanted, which I strove to discover and supply. But soon enough I came to see that nothing I could do would charm or impress these Wall Street types into employing me for the summer. In one interview, two fairly young men met with me briefly and made a series of unanswerable remarks, such as "These are grades any man would be happy to have." As we walked out into the law school courtyard on a brilliant spring day, one of them commented that the firm was "in a downward cycle in the hiring of women." I asked, "Is that because you have so many?" "No," he responded, "we have never had any." "That's not a cycle," I laughed, touching his arm in my Southern style. He jumped back, and I saw that he was both startled and slightly repelled.

That incident, hardly a dramatic example of sexism, was typical of the type of discrimination women met at the elite law firms. We were not barred from being considered: we had the job interview and apparently the opportunity, but when it came down to it, we were not going to get any further. Within the world of Yale Law School, no woman had ever been president of the law journal or become a Supreme Court law clerk. And there had only been one woman professor.

Though I never made it to Wall Street, I did work at a prestigious law firm in the summer of 1962 after my second year. I'm not sure how I came to be hired as a summer clerk at Arnold, Fortas & Porter in Washington, D.C., but I know it was outside the regular interview process. Probably someone in this famously liberal firm with its many Yale connections wanted to give a girl a chance. If so, this was an example of gender working to my advantage. As I have told generations of students who are troubled by being recipients of affirmative action, "It's not how you got the job but how you do it that counts." And not to worry: "You will be unfairly rejected as often as you are given a boost. It all evens out."

I had a great summer at the law firm even though I worked exclusively on an appeal from the denial of a TV license renewal, wrestling with a massive administrative record, while my classmate John Ely, at the same firm, was selected to work on *Gideon* v. *Wainwright*, the case that would establish the right to counsel for indigent criminal defendants. The Supreme Court had appointed Abe Fortas to represent Gideon. I was jealous of John's good fortune, especially in light of my own rare vocation for criminal defense practice, but the choice made sense given not only his gender, but also that he ranked higher than I did in our class, had just been elected an officer on the law journal, and was an excellent legal writer.

At the end of the summer, Paul Porter took me to an expensive French restaurant to thank me for my work on the TV license renewal case, which he said "read like a detective story." They filed the brief pretty much as I had written it and invited me to hear the oral argument in the U.S. Court of Appeals. I think I could have gotten an offer at the firm, but I was still firmly on my path to criminal defense, work they did not do (except for the occasional *pro bono* appellate case like *Gideon*).

At Arnold, Fortas & Porter in the summer of 1962, I met my first woman lawyer, the legendary tax practitioner Carolyn Agger. She had graduated from Yale in 1938, the year I was born, and was married to Abe Fortas. I had heard awed accounts of Agger: how she had risen to partner at Paul, Weiss, Rifkind & Garrison a few years after being hired as the firm's first woman; how she had moved from that firm to her husband's, bringing the entire tax office with her; how she smoked cigars and had a steel trap mind. She took me to lunch and invited me to a dinner party at their Georgetown mansion.

I was excited at the thought that Carolyn Agger might become my mentor. Without being able to articulate exactly what I wanted, I longed for an elder guide. Agger seemed ideal for the role, but in the end she did not relate to me as a fellow woman and disapproved of my criminal defense ambitions. Today, a fund in her name supports women who pursue postgraduate legal studies or who engage in low-paying legal careers. Her bequest makes me think she may have become a conscious feminist after I knew her and that we had met before either of us would have thought that she had a special obligation to aid another woman.

Occasionally interviewers ask about my female mentors. I probably appear ungrateful when I say I did not have any. But I have had many women friends and colleagues who helped me at every turn. A number of men have also advised me, and some have even been my heroes. But my sense of having missed a mentor of my own gender has left me especially committed to helping other women, and it always gives me pleasure when one of them expresses gratitude for my counsel.

After the first year of law school, my formal education was less in the classroom than in the library where I researched cases and on the law journal where I wrote about them. The student-managed and edited scholarly organ had its own subculture within the larger intellectual ambience of the school. Only first-year students with top grades were invited to write for the journal, that is, to become "members." There was also the possibility of gaining membership by submitting a piece of scholarly writing, but very few people made it through that route.

Law journal membership was the next rung on the ladder to professional success, and I was thrilled to be asked. My classmate, Marguerite Schimpff, turned it down; she thought it involved too much drudgery and preferred to devote herself to her studies and other activities. I admired her independence of mind, though I would have been incapable of making the same choice. (Marguerite went on to a brilliant career as a lawyer in Washington, D.C. and to my knowledge never regretted not being on the law journal.)

Each student invited to join was required to write a short "Note," usually an analysis of an important case, or group of cases. If deemed worthy, the Note would appear in the law journal; it was also the main factor in determining whether the member would ascend to the lofty rank of officer. I wrote about the evidentiary effect in subsequent civil law suits of the guilty pleas entered by electrical company executives to criminal charges of antitrust violations.

The government had insisted that the men plead guilty rather than the usual *nolo contendere*—a plea accepting responsibility without admitting guilt. Following on the government cases, consumers brought class actions that offered the chance for treble damages against the companies. It was established law that nolo pleas were not evidence in such consumer cases. But a guilty plea might be different.

When I started I knew nothing about evidence or antitrust law but I learned what I needed, and proposed a theory for admitting the guilty pleas against the executives.[*] The Note made something of a splash because the high stakes suits were ongoing.

Though I find it almost unreadable now, at the time I thought my first legal publication was not only clever but stylish; Edgar Cahn, my classmate and a Ph.D. in English, drew my attention to a quote from *Hamlet* that I could use for an epigraph: "O, treble woe—Fall ten times treble on that cursed head." *Hamlet*, act 5, scene 1. (Maybe Edgar's special contribution was in appreciation for my ceding, out of friendship, my original topic, on prison reform law).

If one hoped to be an officer of the law journal, the Note needed to be finished by January of the second year to be ready for the spring election when the current officers would decide who would follow them. Somehow

---

[*] "The Admissibility and Scope of Guilty Pleas in Antitrust Treble Damage Actions," 71 *Yale Law Journal* 684 (1962).

I completed a draft in time, and after two rounds of review by upperclass Note editors, my piece was headed in December for the Presidential Edit, a process whose capitalization denoted its importance. Alan Dershowitz, the now-celebrated criminal defense lawyer and Harvard professor, was president of the law journal that year and therefore the ultimate judge of my Note. I remember both his patient editing and his main lesson for legal writing: simply say it—no sugarcoating and no pussyfooting.

My enjoyment of the editing was marred because I contracted mononucleosis in the process. To this day, I've never experienced anything like the paralyzing exhaustion, which deep sleep did not refresh. At times, I didn't think I could make it down the narrow steps that led from the law review offices directly into the library to check on a reference (in that dark age before such research is done in seconds online).

After the editing was finished I collapsed in the student health service over the Christmas holidays when most people were gone from campus. I was alone and exhausted in a hospital bed, which made this a very low period. For loneliness and depression, mono was worse than anything before or since. What a difference a cell phone would have made!

By the start of the second semester I was back on my feet, and expecting soon to be elected to an officership on the journal. I saw that it would be an extremely positive credential on a resume, showing the holder to be a hard worker, a good technical writer, and respected by her male peers. On the night of the election, I hung around late at the library waiting to be called upstairs to the journal for congratulations. It didn't happen. All the offices were filled by my male friends and equals. Later someone airily explained that several years back, they had chosen a female officer and it just had not worked out.

For the first time in my life, I felt like the victim of discrimination—but at the same time I experienced the loss as my own fault. Maybe it happened because I was not a good cite checker, but then I realized most of the men chosen were no better, and of course cite checking was not the main skill required of a law journal editor. Perhaps I should have handled the politics better, by lobbying the third year officers, which I knew others had done.

Not being elected had significant side effects. In order to stay on the masthead for the third year, non-officers were required to write a piece longer than a Note, called a Comment. And so I spent much of my third year in law school producing "Limitations on Freedom to Modify Contract

Remedies,"* a survey that would not have been so onerous in the age of search engines. At that time, the breadth of manual, tome-toting research required was startling. I spent many hours in my library carrel reading treatises and state cases (where contract law was located). Today as I look at those forty-six closely reasoned pages on disclaimers of warranty, stipulated damages, and arbitration clauses, I can barely relate to the young woman who found it all so engrossing.

As law school wound down amidst drudgery and dissatisfaction, there were a couple of bright spots. Professor Gilmore nominated my Comment on contract law for the award given to the author of the best published student work. The writing award, together with my earlier advocacy prize, could almost make up for lacking the law journal office on my resume. I was very hopeful.

But John Ely won the prize, and explained to me that his constitutional law entry (on bills of attainder) was more important than mine could be, on the humble subject of contract remedies. I also knew that he had the access of a law journal officer to the faculty members who chose the winner, whereas I was never once in a professor's office in my three years at Yale. I'm not sure what I expected John to do in the name of friendship and gender fairness, but fifty years later, the memory still irks me. If he were alive, I think he would say—assuming he remembered it at all—that he had treated me as he would have treated a man in the same position. And there is some truth to that. After a few months, I forgave his attitude and our friendship resumed.

In late spring, 1963, I finished up my papers, packed up my possessions, took my last exams, and bid classmates goodbye. It all seemed anticlimactic, perhaps because I was remembering the intense excitement I had felt at the beginning of law school. Though I had learned a lot at Yale, in one respect I left as I came: an innocent on the subject of sex discrimination. Not until years later would I wonder about some of the things that happened like not being elected an officer, or nominated for important clerkships, or encouraged to consider a teaching career. Almost a decade would pass before I found the women's rights movement.

I did not attend graduation. The Maryland bar exam—which had among its twenty-three subjects thirteen I had never studied—loomed, and Dad was on a binge and in no shape to travel to New Haven. Eleanor,

---

* 72 *Yale Law Journal* 723 (1963).

staying for a master's degree in American Studies, would not be attending, and my other friends were busy entertaining their families. My wonderful law school adventure drew to an end without proper closure. Since then, I've been to at least forty law school graduations, spoken at six of them, and enjoyed almost all—especially because I missed my own.

4

INTO THE "REAL WORLD": CLERKSHIP AND EARLY PRACTICE (1963-1966)

In my last months of school I had the good fortune to be hired as a law clerk on the prestigious United States Court of Appeals for the D.C. Circuit for the following year, 1963-64. Top clerkships were the most desirable jobs for new law school graduates, especially those who might have ultimate teaching goals. Though the application process was extremely competitive, I thought I had a good chance. I had made Order of the Coif (the top ten percent of the class), and though not a law journal officer, I had two publications that showed my legal writing ability. Confidently, I applied to the several judges I admired on the D.C. Circuit.

The judge I most wanted was David Bazelon, who was especially interested in criminal law, and also regularly sent his clerks on to Supreme Court Justices. (I harbored the ambition to clerk on the High Court though few women had been hired before.) Alan Dershowitz, my friend and supporter, was clerking for Judge Bazelon (and would go on to clerk for Supreme Court Justice Arthur Goldberg). One day Alan called me in New Haven, and I expected promising news about the clerkship. Instead, he told me with his inimitable directness that I did not have a chance—not with Bazelon, not with anyone. When I pointed out that they had all scheduled interviews with me, he replied, "Sure, but they won't be able to go through with it. They are not ready to hire a young, single, attractive woman." I was stunned and half-disbelieved him.

He went on to say I should apply to Judge Henry Edgerton, a senior judge who still heard cases regularly and who had hired a woman in the

39

past, one of the first and few federal judges to do so. Alan said he had already made an appointment for me to see Judge Edgerton when I came to interview with the other judges. I agreed to the interview, while secretly betting that I could persuade Judge Bazelon to take me.

Judge Edgerton was the first on my schedule. At the end of an hour, he surprised me by offering the clerkship on the spot. My mind raced: should I say I would like to meet the others before deciding? But it struck me that I had just had a wonderful conversation with a very great man who wanted to hire me. "Yes," I said. "Yes. I would like to be your law clerk." It was to be one of the best decisions I ever made.

Before clerking, I went home to Hyattsville in late May 1963 and threw myself into studying for the bar exam, which was set for a month later. Most other candidates were from Maryland law schools and had been taking a review course since January. Though I had little time before the exam, I wasn't worried because memorizing heuristics to move quickly through material was my métier. I knew I could do it.

And then all of a sudden, I couldn't do it. My mind grew sluggish, my limbs heavy; I could hardly hold up my head. Our family doctor diagnosed an infected polynodal cyst at the base of my spine and said I needed immediate surgery. But I wanted to take the bar exam first, and he saw my point. He drained the infection and gave me some pills.

Mental acuity returned the next day, and I was able to study hard without panicking. The exam was in a Baltimore hotel and lasted for two days. I was stunned at how foreign much of the material seemed, and regretted briefly that I had not taken more of what some of us at Yale scornfully called "bread and butter courses": commercial transactions, corporations, negotiable instruments, real property. Over drinks after the first day, I discovered that a fellow test-taker knew even less than I did—and he hadn't gone to Yale. Somehow that made me feel better.

At any rate, I squeaked through the exam—second to last on the published and ordered list of those who passed. I tried to think of it as a remarkably efficient performance, expending no extra energy on study. Passing was all that mattered, yet not being in control of the material was an awful experience and one I vowed not to repeat. I joined the D.C. bar by motion based on my Maryland membership and never took another bar examination.

I had the back surgery and lived at home while recuperating, which took some months because it required healing with metal clamps (like big staples) in my back. Even after I recovered and started my clerkship I continued on in Hyattsville. My parents were so happy to have me there that I kept putting off my intended move into town. Dad would take his lawyer-daughter to the courthouse in Upper Marlboro, just to show me off. And Mom loved to help select my professional wardrobe. Shopping was our sport together. I've never really enjoyed it without her. Women lawyers had not yet adopted the dark tailored-suit, silk-blouse uniform most now wear, and especially in court my stylish bright clothes made me stand out from the regimented men.

All three Babcock children were at home on Gallatin Street in 1963-1964. David was twenty-four years old and working in the insurance business in Hyattsville; Starr was a junior in high school. I had always felt close to my brothers, though it had been years since we had lived in the same house.

When Starr was born in 1947, Mom was thirty-seven, and I was almost ten. For much of his early childhood, I was a second mother to him—his "Barboo." Although I had never cared for dolls (except to push them around in a carriage with their naked limbs hanging over the side), I found Starr to be a fascinating creature. Not only was he cute with black curls and dark eyes, but from early on he was a great talker with a rich imagination. Fluffy, his invisible friend, was his constant companion, and for some time he wore a gun and holster set inscribed Smokey Joe and a towel cape secured by a safety pin.

Starr was more complicated than David and I had been as children. He threw tantrums, filled his pockets with worms, and played with knives and with fire. Every meal was a war over vegetables; he would imbibe only milk, tuna fish, peanut butter, and sweets. I can understand now that he felt unwanted and neglected in the middle of Mother's last great battle against Dad's alcoholism. David and I made matters worse by telling him elaborate stories about all the good times we had enjoyed before he was born. (Babcock humor can be cruel.)

When I left for Penn and then Yale, I was not only escaping home trauma but abandoning Starr. Of course I didn't think of it that way—nor would it have changed anything if I had. But when I lived at home again after law school, I was alarmed at Starr's disengagement. He was making poor grades and seemed interested only in baseball. All he read was *The Sporting News*. Mother and Dad were disappointed in him, but they believed in hands-off child rearing. David and I had raised ourselves, and I guess they felt that had worked out fine.

Despite a very high IQ, David had never done well in school. But he found his own way by becoming a skilled mechanic. Years before he got his driver's license, he rebuilt motors in the back yard and drove his old cars in the alley. When he graduated from high school, he joined the Army and chose to operate heavy equipment instead of going to Officer Candidate School, for which he had qualified.

Dad told me how bad he felt when he took David to the bus bound for basic training instead of delivering him to college. He wanted things to be different for Starr and was in a period when he could afford to pay tuition. We located several colleges that would accept him, and Starr chose Davis & Elkins in West Virginia. Mother and I went with him to look it over. It was pastoral and somehow pristine—a great place to make a fresh start.

Starr and David have both had considerable success. After college, Starr attended Georgetown Law School, then joined me in California and practiced in San Francisco. Recently he retired as general counsel of the State Bar of California, the largest bar organization in the world. David continued in the insurance business and rose to a high executive position in the reinsurance field, an achievement all the more remarkable because he did not have the usual educational qualifications.

By the end of the summer of 1963, I was back in full health and ready to start my first full-time legal job: a federal appellate clerkship. I can see Judge Edgerton now in my mind's eye, with his shock of white hair backlit from the window overlooking the Capitol grounds, his shaggy eyebrows raised in amusement or surprise. From the first weeks, we worked extremely well together. Before oral argument, I would read the opinions and briefs and write a short memo summarizing the issues and my own thoughts. Later, if the judge was writing an opinion, I would produce a draft and place the relevant cases on a beautiful heavy wooden rolling cart. He would read the cases and improve on the reasoning and rhetoric of my effort.

Judge Edgerton was a remarkable judicial craftsman—really the best. His writing was unornamented, even plain, and gained "its compelling character from the closely knit cogency of the arguments rather than from the sort of eloquence which is commonly a temptation to judges dealing with infringements of liberty," as one reviewer wrote.* He enjoyed talking about his life, much of it spent on the court where he had served for twenty-six years.

Before his appointment by President Franklin Delano Roosevelt, Judge Edgerton had practiced law and been a law professor. Soon after his start in academia at Cornell, he had been pressured to resign because of his opposition to America's entry into World War I. He returned to private practice in Boston, working for the illustrious old firm of Ropes & Gray. From that period came one of the judge's best stories, which I've told now about as often as I heard it from him.

He had worked for one partner—there was no name in the story—for several years and felt that he had learned a great deal despite the man's gruffness and the lack of personal interaction with him. When the partner retired, his young associate summoned his nerve and said how much he respected and admired him. The partner's face fell and he blurted, "It's not admiration we want, Edgerton. It's affection." When hearing the story, I thought, "Ah yes, but both must be earned."

Judge Edgerton certainly earned my affection—even adoration—partly as the grandfather I had never known. (George Babcock died when Dad was nine; Floyd Moses died when I was six.) The judge was close to generations of his law clerks, as he had been with his students. Our relationship felt so familial that it made me think that I might remind him of his only daughter. He did not speak of her, but a picture on his shelf showed the bridge from which she had jumped to her death.

To each of his clerks, the judge gave three mementos: a glossy 4x6 photograph of him taken in his younger years, a book of his collected opinions on civil liberties, and a reprint (yes, an original reprint from decades earlier!) of his 1937 article "The Incidence of Judicial Control over Congress."† The article showed that the Supreme Court had used its power to overrule legislation most often in favor of the rich and powerful. His analysis of the Court's work through its effects rather than its doctrines was striking, even daring, scholarship at the time. More important for Edgerton's career, the article provided intellectual scaffolding for

---

* Review [by C], 25 *Modern Law Review* 116 (1962). Reviewing *Freedom in the Balance: Opinions of Judge Henry W. Edgerton Relating to Civil Liberties* (Eleanor Bontecou, ed.) (Ithaca, N.Y.: Cornell University Press, 1960).

† 22 *Cornell Law Quarterly* 299 (1937).

Roosevelt's proposal to add progressive justices to the Supreme Court in order to prevent the dismantling of New Deal programs.

It was thrilling to think that by writing a scholarly article, an obscure pacifist law professor with an open commitment to social justice could be appointed to a federal judgeship. Very soon after arriving on the court, Judge Edgerton became a spokesman for civil rights and civil liberties, writing some of his greatest opinions during the McCarthy era. On the rights of the criminally accused, he was all a nascent defense lawyer could wish for.

During his first decade on the court, Judge Edgerton had been intellectually lonely and often in dissent. There had been bright spots when Wiley Rutledge and Thurman Arnold joined the bench. But Rutledge shortly went on to the Supreme Court, and Arnold retired after only two years because he found appellate judging isolating and boring. Things changed for Judge Edgerton with the appointment in 1950 of David Bazelon, and in the ensuing years, a number of other liberals and moderates were added to the court.

As a senior judge, Edgerton could designate the categories of cases he heard, though of course not particular cases. When he learned of my interest in criminal defense, he decided to specialize on the criminal side for the year. He also "loaned" me to Judge Bazelon for criminal work. Judge Bazelon became a second mentor and would be of great help in my career.

Judge Bazelon was a type I came to love: the Jewish man of thought and action, often from Chicago. I think of Lester Crown, Abner Mikva, and Quentin Young, in addition to Judge B (and of course Eli Evans and Eddie Cohen). As chief judge, Bazelon taught me about the politics of running a legal institution and the importance of exercising the power and authority within one's grasp lest it diminish from disuse. I saw how he developed a loyal staff and delegated large responsibilities to them. These were all lessons I remembered when, with his help, I became an administrator myself.

My two mentors were close to each other, almost like father and son, though their backgrounds could hardly have been more different. Edgerton was born in Rush, Kansas of old New England stock, from a learned family; his siblings were both professors (one of Sanskrit at Yale, the other of Egyptology at Chicago). Bazelon was the son of impoverished immigrants; his father had died when he was two. He was the only one of nine siblings to attend college.

Both men told the story of Bazelon's appointment in 1949 when he was, at 39, the youngest person ever chosen for a federal appellate court. He had spent several years at the Justice Department where he was mainly an administrator. Earlier he had practiced in Chicago and had been a prosecutor for five years, hardly a distinguished pedigree. With at least one other member of the court (I can't remember who), Judge Edgerton had made an unofficial trip to the White House to oppose the nomination because he thought Bazelon unqualified for the job, that he was more politico than judge.

The second act of the story of their relationship began with the circulation of Judge Bazelon's first opinion. He remembered that "within an hour" of sending it out, Judge Edgerton was in his chambers: "He was warm in his praise of the approach and generous in aiding my attempt to present the decision compellingly."* Such mutual reinforcement typified the two judges' exchanges about many opinions over the twenty years they served together.

It was ideal to be Judge Edgerton's clerk while working sometimes for Judge Bazelon. "Judge B" was a hard taskmaster, requiring long hours and refusing time off to his regular crew, even for the birth of a child.† But since I was not on his payroll, the judge had to treat me well or I would simply withdraw.

Also, I think my female sympathies and intuitions enabled me to get along better with Judge Bazelon than did some of his full-time male clerks. Early on I realized that he had a bad memory and that he became irritated when pressed for precedent or exact meaning. I would try to grasp his general idea quickly, get out of the room, then put together a text—not a long, learned memorandum, but some language that he would make his own.

At about the time I started clerking in the summer of 1963, everyone was talking about a huge civil rights march that was to draw people from all over the United States to Washington. Eleanor, who was returning to Yale in the fall for the fourth year of her joint degree program, was

---

* Edgerton Memorial Service, 426 F.2d at 11 (1970).

† Alan Dershowitz, *Taking the Stand: My Life in the Law*, 60-64 (New York: Crown Publishers, 2013).

working on organizing it with Bayard Rustin in New York. I wanted to join the march, though most other clerks planned to watch it from the windows of the courthouse, which fronted on the route along Constitution Avenue. The speeches were to be televised.

In the days leading up to the march, there was concern about possible violence. The past year had seen the assassination of Medgar Evers, the jailing of protestors, and the unleashing of dogs and clubs on peaceful demonstrators. Supreme Court Chief Justice Warren had directed court personnel to stay off the mall in case there were arrests that might become cases before the Court.[*] My advisors, Judge Edgerton and my father, were uneasy about my plans to march. But I believed that it would be a great historical event and that I would always be proud to have been present. That's the way it turned out.

On the day of the march, August 28, 1963, I went from Hyattsville with my friend Patsy, who had graduated from the University of Maryland and was working on her doctorate while teaching high school English. We parked in my law clerk's spot near the courthouse and met up with Judy Stein and her mother and brother, down on the train from New York.

The day was not as muggy as August can be in D.C. Thousands of people were already marching by the time we arrived. Having grown up in heavily segregated communities, I had never before been in a place where my white skin made me stand out in a crowd. The atmosphere was like that at a Sunday school picnic—everyone smiling and friendly, including the large numbers of uniformed police and military on hand.

Marching along the historic avenue, singing "We shall overcome" amidst the throng of black strangers, I felt hopeful about the future of race relations in the country. A platform was at one end of the reflecting pool in front of the Lincoln memorial and the program built to the speech by Martin Luther King, Jr. In soaring cadences about equality and freedom, he spoke to the vast crowd. I was moved and inspired, though at the time I thought it was a tactical mistake to speak also of little white girls and little black boys joining hands. I did not think people were ready for that, but in retrospect I see that a speech at such a moment should not hold back from the complete vision.

Working at the courthouse right down the street from the Capitol and the Supreme Court and across from my childhood hangout, the National

---

[*] Dershowitz, *Taking the Stand*, at 73.

Gallery of Art, I felt close to history. For one thing, we found out about current events quickly. I remember hearing within minutes that President Kennedy had been assassinated; Judge Edgerton's secretary had received a phone call.

Her tone reminded me of the only other time a president had died in my lifetime. I was seven years old and helping to hang clothes on the line in Arkansas when a neighbor came out crying that President Roosevelt was dead. I was frightened then because he was the only president I had known. I thought his death might mean the end of the country. Now, about Kennedy, I had adult fears and questions. Who would do such a thing? Could this be the beginning of a war?

Kennedy was the first politician I had campaigned for, going door to door in New Haven and trying to discuss issues with anyone who answered. A classmate was with me, and this was his first time campaigning, too. He kept getting my name mixed up, calling me "Babbara Barbcock," and we would fall into helpless giggles. But we played our part and shared in Kennedy's victory. I felt a sense of personal bereavement three years later as I viewed the funeral procession from my office window.

The courthouse, in addition to its proximity to the political events of the day, had its own community composed of the judges, staff people, and law clerks of the trial and appellate courts; the prosecutors and defenders who practiced there regularly; the uniformed police and detectives who were witnesses; and the laypeople called to serve on grand and petit juries. In 1963-64, there were very few women lawyers in this society. Burnita Shelton Matthews was on the District Court bench, but there were no women on the Court of Appeals. Two women were in the U.S. Attorney's office, and Wendy Weinberg was a permanent aide to Judge Bazelon, writing speeches and helping with the court administration. I was the only woman law clerk.

Although e-mail or even voice mail did not exist, a constant stream of communication flowed all through the courthouse. I enjoyed D.C. culture where everyone read the *Washington Post* in the morning and discussed news stories all day long—critiquing, affirming, or simply repeating. Often in our fifth-floor redoubt, we appellate clerks would hear (how, I cannot say) that there was going to be a hot cross-examination or a good summation somewhere, and we would slip down to listen. The grapevine led me one day to a courtroom where Bill Bryant was closing for the defense.

I have long forgotten the facts of the case, but I can see him now, handsome without being showy, warning the twelve jurors in the box not to "go bear hunting and give the bear the gun." The jury laughed, and I realized that I was witnessing the exact moment when he won the verdict. It may have been one of his last closing arguments, because within the year President Lyndon Johnson appointed him to the federal district court in D.C., the first black man to serve on that bench. Judge Bryant later became my friend and inspiration. His courtroom was an oasis of civility and respect in those cold marble precincts where many other judges resented handling street-crime cases.

I found one group among the courthouse regulars to be especially magnetic: criminal defense lawyers at the Legal Aid Agency, a pilot project whose mission was to design the best way to deliver criminal defense services in D.C. Their leader was Gary Bellow, the most charismatic man of my own generation I had ever met. It was not his physical presence that made him so compelling; his appearance was unremarkable except for beautiful eyes with ridiculously long lashes. Nor was he exceptionally eloquent or in possession of any unusual attributes of voice or speech.

His charisma lay in the intense curiosity he exuded: a universal, inclusive, continuous interest in ideas and people. He never seemed down or too tired to talk about using the law to achieve social justice. Educated at Yale and at Harvard Law School, Gary's job with Legal Aid was his first full-time legal position. From 1962 to 1965, he was the deputy director of the Agency; second to an older local lawyer who recognized Gary's genius and let him lead.

Gary gathered a little band of young lawyers who believed with him that the criminal justice system was in terrible shape and that providing first-rate representation to indigent individuals was a way to improve it. Of his early days at the Agency, Gary later wrote: "We discovered that the best legal education America had to offer didn't teach us how to get someone out of a cell block. We figured it out ourselves and developed our own learning and teaching techniques."*

All I wanted to do was to work for Gary Bellow. The path lay before me as brightly as had my decisions to be a lawyer and to go to Yale. But I didn't get a job at Legal Aid then, either because there were no openings or because someone else was hired. I didn't regard the rejection as final, and

---

* Obituary, *New York Times*, April 15, 2000.

indeed, Gary may have told me to get some experience and then apply again (that sounds like him).

I had one other prospect for criminal defense employment: Edward Bennett Williams had invited me to apply to work at his firm. He was already well-known in D.C. legal circles and was on his way to national fame. His newly published autobiography *One Man's Freedom* had inspired me in law school, and in my third year I had actually met the great man when he came to Yale to speak. I was writing a paper about a case he had argued before the Supreme Court and had asked for a brief meeting to discuss his advocacy tactics. I guess he assumed that this was a ploy to get a job interview, and maybe it was, though I don't remember consciously setting about it in that way.

My strongest first impression was of his size: he was large and imposing and surprisingly catlike on his feet. From the outset I also sensed the restless dissatisfaction that was a chief feature of his temperament. After about twenty minutes of my prepared questions and his straightforward answers, I rose, thanked him, and gathered my books and papers to leave. Evidently surprised at my abrupt exit, he asked, "What are you planning to do when you graduate?" I told him about my desire to practice criminal defense after clerking, and he said to give him a call.

That had been almost two years earlier, and I'd had no further contact with him. But I must have found a way to remind him—through a call from Judge Bazelon, or maybe Wendy Weinberg's husband, Bob, who worked for Williams, put in a good word for me. Perhaps I sent a letter and included my grade-A paper about his case. At any rate, I ended up with an interview and a job offer, which I accepted immediately.

The Williams firm was on a corner that commanded handsome views of Farragut Square and Connecticut Avenue. It was a long way from the gritty neighborhoods and cheap eateries around the courthouse, though the atmosphere inside was even more relentlessly male. I wonder if any law firm anywhere is like it today. Men wore suits and ties even when dictating letters; they talked and laughed loudly; they drank martinis at lunch. A couple of men didn't fit the description: the resident intellectuals, the writers. It was tacitly understood that these men would not go to court or meet clients (though they, too, usually wore ties while doing their cerebral work). I saw at once that I must not become a writer.

I longed to speak to juries in my own voice for a client who depended on me. Of course, I knew that wouldn't happen right away, but I also knew that apprenticing as a writer would not take me there very fast or perhaps at all. As things turned out, I had a great experience—observing and helping Williams prepare and try criminal cases in Florida, Denver, and Washington, D.C. Also, I was second chair to his chief lieutenant, Vince Fuller, in several trials. I learned how to deploy large defense resources, and I internalized a work ethic of extreme preparation.

Though I was often in the courtroom over my two years at the firm, I was mostly silent there. Instead, I prepared witnesses and defendants for their testimony, wrote motions to dismiss the charges on various grounds, and produced tailored jury instructions and instant trial memoranda. If we lost, I might do an appellate brief or petition for certiorari. Often I worked with the brilliant Bob Weinberg, who was an excellent teacher and who, no matter how pressed, always took time to explain a fine point.

Once, Bob enlisted me to represent some anti-war demonstrators in the local courts with him. To my dismay and surprise, Williams was enraged when he found out we had taken on the "sign carriers." When I explained that we had acted in our own names and on our own time, he yelled, "You don't have your own names, and you certainly don't have your own time. When you need more work, just let me know."

An angry Ed Williams was a scary sight: icy eyes, twisted features, reddened face. His rages were a constant background fact, like the weather, at the firm. When he was upset, the lights grew dim and there was trembling in the halls. He was Jove incarnate, whose outsize temper his followers simply accepted as normal for a god. On the other hand, when he was in a good mood, everyone smiled and things went smoothly.

I saw that he was mad at Bob and me not so much because we were representing "sign carriers" but because we had done it without his knowledge or permission. Actually I thought he had a point. Bob quietly insisted that our in-court experience would be good for the firm in the long run.

Since Williams himself made every major decision about employment as well as about cases and clients, I credit him for hiring me in 1964, a time when most firms were flat-out discriminating against women. He had no apparent reservations about my gender and hired Judith Richards that year as well. We were not the first women; some years earlier, his wife, Agnes, had been his associate. (After a few drinks, Williams would regularly explain that Agnes considered being a full-time mother and homemaker a much better job; he intimated that I would probably make the same choice someday.)

Judy tells a wonderful story of how she landed the job with Williams. She arrived at the firm without an appointment early one morning and sent her resume in to him. When told that he was very busy, she insisted on waiting to see if he might have a moment. Several times Williams' assistant returned to discourage her, once even explaining that he had already hired a woman, Barbara Babcock, who was coming soon.

Lunch time arrived, and Williams couldn't get out without passing through the reception area. He waited around the corner as his assistant tried again to get rid of the persistent young woman. This time Judy said a few words about his hypocrisy in advocating for the underdog in his book but not even giving her a chance. Williams came out of hiding and took her to lunch. By the end of the day, she had a job offer.[*]

When Judy and I first met, I was uneasy about the arrival of the "blonde from Harvard." (I was already designated "the brunette from Yale.") Hailing from small-town Ohio (Defiance) and holding degrees from Wellesley and Harvard, Judy drove a dark blue sports car with personalized license plates and owned a piano, both of which seemed incredibly glamorous and grown-up. She did not have the intellectual airs of a Yale Law graduate, making me think (wrongly) that I was smarter than she. But she had a confident, high-roller self-presentation and a keen insight into human motivation. Judy has had a distinguished career practicing in Los Angeles as well as D.C.

At times it seemed that Williams tried to pit us against each other. He was often critical of her to me and vice versa, I'm sure. But with the ancient instincts of female friendship and our own capacities for bonding, Judy and I became true comrades. We had a long lunch at the fancy French restaurant across the street (Sans Souci) and made a pact to share information and support each other. Our relationship was enhanced because I also liked her boyfriend, Joshua Lane, her classmate from Harvard, who was working in the same building. It was not unusual for the three of us to have a late dinner together, often cooked by Judy—like a little family.

Judy and I were fortunate to have each other because the firm could be a rough place emotionally as the men fought for Williams' favor and

---

[*] Judith Richards Hope, *Pinstripes and Pearls: The Women of the Harvard Law Class of '64 Who Forged an Old Girl Network and Paved the Way for Future Generations*, 171-72 (New York: Scribner, 2003).

occasionally vied for independence from him. Though neither of us was ever a contender for Ed's special friendship, we tried, not always successfully, to stay out of the way of the latest struggle among territorial males. He constantly developed new favorites, which unsettled his subordinates' expectations about the coin of current regard—lunch invitations and Redskins tickets as well as juicy assignments.

Williams was very taken with Michael Tigar, who came to the firm a few months before I left. Tigar had been a top student at Berkeley and a leader of the Free Speech movement. Justice Brennan had offered him a clerkship but began to worry about the political fallout from having such a radical in Supreme Court chambers. Reneging on his offer, the Justice called Williams and persuaded him to hire Tigar. In his memoir, Mike noted that Judy and I were not part of the inner circle: "Ed could not see either of these good lawyers in the same way that he did the males."* No kidding.

Despite his liberality in hiring Judy and me, Ed had a deep prejudice against women as trial lawyers. He attributed this attitude to the clients, claiming they would never tolerate a woman lawyer. That did not prove true in my experience, representing as I eventually did all kinds of accused people: rich and poor, ignorant and educated, old and young, men and women, white and black. They were all satisfied if their lawyer worked hard and kept them informed of their options.

I learned a lot with Williams and saw a part of life and practice that was entirely foreign to me. I'm glad I was able to spend two years absorbing the basics with a true master, and I hold Edward Bennett Williams in grateful memory for hiring me when he did.

---

* Michael E. Tigar, *Fighting Injustice*, 70 (Chicago: Am. Bar Ass'n, 2003).

5

MOB MEMORIES (1964-1966)

"Icepick Willie," "Milwaukee Phil," "Charlie the Blade," and my special favorite, "Joe the Possum" were the aliases of some of our clients at the Williams firm. Not only nicknames but certain images come to mind when I recall those days, like the ankle-deep purple carpets in the Miami home of Santo Trafficante, Jr., ("one of the last of the old-time reputed Mafia dons"*) and the icy stare of Marshall Caifano one freezing day in Chicago.

In my two years at the firm, I didn't represent anyone from the "straight" world, as our clients called it. And few of them were local, which meant a lot of travel between D. C. and places like Miami, Chicago, and Las Vegas. Previously I had flown only once in my life, so setting off on several business flights a month made me feel incredibly worldly. Ed Williams directed that we always go "first cabin" because that impressed our clients. With my mother I would plan my travel outfit, heels and tailored dresses or suits carried me from the runway to a business meeting or fancy restaurant.

I made several splendid trips to Houston on the firm's behalf, leaving from Dulles Airport, then only two years old and an architectural wonder. Designed by Eero Saarinen, the building itself seemed poised for flight; the light pouring through the vast windows was uplifting. I flew on Braniff, whose colorful planes and stewardess (sic) uniforms were designed by Gucci to match. Breakfast was served on white linen with real silverware, fresh-squeezed orange juice, and champagne. I would read the *Washing-*

---

* Obituary, *New York Times*, March 19, 1987.

ton Post and watch the country spread out below.

Upon arrival in Houston, I would hail a cab to meet with our client, a bookmaker, in the dimness of a nightclub in daytime. We would consult for several hours over lunch, ensconced in a crimson-plush-upholstered booth. My sole task was to reassure him that the firm was busily at work on his case. After lunch, I would take another glamorous flight back to Dulles. It did not feel like work.

For much of the time that I was with Williams, I lived in an apartment right off DuPont Circle on Connecticut Ave. It was the place I had imagined in my long-harbored dreams of living alone. The door opened to a beautiful large room, with crimson carpets, bamboo-weave wallpaper, and high sky-lights; the bedroom overlooked Massachusetts Avenue. I was told that the author Tom Wolfe had lived there and chosen the rugs and bamboo paper.

I walked the nine blocks to and from the Williams firm at 17th and K. twice a day. At night, I played the news and folk music as loud as I wished, sank into my lounge chair with a glass of gin and read for pleasure: no one was waiting or needed anything from me. The whole world was closed out or closed in by simply shutting the front door. My phone did not even have an answering machine.

Moreover, the rent was reasonable because for all its attractions, the apartment was up three narrow flights and above a bar. The door at the bottom of the stairs opened right on to Connecticut Avenue, and early one Sunday morning, I stepped out to see Earl Warren walking by only a few feet away. "Good morning, Mr. Chief Justice," I said and he gave me his sweet grandfatherly look, tipped his hat, and strode on. The serendipity thrilled me—something that could only happen when living in Washington, D.C.

And it was my singular experience, like so much of my life in this period: walking from Dupont Circle to Farragut Square and back several times a day; going to galleries and the ballet; partying with old friends and making new ones all the time. I was dating two attractive men, both lawyers, both fun in different ways, neither wanting to give or receive any kind of commitment, which made it easy to manage dual affairs. I felt I was living the Wordsworth poem I had quoted in my high school graduation speech.

> Bliss was it in that dawn to be alive.
> But to be young was very heaven.

I even liked the hard, emotionally wearing work that preceded our cases in court. Pretrial, Ed went into an altered state: he suspended the hard drinking that was his custom (and that of most trial lawyers), started regularly exercising, and focused intensely. He left nothing to chance or improvisation, and from the master, I learned how to create a theory of the case and fit the facts into it at every stage.

Besides writing pretrial motions challenging the indictments on various constitutional and technical grounds (there always seemed to be some), one of my main contributions was client relations. With a few exceptions, Williams did not much like our mob clients or even find them interesting. He collected astronomical fees for his work and gave unparalleled representation. But he seldom explained his tactics to them or held their hands.

That was *my* job, and it was never more memorable than in our defense of Chuckie Delmonico, son of Charlie "The Blade" Tourine. Chuckie said he had spontaneously changed his name from Tourine to Delmonico one night when the police threw him against an alley wall and demanded his identification. Looking up, his eyes lit upon the glowing neon of the famous steakhouse he had been headed to in lower Manhattan.

Chuckie was charged with robbing a bank in Evansville, Indiana. His father had referred him to the firm, assuring us that "Chuckie don't have the guts to rob a bank." "The Blade" knew what it took because he had knocked over a few banks in his day. I noted the father-son rivalry, but it did not occur to me that Chuckie might actually be factually innocent of the crime. I had already internalized the creed that the client deserves an effective defense whether innocent or not. My duty was to uphold the Constitution by forcing the government to prove guilt by lawful evidence beyond a reasonable doubt.

Nevertheless, in talking to Chuckie over the next months, I was struck by his outrage at the indictment, not a usual attitude among our clients who mostly took criminal charges as a cost of doing business. He kept saying, "I've never even *been* in Evansville, Indiana." But of course he had been to Chicago, not far away, and he was involved in betting and bookmaking on sports, which could easily have taken him to the college basketball hotbed of Evansville. Nevertheless, as the weeks passed and I got to know him better, I became convinced that though Chuckie Delmonico was not a virtuous man, he had not robbed the Evansville bank.

Yet arguing factual innocence was not necessarily going to win for Chuckie. No jury was likely to take to him, with his lengthy criminal record and thuggish swagger. To prosecutors, he was equally unappealing and was unlikely to be a persuasive candidate for dismissal of charges. Even if he hadn't robbed the bank, he had committed plenty of crimes in the course of his work which regularly included loansharking and extortion. But the victims of those crimes were usually not available to testify, whereas eleven witnesses swore that the man who had robbed them at gunpoint was Charles Tourine, Jr., a/k/a Chuckie Delmonico. The police had not recovered fingerprints, weapons, or cash, but the sworn testimony of nearly a dozen upstanding citizens with no motive to lie would convict in most courtrooms.

Somehow we had to find a way to bolster Chuckie's credibility. Also on the case was Peter Taft, another recent law graduate who was a Williams favorite. I'm not sure which of us came up with the idea of trying to prove Chuckie's veracity scientifically, but I executed it. We started with a lie detector test. Though polygraph results are not usually admitted into evidence, such tests were—and still are—widely used in criminal investigations as interrogation tools and by prosecutors in deciding whether to bring or to drop charges.

The test is based on the fact that many, perhaps most, people betray a physiological response when they lie about important matters—increased heart rate or sweating, for instance—which can be measured and charted. With electrodes attached to his body, the subject is hooked up to a machine that produces a continuous graph of his body's responses to questions. A specially trained operator deciphers the graph, and in the hands of a skilled interrogator, the polygraph has undoubtedly scared a lot of people into telling the truth.

The test's scientific validity is contested, however, and numerous studies point out that a sociopath may be a cool liar without the usual physical symptoms, and that a truthful but nervous subject can produce false signs of deception. But in Chuckie's case the question to be put to him was straightforward and not likely to have accrued guilty associations that would skew the results: Had he ever been to Evansville? Yes or no? It was the perfect circumstance in which to use a lie detector. We planned to offer Chuckie for testing by a government operator, but we had him examined privately first. He passed with flying colors while I watched through a one-way mirror.

Next we turned to narcoanalysis, where the subject is questioned in a semiconscious state after being injected with "truth serum," i.e., sodium pentothal. The free-form uncontrollable responses the test can generate make this a potentially risky proposition for a criminal defendant. Again, we ran through a private preview of the procedure with our own hired doctor, which Chuckie again passed on the Evansville question while confessing to a number of other crimes.

Meanwhile, the trial date was drawing near, and we were filing our pretrial motions. We argued that the flaws inherent in eyewitness identification required that such testimony be corroborated, and we produced memoranda contending that the unusual circumstances of the case justified making an exception to the evidence rules excluding lie detector and truth serum results. We prepared alibi witnesses from Miami, where Chuckie claimed he was on the date of the robbery, and developed our strategy for undermining the eyewitness testimony.

Our theory was that the bank president had seen Chuckie's picture in a Chicago paper, had become convinced he was the robber, and had influenced his employees to make the same identification. The prosecution's original eleven eyewitnesses actually boiled down to only one: the bank president who had, wittingly or not, manipulated ten others. (I used this same defense in a multiple-witness robbery of a beauty parlor several years later.)

Ed Williams and Peter Taft went to Evansville early, leaving Chuckie and me to paperwork and witness preparation in the east. The federal prosecutors in Indiana sneered at the claims of innocence. But Williams went over their heads to Attorney General Nicholas Katzenbach himself. Somehow he convinced Katzenbach that a miscarriage of justice would occur unless he intervened: the Attorney General agreed to drop the charges if Delmonico passed narcoanalysis administered by a doctor of Katzenbach's choice.

By then it was the eve of trial. The doctor whom Katzenbach had selected was affiliated with a state mental hospital in New Jersey. Williams called me and said to get Chuckie there pronto. Chuckie borrowed what he promised was a reliable Rolls Royce, and we set out early the next morning. The car certainly looked impressive, but once we reached freeway speed, the doors started popping open, sometimes one at a time, sometimes all four at once. Chuckie laughed; I was terrified. All I could think was that I was about to perish on the New Jersey Turnpike in the company of a two-bit hood.

I was quivering with anxiety by the time we rolled into the mental hospital's parking lot. But we met the doctor at the appointed hour. We had established ground rules in advance for the questions and the test was audio-taped. Only the doctor and I were present with Chuckie, who quickly went under to the "truth serum," as he had in our private test of him. But this time instead of bragging about his various crimes, he started to free-associate about his sexual fantasies. This was fine with me until suddenly he said, "I'm in love with my lawyer. I want to fuck her so bad— she has a big ass, but I like that" and more in this vein. Every time the doctor tried to bring him back to Evansville, there would be a similar outburst.

"Chuckie," I intervened urgently, "tell us about Evansville, Indiana." He said, "I don't know, I never been there, but I think my lawyer is going," and off he'd start again about his desire for my body. Yes I was embarrassed but, hey, it was also pretty funny. The doctor thought so, too, and we worked together to steer Chuckie toward more relevant truths under the serum's spell.

It took about an hour for the doctor to satisfy himself that Charles Delmonico had never been to Evansville, Indiana—where Chuckie and I then flew the weekend before the trial was scheduled to start. Williams now had Attorney General Katzenbach's word that he would order the case dismissed on Monday morning. Meanwhile, the media were watching with some puzzlement the famous out-of-town lawyer and his entourage—we were spending most of our time in Evansville's better bars.

And indeed, on the first day of trial, the prosecutors got a command from the Attorney General to dismiss the Delmonico indictment. They were shocked and angry that a case they believed in had been squelched from above. The bank president's reaction was a succinct: "It stinks." Ed Williams's biographer used the case to illustrate the good relations Williams enjoyed with the Justice Department during the Johnson administration.[*]

As a neophyte lawyer, I hardly knew what to make of it all: months of preparation on both sides, followed by a low-comical interrogation under

---

[*] Evan Thomas, *The Man to See: Edward Bennett Williams, Ultimate Insider; Legendary Trial Lawyer*, 194-95 (New York: Simon & Schuster, 1991).

drugs in a New Jersey mental hospital, culminating in a public result in Indiana that had been hatched away from the public eye in Washington, D.C. It hardly presented an illuminating picture of the criminal justice system, and the outcome had established no precedent for the wrongly accused. On the other hand, cases against innocent men *should* be dismissed rather than tried, and no corruption was involved.

Fifty years later, I'm still not sure what to think. On a personal level, I felt sympathetic toward Chuckie because of his brutal upbringing, which left him without a chance to be much better than he was. The truth-serum tale became part of my permanent repertoire, and what I learned about the vagaries of eyewitness identification served me well later in representing poor clients who had no private channel to the Attorney General. Another man was eventually convicted of the Evansville robbery, and I don't know, but I would bet he resembled Chuckie.

Delmonico himself was successfully prosecuted for other crimes, and he died in the federal penitentiary in Atlanta while serving a long sentence. I don't think I saw him again after we left Evansville the day the case was dismissed. His father, Charlie "The Blade," continued to come around the firm because he was a co-indictee of another of our clients, Joe Nesline.

Among the mobsters I met while working for Williams, Joe was my favorite, partly because he really admired my lawyering skills. While newspapers designated him "The Boss of D.C." and alleged that he had ties to New York's Genovese crime family, Joe maintained he was an honest gambler and "gaming consultant"; he said his tables were fair and that he paid off when he lost. Joe loved high-stakes play at one-on-one card games and craps, but he also bet on sports and just about anything else. He was a local, and though at times his business extended to Las Vegas, Antigua, London, and Dubrovnik, his base was the District of Columbia, where he was known and felt comfortable.

Like many of his associates, Joe had started out running liquor during Prohibition, bringing rye and bourbon from the stills of southern Maryland into the District. It was a lucrative business and a dangerous one. When I knew him, he was on daily medication to control seizures resulting from a head injury he had sustained decades before, crashing a car full of booze in a high-speed chase.

Also early in his career, Joe had killed a man, another gambler, shot in a Georgetown restaurant in front of onlookers, at least some of whom supported Joe's claim of self-defense. He had hired the best criminal defense lawyer in D.C. at the time, Charlie Ford, and won an acquittal on the murder charge but was convicted of carrying a gun; there was no way around that. In a long life lived over the line, the year Joe served on that gun charge was his only prison sentence for a criminal conviction, though he did languish for some months in a Miami jail on a civil contempt-of-court citation for refusing to testify before a grand jury.

Joe told a story of his defense in the murder case that I could never quite understand, though I heard it many times. The lawyer had a special suit of clothing made for a winning demonstration—of what? That the deceased had carried a weapon? Had drawn first? I took from the tale not the sartorial details but Joe's gratitude for his lawyer's effort. Such understanding appreciation for attorneys was not typical of organized crime figures, who did not always value the motions we filed, the appellate points laid into the record, and the long hours spent in preparation.

They preferred the quick "fix" they imagined would follow from bribing the decision makers or intimidating the witnesses. Joe told me about mob lawyers who took money meant to bribe the judge and kept it for themselves on top of their fees, claiming, when they lost the case, that the judge would not "stay bought." Crooked lawyers could get away with it because mob clients were generally uneducated and ignorant about the actual workings of the system. They did not realize that the American judiciary is strikingly honest: judges may be biased or rude or stupid, but they are almost never corrupt.

Williams could not personally represent all the clients who retained the firm. He tried to pass the cases on to his associates, but often the clients resisted. It was a matter of pride for them to have the top attorney, and since they had paid for Williams, they demanded his services. But Joe Nesline, perhaps because he understood what was involved in good lawyering and saw that he was getting it, readily accepted the hand-off to Vince Fuller and me.

Vince was one of the first to become an associate of Williams. He was a superb trial lawyer, businesslike and sincere, and had a magnificent voice. He did not share Williams' prejudice against women speaking to judge and jury, and he gave me several opportunities to do so. In our two gambling trials for Joe Nesline, Vince and I won an acquittal in one and a hung jury in the other, after which the prosecution was dropped.

One of the trials had to do with a casino on the Eastern Shore of Maryland, the other with the glossy Amber Club within blocks of the

Capitol, said to be popular with members of Congress. My main job was to prepare Joe to take the stand. It was Williams' view, which I came to share, that the accused should always testify if he possibly could do so without perjuring or otherwise incriminating himself.

Jurors want to hear the defendant deny the charge under oath, and even if his story is far-fetched, seeing and hearing him might dispose them toward sympathy and hence toward finding a reasonable doubt. I have spent many hours preparing clients who did not ultimately testify because there was a guilty plea or some other outcome (as with Chuckie Delmonico). Joe Nesline was the first client I represented who actually took the stand. He gave me the credit for his star performance.

My job was to help Joe present his best self—to ease up on his slick wise-guy persona and bring out his Rotarian charm. He had it in him to appeal to a wide social range, including the middle-class blacks who were likely to be on the jury. Joe was at ease with African Americans, and I heard later that he had a good reputation among black gamblers, partly because he had used his influence to keep organized crime out of the local numbers game. In D.C., people from all walks of life participated in this form of illegal gambling. Nesline, for instance, played a number every day, like his mother and grandmother before him. So did many of my clients at the Public Defender. (Once or twice I tried to show that sudden prosperity suggesting theft actually resulted from hitting the number, but found that there were no records or witnesses to subpoena for proof of the number and what it paid, or for that matter of who won on any day.)

When Joe heard that Chuckie Delmonico's indictment had been dismissed, he wanted to take a lie detector test, too. I explained that the facts in his case were more "nuanced" and that even if he passed, we probably couldn't use it. But Joe liked long shots. He took a test successfully, though we suspected the operator may have fudged the result to please the Williams firm. We did not try to introduce the test or even mention its existence to the prosecutor. But when Joe was being fiercely cross-examined about the conflict between his testimony and that of the key government witness, there was this exchange:

Joe: I took a lie detector test; he didn't.

Prosecutor: Oh, did your lawyers arrange that?

Joe: They did.

Prosecutor (sneering): So they didn't believe you either.

Joe (calmly): Now they do.

The jurors swiveled as one to look at Vince and me at counsel table, and we knew we had scored.

I handled my first criminal appeal while I was working for Ed Williams, and on my own, I devised the theory, wrote the brief, made the oral argument, and lost the case—though in some ways, it turned out to be a victory. Here's how it happened. The D.C. Circuit Court of Appeals had appointed a partner in our firm to represent an indigent appellant. The partner proposed to file a motion claiming that his study of the record had revealed no valid grounds for appeal.

An obviously torn Williams called me in and asked my opinion. Apparently he suspected his partner of trying to get out of the case because he was busy and did not like appellate work, and Ed was afraid the firm might be criticized for inadequate representation in an appointed matter. I think he wanted me to sign off on the conclusion that there were no legitimate appellate points. But we both knew that there would be some for a paying client. Moreover, I had seen so many mistaken rulings in trials of indigent defendants when I was clerking for Judge Edgerton that I claimed I could find reversible error in any trial transcript.

The client, James McCoy, had been accused of unauthorized use of an automobile—joy riding. The government had put on its proof in just a couple of hours. It came in as a weak case, and the prosecutor offered McCoy a plea to a charge even less severe than joy riding: taking property without right, a misdemeanor carrying a maximum six-month jail sentence.

Because McCoy had already served that much time awaiting trial he jumped at the chance to plead. But in answering the questions the judge was required to ask before accepting such a plea, McCoy refused to admit guilt. He said he had merely been sitting in the car awaiting a ride home from a friend, a common defense to joy riding. His insistence on his innocence while trying to get the benefit of the reduced penalty seemed to have infuriated the judge, the prosecutor, and McCoy's appointed lawyer. The judge rejected the guilty plea, the trial resumed, and McCoy was convicted and sentenced to serve eight months to three years in prison—his first felony conviction and likely to set him on a familiar, tragic path for a poor black man in D.C.

It was the holiday season when I got involved in the case, and just as I would for a paying client, I turned first to getting McCoy out of jail pending his appeal. The trial judge had set a $1,000 bond, then reduced it to $500 in response to a motion that McCoy himself had filed without a lawyer. I worked up a quick motion to have him released on his own recognizance, pointing to his lack of a prior criminal record and his substantial family ties in the District.

It would have been faster and easier to get a professional bondsman, but they would not write it because of the belief that "once a man has actually served some of his time in prison . . .he will, [if his appeal is unsuccessful] flee the jurisdiction."* The "taste of jail" standard was one of a number of the unofficial guides to bond setting in the District. A star-studded panel decided McCoy's fate for the holidays. My friend and mentor Chief Judge Bazelon was one; Judge Harold Leventhal wrote the opinion granting McCoy a bond "to be signed by [him] and any two of his close relatives—mother, father, grandfather, two aunts."†

The judge pointed out the injustice here when "the appellant is young, is not 'well known' to [the bondsman] through past involvements, and offers only modest opportunity for gain due to the low amount of the bond."‡ And so, on the late afternoon of December 31, 1965, I met McCoy in the clerk's office of the D.C. Circuit Court of Appeals, where he signed for his release and his relatives took him home to celebrate the New Year.

In the following months, I wrote a brief raising what was then a novel point: that an indigent accused should have the same opportunity as a rich defendant to enter a plea without admitting guilt. For corporate executives it was called a plea of *nolo contendere* ("I will not contest"), that is, I accept the consequences but do not admit guilt. I had thought about the benefits of a nolo plea when writing my Note for the law journal back at school, and now I was trying to obtain some of those for James McCoy.

I acknowledged that the judge was not required to accept such a special plea but maintained that he had abused his discretion by not exercising it in this case; instead he forced McCoy to confess guilt or proceed with the trial. Though Williams didn't say it to me, I heard that he thought my argument was stupid and therefore refused to put his name on the brief. I orally argued McCoy's appeal on March 23, 1966, in front of another three-

---

* *McCoy v. United States*, 357 F.2d 272, 272-73 (D.C. Cir. 1966).

† *Id.*

‡ *Id.* (citations omitted).

judge panel, this one led by Bazelon, who dissented from the opinion denying the appeal.[*]

Nevertheless, I've always counted the case to be a personal victory. In the first place, McCoy used his time out of jail while the appeal was pending to get a job and get married. I moved to reduce the sentence, and he pled guilty to a misdemeanor and was sentenced to time served. Second, just four years later, the United States Supreme Court in *North Carolina v. Alford*[†] decided a case that largely mirrored my reasoning about the right of defendants to take responsibility without admitting factual guilt. My appeal for McCoy was cited by both the majority and the dissent in *Alford* in their discussions of how lower courts had dealt with the issue. Today such pleas are commonly accepted in state and federal courts.

The McCoy case added to my growing doubts about working at the Williams firm. Nothing I did for the paying clients compared with the thrill of freeing James McCoy on New Year's Eve. And I had done it alone, using my skills on behalf of a person who had never before had the services of a real and passionate lawyer. As the months went by, I could see fewer chances for repetition of the McCoy experience within the firm. I wanted my own clients and my own cases.

It was time to move on.

---

[*] *McCoy v. United States*, 363 F.2d 306, 308 (D.C. Cir. 1966).

[†] 400 U.S. 25 (1970).

6

Precious Freedom: Favorite Cases (1966-1968)

Things did not go smoothly in my last days at the firm. I felt that I was doing good work, but Williams seemed unaware of it. Like a couple in a disintegrating marriage, we hardly spoke for weeks on end. The rumor was that he wanted to change the character of the place, cutting back on the organized crime and turning to white collar and political corruption cases, as well as expanding the non-criminal trial work. He was negotiating with Paul Connolly, who was a partner at a prominent civil law firm, and shortly after I left, the law firm of Williams and Connolly was born.

I was ready to make my move, but things were in turmoil at the place where I was set on going next: the Legal Aid Agency. Gary Bellow, the Agency's compelling leader for whom I had wanted to work for more than two years, had left to secure civil services for the indigent in the War on Poverty. With the passion and arrogant certainty of youth, I accused him of betrayal because there was so much still to do on the criminal side. But betrayal is in the eye of the beholder, and looking back, I see that Ed Williams may have thought I was a traitor when he heard I was planning to leave without having consulted him in advance.

In my naïveté about how D.C. operated, I did not realize that he would know immediately that I had applied to Legal Aid. The new director was on the phone to inform the great man almost before I was out the door after the job interview. Williams was furious, and when I went to tell him my plan, he said, "If you're going ['There is no *if*,' I wanted to shout], leave now. Get out. Don't hang around." I was in the midst of drafting a complicated petition for certiorari to the Supreme Court, the holiday season was upon us, and the yearly bonus was due, so that was a harsh fare-thee-well.

I finished the petition, packed up, and left without seeing Williams again—and without the bonus. But I did hear later that he subsequently had spoken well of me; this was confirmed by his FBI interview in 1977 when I was nominated to be Assistant Attorney General during the Carter administration. At that point, he said I had done a great job and had left the firm because I could not get the litigation experience I desired given the clients' preference for male lawyers. At any rate, the bitterness of the parting, though I recall it vividly, did not really dim the excitement I felt at starting my true career: defending poor people who had never had a real lawyer.

The Legal Aid Agency was located in the back streets of the courthouse neighborhood. On some early mornings, I would find a man passed out over the heating grate near the front door. Once, he was clutching a broken roll of Life Savers mints in his outstretched hand, apparently his last futile effort to mask the liquor on his breath. My desk was in a windowless passageway that two other lawyers traversed to get to their shared office: no privacy, no quiet, and no view. The luxurious offices of the Williams firm on Farragut Square, though only a dozen blocks away, seemed very distant.

The spirit and enthusiasm that originally had drawn me to the Agency was considerably dampened by Gary Bellow's departure, and the office was in a kind of uproar with people coming and going. The director, Charlie Murray, had left, too. The new director, Ken Woods, was, as Murray had been, a local criminal defense lawyer with a good reputation; Addison Bowman, one of Gary's protégés, had taken Gary's place as the deputy.

Both Murray and Woods came from a group of lawyers known as Fifth Streeters (their offices were near the bail bond agencies and the misdemeanor courts on Fifth Street). These lawyers were the backbone of the D.C. criminal defense bar, picking up court appointments for the indigent as well as paying cases. Theirs were not the high publicity, big criminal matters, but many of them made a decent living at the work.

Some good lawyers among the Fifth Streeters prepared their cases well. But too many were hacks, who took advantage of their clients' ignorance and routinely pled them guilty without doing much, if anything, to prepare a defense. It was rare for a Fifth Streeter to file something as basic as a motion to suppress evidence, or indeed to file any motions at all.

A few blocks from the local misdemeanor court was the federal courthouse, which housed trial courts and the D.C. Circuit Court of Appeals. Felonies, including violations of the D.C. Code for common-law crimes such as rape, robbery, and murder, as well as federal crimes, were tried in that more august setting. Because there was not a true local court system at that time, the federal courts thus served as the equivalent of primary state courts for the District.

Federal judges' desire for improvement in the quality of defense lawyering in their courtrooms was one motive behind founding the Legal Aid Agency in 1960. Most of the judges wanted an efficient organization that would guarantee that (the few) possibly innocent defendants would be adequately defended, given a fair trial or have charges dropped, and that the rest would be persuaded to plead guilty. They were not looking for crusaders dedicated to due process and a fair trial for every accused person who wanted to contest the charges.

Legal Aid's new director did not have that in mind either. His major goals were to please the judges and to help the courts run smoothly. He also was unwilling to leave hiring and training of new attorneys to deputy director Addison Bowman, as had been the arrangement when Gary Bellow was in that position. Within months, Bowman resigned to teach at Georgetown Law School and run the clinical E. Barrett Prettyman Program, which trained attorneys to teach and practice criminal law. (Addison had been a Prettyman Fellow himself.)

This left a vacuum in leadership and a public defense agency facing an uncertain future. As uneasy as I felt about the scene, I resolved to throw myself into the trial work for which I had come rather than try just then to reform my new world. There were still good lawyers at Legal Aid who could advise me and plenty of meaty cases to try.

My first victory on my own, rather than as the second chair and unsung motion writer I had been with Williams, was especially sweet. It was the moment I had been waiting for, all my life as it seemed to me: a jury of twelve, the judge on the high bench, fate in my hands, and freedom in the balance. The scene was very different from when I had gone to court with Williams. Then, with spectator seats packed, the press gallery filled, and extra marshals present to manage the crowd, the great lawyer, surrounded by his attractive acolytes, towered over the whole scene.

By contrast, my rather small client and I were alone at an immense mahogany table, and we had only one spectator: Joe Nesline, my favorite Williams client, sitting in the back row where he stayed for the whole trial. By noon of the first day, though, the rest of the seats had filled up, and I learned that word had spread on the street that "The Boss of D.C." (as Joe was known) was observing the trial, resulting in an SRO crowd trying to find out what was going on that was so special.

My client, a young African American man, had been arrested in an alley near a silver Jaguar he was allegedly taking apart. The charges were grand theft of an automobile and a few added counts of dismantling it to sell the parts. Our defense had to do with the police having lost the incriminating tools they said had been near the car. With full-throated passion for victory, I pleaded with the jury for a verdict for me and for my client. That night Joe Nesline was recorded on Mafia wiretaps bragging that the "girl lawyer got the little n***** off."

My first case was not the only one that Joe attended. He stayed in touch, followed my career, and became central to a plan I was hatching to start a firm with a few like-minded defense lawyers. I envisioned a kind of Robin Hood practice where we would represent Joe and his friends for hefty fees and the indigent accused for free.

In the interim between leaving the firm and starting at Legal Aid I had a taste of the kind of business Joe might generate. He asked me to handle a contract for the promotion and training of a fighter he liked, Bobby Foster. Joe felt he had been mismanaged and had bought out his previous contract. Having never previously drawn a contract, I enlisted my father's help, and the business was done in his office in Maryland.

Several years later, I found myself at ringside at Madison Square Garden, standing on a chair screaming "Kill him! Kill him!" as Foster fought Dick Tiger for the light heavyweight title. Our man won, and afterwards we partied with Bobby and Joe at Dempsey's, a famous New York sporting bar and restaurant. Recently I heard from a man who is writing an "as-told-to" story of Foster's life. There is a chapter about Nesline which mentions my role and says: "She was one of the best lawyers in all of D.C., and she had helped Joe stay out of a lot of trouble."

My dream of starting a Robin Hood firm faded as I turned into a whole-hearted public defender. I don't have a record of all the indigent criminal defendants I represented, and only a few transcripts survive from cases I lost that were appealed. But I remember many of the trials, especially those I won—and I won a lot. Over my years of teaching criminal procedure, I've told and retold the stories, which survive emblazoned on my brain and in my class notes.

Of course, I pled many people guilty, too—including some whose cases I thought I could win with a jury. But those were often the cases where the prosecutor offered a great bargain and my client wanted to take it. I always felt a little sick when a client with a plausible defense pled guilty, no matter how good the deal. He faced years in prison without the hope, consolation, and distraction of an appeal or a *habeas corpus* petition.

Pleading guilty was hard and oddly enough, so was representing a client who was factually innocent. I don't mean someone with a credible defense, but one who simply had nothing to do with the crime. Such cases were rare and tended to look just like those of guilty defendants. Victims and eyewitnesses swore he had done it; he said he had spent the night with his grandmother or his girlfriend, at a bar or a birthday party.

Twice I went to trial with accused armed robbers whom I believed were totally innocent, though my efforts to convince the prosecutor to drop the indictments were unsuccessful. In one case, I was able to destroy the credibility of the eyewitness identification on cross-examination. At the close of the government's case, the judge abruptly ordered the surprised jurors to stand, told them what to say, and then asked for their verdict. "Not guilty," they murmured in unison. That was the only time I ever won a motion for a directed verdict or, indeed, saw one happen.

The case of my other alleged armed robber went all the way to an actual jury verdict. The government's witnesses had been convincing, and my client's alibi was not well delivered by his frightened Haitian-immigrant family. I was not allowed to tell the jury that of all the people I had ever represented, Ernest was the only one I was certain had had nothing to do with the crime. Lawyers may not express their opinions of the evidence in the case (a rule prosecutors often violate).

Usually I approached summation with the calming private thought that losing would not result in terrible injustice. But in this case I was so nervous that I spilled a pitcher of water in the lap of my pink suit and had to conceal it by standing immobile behind the podium. We won, but some-how, securing acquittal for an innocent man seemed a lesser triumph than most of my jury victories. So yes, ego can be a more powerful motivator than the love of fairness.

One of my most satisfying wins was in the case of another Ernest, this one charged with second degree murder. He was a sanitation worker, twenty-five years old, a D.C. native, who had never been arrested until the day his opponent in a street fight died. Their altercation had started in a bar, where Ernest had stopped after work. He had driven a new collection route that day, and was unfamiliar with the neighborhood, so he did not realize until well inside that he was the only black patron.

But it was a hot day, and he had been working hard and was thirsty. Ernest ordered and paid for a beer, and then went to the rest room, and upon his return found a large white man drinking it. The bartender refused to give him another one, and told him to get out; the atmosphere felt menacing and Ernest reluctantly departed. His testimony was that the beer thief followed him outside and struck him hard on the back. Whirling around, he hit the man, who fell to the sidewalk and died. Several witnesses told the police that Ernest had delivered a powerful karate chop to the victim's head; Ernest swore he did not know karate.

I started investigating how it could happen that the victim died from a single blow. When I showed the coroner's report to a neurosurgeon friend, he said it indicated that the deceased suffered from hydrocephaly, water on the brain, a congenital condition with a negative effect on the temperament, making many hydrocephalics angry and aggressive. Next, I subpoenaed the deceased's Army records, and learned that he had been dishonorably discharged for a number of unprovoked assaults on fellow soldiers. Our approach—my favorite in a self-defense case—was now set: in the celebrated formula of the famous Texas criminal defense lawyer Racehorse Haynes: did the deceased deserve to die, and was my client the right person to kill him?

We were sent out to trial before Judge Gerhard Gesell, who had left a partnership in a prestigious D.C. firm for the federal trial bench and who sometimes seemed to view criminal cases from the mean streets as beneath him. But he perked up when I put the neurosurgeon on the witness stand; the doctor testified about hydrocephaly and said that the blow Ernest had struck would not have killed a normal person, thus negating malice, the critical element of second-degree murder.

The high point of the defense presentation was Ernest's testimony. When I asked him if he had noticed anything unusual about the deceased, he said, with his deep accent, "Yes, ma'am. He had a big haid [gesturing]." A pause, and he looked up at Judge Gesell and added, "Like the jedge."

The jury roared because the judge did have a disproportionately large head, and was also quite irritable. Indeed he was irritated by the unintentional joke at his expense.

He also saw that we were going to win unless the somewhat charmless prosecutor got some help. Overnight, the judge decided that he would instruct the jury on a theory of misdemeanor manslaughter modeled on the felony murder rule, which holds that the evil intent to commit a serious crime, say, armed robbery, can carry over to a death resulting from the incident even if the defendant did not intend to kill. By analogy to Ernest's case, his intent to assault the beer thief could make the victim's death into the less serious degree of homicide that is manslaughter.

The judge was beaming and seemed to think he deserved accolades for his acumen, but he did not get them from me. I believed he should have been a neutral referee and suspected that he would not have stepped in to shore up a defendant's case in the same way. Mainly, I was worried because now everything rested on our ability to prove self-defense, which would negate the criminality even of the assault. I had not been able to locate anyone to back up Ernest's word that the dead man was the aggressor.

Closing argument was my forte and though I had been giving all kinds of speeches since girlhood, nothing compared to the thrill of talking to a jury. In D.C., the prosecutor spoke first, and also last in rebuttal. The defense had only one chance. In my first trial, Judge Bryant's marshal, a kindly older man, who had watched over many sitting juries, advised me: "Be sure to tell them that you are not allowed to answer the prosecutor's rebuttal. I have heard many jurors comment that the defense failed to respond to a critical point." With that advice I developed my signature closing argument.

I told the jury "this is my last opportunity to address you on behalf of my client, (insert defendant's full name). The prosecutor, if he wishes, may attempt to respond to what I say, but I cannot answer him. This is not only because arguments must come to an end, which lawyers might never reach on their own, but because the government bears the very heavy burden of proof in a criminal case, and is given every opportunity to meet it, including speaking first and last."

Then I would launch into a definition of reasonable doubt, the greatest weapon in the arsenal of the defense, and tell the jury that there were many grounds for doubt in this case. Looking each of the twelve in the eye,

I would give him or her a specific reason to carry back to deliberations—one I thought from my observations of them would appeal to the particular juror. Twelve reasons, any one of which would be grounds for acquittal, but when taken together ... and so forth. I started planning possible reasonable doubt examples from the first client interview.

By the time I stood before the jury in a case, I was consumed with the uncomplicated atavistic desire to win. I wooed them like a lover, whose heart they would break by the wrong decision. Referring always to "my client," I used his full name, and used it often, pleading not for mercy, justice, or a fair verdict, but for the words "not guilty."

Unlike some clients who were buoyed by my rhetorical skills, Ernest took them for granted and seemed largely unaware of his peril. While I paced the halls, he calmly planned his next day's work schedule. After a few hours, the jury returned—that most dramatic moment—and the judge directed Ernest to stand and face them: Not guilty of second degree murder; not guilty of manslaughter; not guilty of assault. At that point Ernest gave a little bow to the twelve in the box and said simply: "Thank you very much, ladies and gentlemen. I really appreciate that." Never before or since have I seen a client do that. He walked out of the court-house a free man.

As I tell it, the case may appear to be the slam-dunk Ernest apparently considered it. But it was not that easy. A black man had killed an unarmed white man on the street. White flight from the nation's capital because of the crime rate was the source of much political handwringing at that time, a concern reflected in prosecutors' charging decisions and sometimes in jury verdicts. Ernest might have been charged differently or even not at all if the deceased had been a black man with a criminal record.

Most poor people accused of crime in D.C.—my clients—were black, and so were many crime victims. Most judges and lawyers, court personnel, and even the police were white, as were a majority of other government employees. Though the city's racial composition and job distribution gave a colonial feel to the courthouse, they made for wonderfully integrated juries, probably more so than anywhere else in the entire country. I loved those D.C. jury pools because they always contained blacks who understood the subtexts, for instance, how rare it was that Ernest, growing up in his neighborhood, had reached manhood without a single previous arrest. In addition, plenty of white women government workers, who were especially responsive to me and my arguments, were also in the mix.

For years it was common practice in many places for prosecutors to strike all or most members of the defendant's race or gender from the jury. I'm not talking about eliminating those obviously unfit—relatives and friends of the trial participants, for instance, or victims of similar crimes. The court itself often weeds out such potentially prejudiced jurors for cause. But each side has a set number of peremptory challenges in addition, enabling dismissal of jurors without stating a reason. Though the U.S. Supreme Court held in 1986 that peremptory strikes could no longer be made on the basis of race (and later, of gender),[*] it still happens frequently.

Trafficking in stereotypes also occurs when potential jurors falsely claim prejudices and beliefs that they hope will lead them to be excused. The whole process of arbitrarily selecting and excusing made me uneasy. But I was afraid not to engage in it for the sake of the client. It was, after all, his jury, and he should be satisfied with its appearance.

For rich defendants, moreover, jury selection experts and consultants are routine though Edward Bennett Williams inveighed against their use, claiming that his own instincts were superior to their so-called science. "Just put the first twelve in the box, he said. If you do your job, they will do theirs." He never tried it as far as I know, but I did once accept a jury without using any of my peremptory challenges.

It happened when I represented a woman, call her Geraldine, who was accused under a draconian federal drug law of her third offense for possessing heroin.[†] A conviction would send her to prison for twenty years with no possibility of probation or parole. Geraldine was forty-two years old, black, poor, and uneducated. During the few years of her adult life when she was not incarcerated by the state on her previous possession charges, she had been imprisoned by heroin addiction of the most awful sort.

But even for one as beleaguered as Geraldine, the general practice in D.C. was to allow a guilty plea to a local drug charge, which did not carry

---

[*] *Batson v. Kentucky*, 479 U.S. 79 (1986); *J.E.B. v. Alabama*, 511 U.S. 127 (1994).

[†] See Barbara Allen Babcock, "'Defending the Guilty' after Thirty Years," in Abbe Smith and Monroe Freedman, eds., *How Can You Represent Those People?*, 1-13 (New York: Palgrave Macmillan, 2013).

the harsh mandatory federal penalties. In this case, the prosecutor refused the usual plea. Casting about for a defense, I sent her for a mental examination. The doctors at the public hospital reported that Geraldine had a mental disease: inadequate personality. When I inquired about the symptoms of this illness, one said: "Well, she is just the most inadequate person I've ever seen." So there it was—at least a defense: a disease or defect listed in the *Diagnostic and Statistical Manual of Mental Disorders* of the day.

The case was set for trial before Judge William B. Bryant, the first African American judge on the U.S. District Court in D.C.—as he had been the first black federal prosecutor there, a job he left to become a criminal defense lawyer. Judge Bryant alone on that court fully appreciated the difficult work of a defender, and he listened to both sides with sympathy, intelligence, and, best of all, a certain enjoyment of the human predicament in which we were all enmeshed.

Drawing Judge Bryant from the random case assignment system was one of the few lucky things that had ever happened to Geraldine. To her lawyer, it felt like a form of insurance. I was sure the judge would avoid imposing the mandatory twenty years of hard time by taking the case from the jury and granting a judgment of acquittal. I knew there would be plausible grounds for his doing so because under the law at that time, once the defense presented evidence of mental disease, the burden shifted to the government to prove sanity beyond a reasonable doubt.

My confidence in the judge's compassion led me to experiment with jury selection. As soon as the first twelve potential jurors were seated, I announced, without having asked them a thing, "The defense is satisfied with this jury." That dramatic move threw the prosecutor off his game. Expecting that jury selection for an insanity defense would take some hours, he had no witnesses ready to call and only a rough opening statement in hand.

Our early tactical advantage seemed to vanish during the trial. This unselected jury just looked so bad. They were diverse enough, but regardless of race or gender, they shrugged and sneered and slept as I presented the evidence of my client's horrendous childhood and of the toll of many years of heroin addiction on her personality development. In particular, Juror #6 distressed me—a large Germanic woman with thin lips whose hair looked like it had been cut around a bowl. Every time I glanced at her, she was rolling her eyes and shaking her head.

Throughout the trial, I was fairly choking with rage at the prosecutor's refusal of the usual plea, and his willingness to send my client to prison for so many years. He claimed that she was not just a junkie but a seller and deserved a long sentence. Without actual evidence to prove his theory, he tried through his questions and insinuations to get it before the jury. At several points, I felt like slapping him and I did curse him under my breath where only he could hear. It was the angriest I have ever been in court. The only thing that sustained me was the expectation that the judge would direct the verdict. Instead, he sent the jury out to deliberate, telling me privately to "keep the faith."

Geraldine had observed the seven days of trial with only mild interest, but when after many hours of deliberation the jury returned a verdict of "not guilty by reason of insanity," she burst into tears. Throwing her arms around me, she said, "I'm so happy for you." Judge Bryant started laughing at that. He was still laughing when the Germanic juror joined Geraldine and me. "Well, we went out 11-1 for conviction, but I was finally able to bring them around," she declared.

Singlehandedly she had led the jury to see that Geraldine should have treatment, not punishment. Her eye rolls and head shakes had been indications of empathy, not hostility. Geraldine would go not to prison but to a mental hospital until she could be certified as not dangerous to herself or others—which was likely not to be very long, given that her "disease," such as it was, did not include violent tendencies.

With that verdict, I joined my hero, Judge Bryant, in believing in the ultimate wisdom of the jury and in its often mysterious deliberative process. I have written Geraldine's story as one about juries and jury selection, but it also illustrates the excitement and satisfaction of public defense as a vocation. By direct application of my skills, I saved a woman from spending the rest of her adult life in prison. In constructing her defense, I had become intimate with a life as different from my own as could be imagined, and I think Geraldine's friends and relatives who testified and who talked with me were impressed by the fact that the system had provided her with a real lawyer.

In the last analysis, however, Geraldine was right when, at the moment of the verdict, she saw that my life, too, had been saved. Her case had become my case. And it had given me what I treasured most: the unalloyed pleasure of "not guilty." In life I have found few joys so pure.

7

TAKING CHARGE:
THE D.C. PUBLIC DEFENDER SERVICE (1968-1972)

For my first two years at the Legal Aid Agency, I spent most of my time preparing to plead my clients guilty or try their felony cases in federal district court: mostly rapes, robberies, and murders. Though drugs and alcohol were often involved in what we defenders always called the "incidents," narcotics charges were not the bulk of the caseload in those days as they are in many places now. I worked without supervision or direction, but some of Gary Bellow's people were still at the Agency, and even after Addie Bowman went to teach at Georgetown, he was still nearby and available for help. Addie was a superb trial lawyer who taught me a lot about examining witnesses and, more important, encouraged me to be bold and fearless in court, which did not come naturally.

Our trial skills tutoring sessions took on another dimension when we fell in love and were married in December 1967. Judge Edgerton performed the ceremony at the Cosmos Club, which did not admit women to membership or through the front door. But in my pre-consciousness state, I hardly noticed. Similarly I did not hesitate to change my surname; though I was glad my initials and the sound of it stayed the same. I was nearing thirty; Addie was thirty-three and had been married twice before. That fact alone should have made me pause before leaping into matrimony, but I was madly in love and also thought it was time to get married. Addie Bowman was the first man who had asked me.

He was unlike the men who had attracted me before. A graduate of Dartmouth and of Dickinson Law School, Addie was intelligent but not intellectual. His general lack of interest in ideas made him seem almost the opposite of Eddie Cohen, my other great love until that point, though they shared one thing: my mother was very dubious about both of them. To my sorrow, Addie did not care for her either and resented the amount of time I spent with her. I, on the other hand, was very fond of his mother, who was widowed and lived in Mechanicsburg, Pennsylvania. Addie's father had been a much-beloved small-town lawyer, fun loving and handsome like his son. Family legend had it that a speech impediment had prevented his being a jury lawyer and that Addie was living out his father's dream.

Many of my friends, especially the Yalies, disapproved of Addie for me, finding him insufficiently serious, I think. But from the first, Gail Saliterman was an exception to the general negative opinion. Gail was my third BFF (best friend forever), after Patsy from grade school and Bunny from college. We met at a party at Gary Bellow's house in 1963. Though we did not at first like each other much, I saw her a second time on a cold, rainy D.C. night, and she mentioned that she had found a deal for a trip to Puerto Rico and the Virgin Islands in February. I had never been to the tropics and impulsively suggested going along, and just as quickly, she agreed. We were both risk-takers.

Our friendship blossomed overlooking the turquoise sea, with papaya for breakfast and soft zephyrs all day. Shortly after our return, we rented an apartment in Georgetown together and kept having fun. The main mode of entertaining in the '60s was the dinner party. I learned from Gail to be easy about it—have simple, fresh food and lots to drink; mix up the guests to create the possibility of sexual tension. Unlike at college and law school parties, we didn't dance but carried on Washington-worthy conversations—gossip, speculation, and law talk.

At first Gail seemed exotic to me, what with her Minneapolis Jewish origins. Over the next fifty years, we traveled and lived together so often, picking up each other's gestures and stories, that people often mistook us for sisters. What I liked best from the beginning was her daring and capacity for fun now whatever else might be on the schedule for later. On my own, I tended to overstudy a situation and sometimes fatally delay gratification.

When we became apartment mates, Gail was at loose ends about her career. She had started a Ph.D. program at Yale in political science and international relations but had left after a year when her first serious love affair fell apart. In D.C, she was working at a research institute connected with American University, a job she regarded as temporary. My career advice generally is: go to law school; it takes only three years, and there are so many different things one can do with a law degree. But Gail was not keen on this option (though a few years later, that is what she did). Then Judge Bazelon, this chapter's hero, came on the scene.

One day he phoned me sounding quite pressed about an upcoming speech he had in Israel comparing the treatment of juvenile delinquents there and in the United States. He wanted my help, but I was busy with law firm work, knew nothing about the topic, and had little interest in it. I thought of Gail, who had at least been to Israel and could absorb a subject quickly and write fast and well.

They hit it off instantly. Gail's father could have been the judge's brother, so similar were their ethnic immigrant backgrounds in Chicago. After the Israel speech, Gail and Judge Bazelon worked together for the next two years. She staffed a committee he headed to investigate and aid the D.C. public schools. It was Gail's kind of project, bringing together the experts and the doers. I'm not sure anyone else could have succeeded in the work, without a title or clear-cut authority attached to it. But she managed to speak for the judge while taking responsibility herself if anything went wrong.

Early on, Gail and the judge met with educators at the University of Chicago to talk about the possible contribution of sociological studies to school reform. She came home and announced that she was especially drawn to a brilliant professor she had met that day, Fred Strodtbeck. I did not understand the attraction; he was twenty years older than we were and no one would have called him handsome or even distinguished looking.

But Gail found him fascinating for his mind, which entranced me less because it was not of the legal turn. I *was* impressed with his handiness, his verbal agility, and his energy, which enabled him to keep up with Gail. Not many men of any age were able to do that. Gail and Fred both enjoyed Addie, and the four of us had some great times sailing in the Virgin Islands, camping on Chincoteague Island, and, when Gail moved to New York, spending weekends at her wonderful apartment across from Bloomingdale's on the Upper East Side.

Another close friend who liked Addie was my Yale classmate, Eli Evans. He was working for the Carnegie Foundation in New York and on a Washington visit came by to see me at the Legal Aid Agency. As he walked down the hall, Addie was coming the other way, and they fell into each other's arms. They had been Navy lieutenants together, stationed on a ship in Japan. Each had often mentioned the other (though not by name) and had told me stories of their adventures together. (My favorite was the time Addie sold Eli to the bar maids at a Japanese country inn.) This was the first time they had seen each other in years.

Addie and I rented a cottage on Terrace Court off A Street N.E., right behind the Supreme Court. Once again, I could walk to my office, this time along Constitution instead of Connecticut Avenue. Work and play blended as we partied with courthouse and Georgetown people and enjoyed the special camaraderie of defenders. We had our own neighborhood watering hole a floor below the office, The Golden Bull, a name appropriate in so many ways. My daily diaries from those years show lots of dinner parties, out and in; regular family visits; movie-going and occasional theater; sailing in our little boat; playing bridge, poker, and charades; late nights and lovemaking—all done in a whirl of hugely hard work leavened by large quantities of gin and champagne.

Though I was happy with my personal life and absorbed in trying cases, I was growing more concerned about the state of the Legal Aid Agency. No one was training the lawyers or thinking about the future of the institution. Instead, it was drifting along as a glorified guilty-plea mill, mired in Fifth Street go-along get-along attitude. Addie and I decided to do something about it and turned to Judge Bazelon for help. As chief judge of the U.S. Court of Appeals, he was head of the governing board of judges that chose the Agency's seven Trustees, who were mostly prominent lawyers making a *pro bono* contribution.

The whole story of how we conspired to restore the Agency to its original vision is too long to detail, but it primarily involved Judge Bazelon's wielding his consummate political skills from a place of lifetime tenure. His first move was to persuade the board to commission an objective outside report on the functioning of the Agency, which had existed for almost a decade without any serious performance evaluation. A panel of three distinguished lawyers was appointed to make the study, and the Office of Economic Opportunity provided funding.

The panelists interviewed over a hundred people from all sectors and factions and their thorough final report was a devastating documentation of the Agency's poor quality of representation. Though he had no official role in the report, Judge Bazelon took all the blame from those who wanted a defender agency that existed mainly to serve as an efficient vehicle for moving most accuseds from arrest to incarceration. One local judge called the report "a bunch of lies" and "the culmination of an effort to thwart and twist the direction of the Agency to an unusual personal legal philosophy of one man."[*]

Soon after the report was submitted, the Agency's director resigned without comment or explanation. He had no stomach for a fight, especially one in which Judge Bazelon led the opposition. The search for a new director began. The main problem was that the statute establishing the small experimental agency had set the director's salary at $16,000 in 1960. Even then, it was not enough to support a family; eight years later, it was almost laughable. We planned to propose a new bill, but for the present the director would have to chance being permanently underpaid. As promising candidates dropped out of the competition, one after another, we became increasingly worried.

One day I was trying to persuade Addie to apply, but he did not want to appear to have engineered a coup so that he could take over himself. Also, he was enjoying teaching at Georgetown and running the criminal defense clinic there. As we talked, it suddenly occurred to me—really out of the blue—that I could, and that indeed I should, do the job.

Addie agreed and suggested that I produce a campaign document stating my ideas for the Agency's future. The resulting *Prospectus: Making the Legal Aid Agency a Model Defender Office* briefly summarized the Agency's current parlous state, and followed with seven pages stating what I would do if appointed director: hire top lawyers, recruit minorities (there were none), integrate social workers into the Agency's work, train people systematically and rigorously before they represented any one in court, and finally use our many cases as springboards from which to try to reform the law.

When I showed the prospectus to Judge Bazelon and said that I thought I could do it, he did not flinch or object to my gender or youth. Instead he lobbied the board members on my behalf. When I was formally interviewed, I sensed that a few were stunned by the audacity of the application, but even they were apparently impressed by my confidence. One of my supporters was Sidney Sachs, a well-respected local attorney. At the interview, he gently asked whether I could run the Agency and raise a family at the same time. Without missing a beat or resenting the question

---

[*] "Blast at Legal Aid Unit Held 'Bunch of Lies,'" *Washington Post*, September 14, 1968.

(partly because it came from Sidney), I replied that we were not planning on children in the next few years: another example of my pre-feminist state.

I learned later that Sidney had a lot to do with bringing the other uptown lawyers on board for me. On October 10, 1968, I was appointed director. The next day my picture was on the front page of the *Washington Post* with a smile so broad that my dentist wrote to say he had used it to make a yearly check-up. The first line read: "Barbara Bowman, thirty-year-old trial attorney, named. . . ." I agreed that "trial attorney" described my achievement so far. Next I wanted to lead and inspire.

The joy of winning the job was soon overtaken by the immensity of the leadership task. There were many attorney vacancies and little able support for those who had persevered through the scathing reports and bad press. It was natural that morale was low, and the appointment of a young woman with big ideas and little administrative experience did not improve matters in the eyes of many of the Agency's constituencies. I needed help.

My first major decision, one of the best I ever made, was to persuade Norman Lefstein to leave the Justice Department and come to the Agency as my deputy. Norm was a friend of Addie's and had become an Assistant U.S. Attorney after a Prettyman Fellowship at Georgetown. He had applied and then withdrawn from running for director because the salary was inadequate to support a family of four. I promised him that getting the cap removed would be our first priority and pointed out that the deputy's salary was not statutorily set, so we could pay him more than I made. My recollection is that we did that, but he still came to the Agency at considerable financial sacrifice.

Norm and I were a team for four years, and when I left, he became the director. He had not only a taste for administration but also tremendous talent at it. First on our agenda was to put the Agency on sound statutory and budgetary footings. He drafted a public defender bill and led the effort to lobby it through a Congress notably unsympathetic to the needs of D.C. citizens. Norm's self-presentation was more careful bureaucrat than crusading defender, and he spoke less of constitutional and civil rights than of cost-containment and efficiency; he made his case not with rhetorical abstractions but with charts and projections. Congress responded to his politic ways, and the Agency grew and prospered. Once more, as in Gary Bellow's day, we attracted top legal talent, and we could again take pride in an effective adversary system in the District's trial courts—poor people began to have real defenders.

Many of our ideas were novel for the time, but today they are the recognized best practices for defender programs. We named the new organization the Public Defender Service (PDS), though the old hands continued to call it "the Agency." It may have been the first such office to have the word "service" in its title, reflecting the insight that for public defenders, the strictly legal work is only part of the picture. Public defenders need social workers at hand to find treatment and employment opportunities for their clients, and investigators to help them to prepare effective defenses in court, and to shape remedial responses at sentencing. Norm built the Agency's pilot Offender Rehabilitation Program, as well as a provision for trained defense investigators, into the PDS statute.

From the first, we insisted that PDS should not be responsible for all indigent criminal cases; we thought the private bar should stay involved in the system, and we knew that funding would never keep pace with case-loads. We had seen other public defenders become overwhelmed and un-able to provide adequate assistance of counsel. Individual representation was our ideal, and we resisted the traditional practice of assigning a lawyer to a courtroom rather than to a client.

Because Norm was so good at negotiating the minefields of D.C.'s budgetary process in Congress and at systematizing our work, I was able to maintain a small trial caseload, specializing in second-degree murder, a charge which required malice but not premeditation. Since the prosecutors routinely overcharged, a second degree indictment usually showed a weakness on their side, hence a good chance that the case was, as we used to say, "triable." Often such cases had credible self-defense claims. It was one of my favorite defenses though difficult to mount, because it was necessary for the client to testify that he was afraid for his own life. Many defendants had trouble admitting primal fear, much less describing it.

Norm did not object to my devoting time and energy to trying cases, and the administrative load was otherwise divided fairly and according to the interests and talents of each of us. Big decisions such as hiring and firing we made together. On May Day 1971 we were even in court together. Antiwar demonstrators had threatened to shut down D.C. and were marching at rush hour on various government buildings. Hundreds of people were arrested throughout the morning; we saw it happening as we arrived at the office. In a true dragnet, many of these people were scooped up just walking to work, especially if they were young or had long hair and love beads.

We realized that we were going to need a lot of lawyers, and we put the whole staff on standby while also contacting the bar associations and the ACLU to have volunteers at the ready. But hours passed, the smell of tear gas faded from the streets, and still no one had been brought to court for arraignment, nor could we find our potential clients in the usual places: the jails, the police stations, the houses of detention.

Public defenders on motorcycles fanned out across the city and finally located a thousand people locked up in the football stadium without adequate medical, sanitary, or other provisions. Night was drawing near, and there was a chill in the spring air. Norm speedily drafted a petition for a mass writ of *habeas corpus* and called a judge at home to come back to town and hear it. Moonlight was streaming through the courtroom windows as I cross-examined police officers and Justice Department officials and Norm successfully argued the law supporting the immediate release of the thousand John and Jane Does. In the next few days as more people were arrested and we continued our labors to get them released, it was like a great battle on a number of fronts. It was exciting, and we knew we were doing good work.

At one point, police were not respecting a judge's order to allow defense lawyers into the cellblock to interview their clients. By then, some people had been held for thirty hours without outside contact. Cross-examining the general counsel of the police department, I looked deep into his eyes and asked:

> Q. When you received the information that [the judge] had is-
> sued the order [admitting attorneys], your main concern was
> for a reasonable way out of that order, was it not?
> A. Yes, ma'am.[*]

It was a Perry Mason moment. The judge made his subsequent orders clear beyond the possibility of police misinterpretation.

I loved being the public defender with Norman Lefstein as my deputy. We worked so well together partly because we were old debaters (indeed,

---

[*] *Legal Services During the 1971 May Day Demonstrations, A Special Report of the Board of Trustees* (Washington, D.C.: District of Columbia Public Defender Service, 1971), p. 19.

Norm was a national champion) who saw both sides of most issues, and both of us were calm and balanced in temperament. Also, we shared a sense of humor and knew what was really important to the other. Running the Agency under high pressure for years, we did not have a single quarrel or serious falling-out.

Another source of help in administering the Agency was a law-professor-in-residence program that I started inadvertently. Soon after I became director, Phil Heymann came to see me with a proposal. He was leaving the State Department to teach criminal law at Harvard and wanted some hands-on experience. Harvard would pay his salary for a year to work at PDS. Phil had a dazzling resume; he had finished first in his class at the best schools, had clerked for Supreme Court Justice Harlan, and had served in the Solicitor General's office. Still, I said no—I was afraid he would consume my time discussing academic questions and issues. Also, we had just instituted a requirement of a three-year commitment to the job, which he obviously could not meet.

When he persisted and promised he would not encroach on my schedule and said he was willing to occupy a desk in a room with three or four other lawyers, I grudgingly said OK. Phil turned out to be a wonderful addition to the office. He knew how to find out what he did not know and was a natural teacher for the younger lawyers. Most important, he was deeply empathetic with our clients.

One of them wrote an autobiography in which he described his relationship with the future Harvard professor: "Right from the beginning there was something about Phil that made me trust him more than any other lawyer. He never really said, but it was a thing like: understand that you're my client; all I have is your best interest at heart."[*]

He described Phil in action in the courtroom, first noting that the prosecutor had shouted and slammed his fist on the table. Then Phil "got up kind of slow, straighten himself up, and begins talking plain and average, but he was getting his points across. He didn't yell once. He talked so that the jury, judge and D.A. could hear him with no trouble, and they all understood what he said. . . . [H]is words seemed to roll out with great tenderness, but a greater respect."

---

[*] John Allen, *Assault with a Deadly Weapon: The Autobiography of a Street Criminal*, 149-51 (New York: Pantheon Books, 1978).

At the end of his stint at PDS, Phil told me he thought I was "a dandy director," one of my favorite compliments of all time. The next year when Mike Wald wanted to come to the Agency on leave from teaching at Stanford, with the school paying his salary, I was delighted to have him, and he, too, was a great asset, working especially to upgrade our juvenile court representation. When he was about to leave, as a reward for his contributions I assigned him a jury case that had been reversed by the appellate court and remanded for a new trial. I thought the case was unwinnable and so couldn't be botched up by a lawyer without much trial experience. To my astonishment and his own dazed delight, he won a not-guilty verdict. Mike's trial confirmed for me what I've always believed: that juries will acquit in a lawyer's first trial because they sense how much he cares.

Recently we had a reunion of the PDS lawyers who had become academics, and people related their favorite stories. Mike sent in one that involved "a client who was accused of robbing two High's Dairy Stores which were across the street from each other. There were eleven robberies in eleven days, with the robber alternating stores. The robber had not worn a mask and the clerks identified my client: he had gone to high school with them.

"The only way I saw to get the client off was to plead insanity, which my client did not want to do. I ultimately persuaded him to do so (another ethical story since I pushed him very hard) and we went to trial. I believe it was the first contested insanity case tried by the Office. The trial took five or so days. As I was leaving the Courtroom at the end of the third day, an elderly juror, probably in her late 70s, said to me 'You are doing great.' I was delighted, but of course troubled. That night I called Barbara B. to tell her what had happened and to discuss whether I had to tell the judge. We debated for over an hour and I reluctantly agreed with her conclusion that I had to tell the Judge—George Hart—a very prosecution-oriented judge, who kept guns in his chambers.

"So I dejectedly went to the Courthouse early the next morning and asked to see the Judge in chambers. To my surprise, the prosecutor was there. He immediately told me that he had to tell the Judge something. The same elderly juror—my juror—had come up to him after court the previous day and said 'You are doing great.' When I told him why I was there, we both had a good laugh and proceeded with the trial. My client was found not guilty by reason of insanity—and walked off from St. Elizabeth's [the public mental institution] several months later."

My role in Mike's story brings back powerful memories of being director of the Agency: the night calls, the hard decisions about duties to the client and to the court, the funny things that happen in jury trials. For several years after my appointment, both my personal and professional lives went well. One of my fondest memories is a sail out of Annapolis with Eli and a woman he loved at the time. Eli took pictures of the three of us that summon up that special bright day. Less than a year later, Eli and I met in the Florida Keys on January 1 to console each other. Both of our loves had left us. My marriage of four years ended in an amicable divorce.

Besides Addie's extreme flirtatiousness with other women, which I had almost come to accept as an unconscious reflex on his part, two other difficulties contributed to the break-up. When I started winning cases and defendants would regularly ask for "the Baaad Cock," my reputation as a trial lawyer began to surpass his. Then I was named director of the Agency, leading to insensitive remarks like that from a partner at a prestigious firm who introduced us as "this remarkable woman who runs the public defender and the son of a bitch who is married to her." Addie was not amused.

More serious than the shift in status between us was his (to me) peculiar desire to be a "movement lawyer." It started with a case of former and current priests and nuns breaking into Dow Chemical Company, destroying furniture and files, and pouring a blood-like substance over records. The group became known as "the D.C. Nine." Addie was thrilled to be one of their attorneys; I thought he was wasting his time and his great skills.

These clients saw their trials as part of their protest against the use of chemical weapons in the Vietnam War. At first, at least, they were not particularly interested in winning, since victory might be taken as evidence that the despised "system" worked. And they cared nothing for skilled lawyering; indeed, they clamored to represent themselves so they could speak to the court and the press more freely than an attorney could do. In an ironic and (to me) amusing by-play, the court appointed Ed Williams to represent one of the nine, who in effect fired him, expressing "emphatic, indeed vitriolic, dissatisfaction with [his] representation."* I suspect that

---

* *United States v. Dougherty,* 473 F.2d 1113, 1118 (D.C. Cir. 1972).

Williams tried to negotiate a good plea in the case, or work on a technical defense.

While the D.C. Nine trial was in progress, attended by many supporters and much press, replete with political theater and dramatic clearings of the courtroom, I was quietly defending a first-degree murder case across the hall. As I struggled to save a young man from life in prison, I felt that Addie and the other good lawyers should be doing the same for clients who were in grave need of their talents. Though I marched against the war, I disapproved of destruction of property as a form of protest and was appalled to watch trial strategy being concocted under clouds of marijuana smoke amidst hours of political ranting.

Celebrations over the win of my murder case were muted by the D.C. Nine's loss. (Ultimately the case was reversed on appeal for the failure to allow defendants the full right of self-representation.) The depressing drama of our dual trials was the effective end of our marriage. Of course, we tried reconciling and talked to counselors and advisors, but I could not compromise my ideas about fidelity and accountability, and Addie wanted freedom.

Unexpectedly, I was hit by a sense of failure and humiliation. I loved Addie and our life together. To a woman raised in the 1950s, losing one's husband felt shameful. I thought maybe I should have tried harder. After all, Mother had stayed with my father through his years of alcoholism, but of course, she, unlike me, had three children and no career for support. Initially I was torn about whether to file for divorce. I consulted a psychiatrist, who asked, "What kind of life will you have without Addie?" "Oh," I said, "I'll have a wonderful life with great work and interesting friends." And that is what happened.

From the first days of the split, I was enveloped with love and support from lawyers at the Agency and other friends. In 1971, Gail moved back to town from New York, and we rented a large house with a deck and garden in the Mount Pleasant area of D.C. I could no longer walk to work, but it was good to leave the cottage on Terrace Court, which had begun to seem dark and oppressive.

As always in troubled times, I buried my sorrows in work, and there was plenty of it to do. My six years at the Agency were exciting and happy but also frazzled and anxious. For the last four years, I had not only the administrative and public duties as the director of the Agency, but also clients charged with serious crimes, often murder. For them, there was always something more that could be done, and filing a motion, finding a witness, or stopping by the jail for a chat on a Sunday afternoon could mean the difference between victory and defeat, between freedom and prison.

The ceaseless nature of the work was one thing; the paranoia it generated was another. Often it felt like everyone was against us: police, prosecutors, judges, clerks, court reporters, and the general public as represented by jurors who sometimes seemed to return guilty verdicts whatever the state of the evidence. Only our little band of lawyers stood between the indigent accused and powerful forces that threatened to overwhelm us all. On our side, we had each other—a comradeship all the stronger because forged in combat with the rest of the world—and there were the jurors, who would sometimes acquit.

And we had our clients. As maddening as they could be, they were the best part of the job. The fragility and difficulty of their lives, the humanity we came to see in each, and our hopes of making a difference for them were the ever-sustaining constants of the work. Though I have spent many rewarding years writing and teaching, I still count my public defender days as the most fulfilling of my career because the need of my clients for my help was so urgent and the demands of my role were so clear.

My talents perfectly matched the task, and for all its strains, fighting for the underdog was deeply satisfying. Reading Clarence Darrow's autobiography when I was young, I had been struck by the simplicity of his justification for his vocation: "Strange as it may seem, I grew to like to defend men and women charged with crime. . . . I was dealing with life, with its hopes and fears, its aspirations and despairs. With me it was going to the foundation of motive and conduct and adjustment for human beings, instead of blindly talking of hatred and vengeance, and that subtle, indefinable quality that men call 'justice,' of which nothing is really known."[*]

I felt the same way.

---

[*] Clarence Darrow, *The Story of My Life*, 75-76 (New York: Grosset & Dunlap, 1932).

8

DEFENDING THE GUILTY

"How can you defend a person you know is guilty?" Everyone asks it—benign old aunts, eager young students, the gardener, and the grocery store clerk. No one else in law or any other profession is, like the criminal defense lawyer, constantly called upon to justify her vocation. Forty years after I last appeared in a criminal case, interviewers still bring up the question.

Most defenders have developed a stock answer for the inevitable existential query, and over the years I've used various responses, ranging from constitutional rhetoric to a rather peevish, "It's not for everyone. It takes a special mindset and soul set to be a defender." In the early eighties, I wrote an article enumerating a selection of rejoinders to give fellow defenders ammunition for designing their own explanations.* It pleases me now to see that the piece has become a standard reference and is widely cited.

I intended the title, "Defending the Guilty," to be sardonic because the question has an accusatory tone that assumes the lawyer knows the client did it. First on my list was the garbage collector's riposte: it's dirty work, but someone has to do it. That was juxtaposed with the constitutionalist's rationale: it is a noble calling to live out the Bill of Rights and make it real

---

* Barbara Allen Babcock, "Defending the Guilty," 32 *Cleveland State Law Review* 175 (1983). See also Babcock, "'Defending the Guilty' after Thirty Years," in Abbe Smith and Monroe Freedman, eds., *How Can You Represent Those People?*, 1-13 (New York: Palgrave Macmillan, 2013) (updating the original article and describing its wide use).

for others. Next is the legalist or positivist who would say that guilt is not a fact but a legal conclusion that can follow only from a prescribed process.

The political activist and the civil libertarian maintain that criminal defense keeps the system functioning fairly for all, and the social worker is concerned with the benefit to the accused and his community that flows from having a lawyer to stand up for him and protect him when he is otherwise helpless.* Then there is the egotist speaking: "Defending criminal cases is more interesting than the routine and repetitive work done by many lawyers, even those engaged in what passes in civil practice for litigation. The heated facts of crimes provide voyeuristic excitement and actual court appearances, even jury trials, come earlier and more often in one's career."†

My own justification is a combination of the social worker and the egotist, and if the inquirer has time, I tell him the story of my client Geraldine (see Chapter Six). By my jury skills I saved her from spending most of the rest of her life in prison. After the verdict she turned to me and said: "I'm so happy for you." We were happy for each other that day and one thing I try to convey in telling the Geraldine story is that criminal defense can be, dare I say it, *fun*, or at least viscerally exciting.

The practice can be intellectually interesting and challenging as well. To illustrate this point, I used to tell my classes about the case of Alvin Hines.‡ He was angry when I became his lawyer soon after I joined the Legal Aid Agency (1966). Having refused to work with the first two private attorneys assigned to represent him in his robbery case, he was not pleased to see a young woman replace them. But he liked me better when I immediately set about getting him out of jail while he awaited trial.

Hines had been locked up for twenty-two months because he could not post a five thousand dollar bail bond, and no one had tried to get him released on his own recognizance. Yes, he was charged with a serious crime and might be thought a risk to flee, but he had never been out of the D.C. area in his life, and his criminal record was short and did not involve violence. He lived with his mother in one of the city's poorest neighbor-

---

* "Defending the Guilty," 32 *Cleveland State Law Review* at 178.

† *Id.*

‡ I use the client's full name when it appears in the case reports but just the first name otherwise.

hoods. Though he was a grade school dropout, Hines seemed intelligent (and indeed he was, as the rest of the story will show).

He was accused of robbing a beauty parlor at gunpoint and taking the jewelry and cash of eight women customers and employees. Several victims picked out his picture from a photo array, and he was arrested the day after the robbery with ninety-eight dollars in his pocket, which he said he had won in a crap game. No gun or stolen jewelry was recovered; no fingerprints or other forensic evidence were found in the shop.

There was little evidence of any kind against him except for the positive identifications of the victims. Bolstering their word was the fact that they were all black like him and some of them had described the robber's "little bitty eyes," a feature Hines indisputably had. Three of the women identified him in court at the preliminary hearing, and five others had been taken as a group to see him in the courthouse cellblock before they testified to the grand jury. The cellblock confrontation became the centerpiece of our defense, thanks to Hines, who told me about it at our first meeting. He thought it was wrong that the five women together had viewed him while he was alone in the cell "like an animal in a cage." He also insisted that a lawyer should have been present when the women had looked at him and discussed his appearance.

His previous appointed counsel had thought that was a ridiculous point, and one of them sent Hines for a mental evaluation because of his insistence on raising it. I didn't think much of it either but agreed to look into it. To my surprise, I found cases in other jurisdictions suppressing in-court identifications because they had been corrupted by suggestive pre-trial viewings. Citing these precedents, I moved to suppress all of the identification testimony in Hines's case. At the same time I successfully argued for his pretrial release.

Alvin was thrilled with the suppression motion and happy to be out of jail. He produced an excellent witness corroborating his story that he had won the money at a crap game, and with the help of our office's social workers he found a job and held it for the many months leading up to trial. The defense turned on mistaken identification, and Hines also had an alibi: he had been at home having dinner with his mother. But he did not want her to testify because, he said, "It would scare her, and I've caused her so much trouble already." I suspected that part of the trouble he caused her was robbing the beauty parlor she patronized, and where he had often picked her up. I don't have a transcript of the trial and my memory isn't certain on the point, but I believe I persuaded him to let me call her; I know she was in the courtroom supporting him at the trial, a sweet-faced woman.

The motion to suppress was set to be heard at the outset of the trial, but once Hines was out of jail, neither side pushed for a court date. Meanwhile, as the months went by, two of the cases I had cited from other jurisdictions made their way to the U.S. Supreme Court. On the day we finally went to trial, June 12, 1967, the Supreme Court handed down three decisions holding that pretrial confrontations were a critical stage in criminal prosecutions, so that henceforth a defendant had a right to have a lawyer present at a formal lineup, and that eyewitness identification testimony rooted in an unduly suggestive lineup or other confrontation would be suppressed.[*] It was my client's point exactly, dressed in constitutional language.

After the judge sent his bailiff up the hill to the Supreme Court to pick up copies of the opinions, which we all took an hour to read on our own, we launched into the first suppression hearing in the whole country based on the new decisions. We all agreed that the question was whether identification testimony should be suppressed because it was the fruit of an unduly suggestive confrontation. For two days, all eight of the government's witnesses testified under oath, and I cross-examined them.

Apart from the possibility of suppressing their identification testimony, it was an unprecedented opportunity to prepare for trial. Because pretrial depositions are not routinely available in criminal cases, and prosecution witnesses often refuse to talk to defense investigators, a defense lawyer's first and only chance to question key witnesses is usually cross-examination at trial. *Gilbert* hearings (as they became known) in effect gave the defense an invaluable chance to preview the prosecution testimony.

My most vivid memory from the hearing was the testimony of a salon employee, a gorgeous woman from Guyana, who was understandably confused about the purpose of the hearing procedure. As I questioned her about her attention to a customer who had fainted, presumably distracting her from observing the robber, she suddenly exclaimed, in her lilting

---

[*] *United States v. Wade*, 388 U.S. 218 (1967) (lineup a critical stage, requiring counsel to be present); *Stovall v. Denno*, 388 U.S. 293 (1967) (*Wade* rule not applicable to lineups held before date of *Wade* decision); *Gilbert v. California*, 388 U.S. 263 (1967) (apart from *Wade* rule, identifications resulting from unduly suggestive confrontations inadmissible; this applicable to pre-*Gilbert* confrontations).

accent: "Oh, you are trying to say he is not the man! But," pointing at Alvin Hines, "HE IS THE MAN!" Needless to say I let her testimony stand without cross-examination when she appeared as a witness at the trial.

After holding this novel hearing, the judge found that the cellblock confrontation had been unduly suggestive, and ruled that the government couldn't introduce any evidence of identifications made at that encounter. He also ruled that two of the witnesses who had seen Hines in the cellblock would not be allowed to identify him at trial because they could not say for certain that they had not been influenced by the suggestive confrontation. That left six witnesses who swore that Alvin Hines was the short dark man with small eyes and a large pistol who had robbed the well-lit beauty parlor. The prosecutor also called the two women whose identification testimony had been suppressed, probably because they were well spoken and could describe the robbery graphically.

The array of citizen witnesses reminded me of Chuckie Delmonico's case when I was working for Ed Williams, where eleven bank robbery victims were certain he was the perpetrator (see Chapter Five). My theory for Hines was the same as in that case: that the beauty shop owner's powerful personality, like that of the bank president in Delmonico, made this a one-witness robbery rather than the multi-witness one it appeared to be. Later at trial, I used what I learned at the suppression hearing to cross-examine the eye-witnesses on the chaos and confusion in the beauty shop that night, which was likely to affect the memories of the people who were there. But though I thought these cross-examinations might have shaken them, the witnesses remained firm in their identifications of Alvin Hines. Several of them even said those fateful words: "I'll never forget that face."

This confidence under cross-examination led me, after all, to introduce the unfair cellblock confrontation myself in an effort to show the jurors that it had tainted the certainty of these witnesses. The confrontation had multiple flaws: Hines had been alone and behind bars, the witnesses knew he had been arrested for the robbery, they had been taken to the cellblock in a group, and the beauty shop owner had told the others that she believed him to be the man. The judge did not understand why I was introducing the evidence: he wrung his hands and wondered why he had spent two days deciding to suppress the testimony about the unfair identification procedures if I was going to turn around and use it.

In closing, I argued my one-witness-robbery theory and told the jury that the police had not really investigated the case; they had not gotten a warrant and searched for the gun and stolen jewelry or even checked pawn shops and fencers of stolen goods. They had only held unfair confrontations that had created the risk of irreparable mistaken identifications. After deliberating for a few hours, the jury came back with guilty verdicts on all counts. The judge gave Hines 18 to 54 months, actually a rather mild sentence that may have reflected his doubts about the correctness of his suppression decisions.

But as I explained to Alvin, we were sure to win on appeal because the prosecutor, enraged at my closing argument about the beauty shop owner's sway over the women's testimony, had countered that two witnesses had not identified Hines from the stand (and thus the owner was not so powerful). Of course, they actually had identified him but the judge had suppressed that part of their testimony. The prosecutor had argued inadmissible evidence.

I objected, but in my heart I hoped the judge would overrule me, which he did. On appeal, the government confessed error, and the conviction was reversed.[*] By the time the case came back on remand, the evidence was stale, and the government decided not to retry Alvin Hines. When I met him in court for dismissal of the indictment, he gave me a big wink out of one of his little bitty eyes.

My suspicion that he probably did rob the beauty parlor did not undermine my satisfaction with the result. I had helped advance the law on challenges to eyewitness identification, and it was fun to litigate on the cutting edge of the law.

Moreover, I liked Alvin Hines because he cared about his mother, he appreciated my representation, and his idea about fairness turned out to anticipate the Supreme Court rulings. Finally, the time he spent in jail pretrial and in prison while his appeal was pending (his case was consolidated with two others to consider a range of identification issues) added up to several years—about right in my opinion for a robbery in which no one was hurt.

The confrontation cases (or lineup cases, as we called them) were, to my mind, the high-water mark of the Warren Court's attention to fairness for criminal defendants, and they came right on the heels of *Miranda v.*

---

[*] *Clemons v. United States*, 408 F.2d 1230, 1243 (D.C. Cir. 2016).

Arizona,* which held that a defendant had a right to a lawyer at interrogation. Few of our cases involved confessions because, I used to comment, our clients were usually caught in the act—no confessions necessary. But the glib joke does not capture the range of unfairness that can crop up in run-of-the-mill cases, even though they are not ones where the police engaged in questioning. On the other hand, the issues raised by unfair and suggestive identification procedures were omnipresent.

In addition to suppression motions, we also represented defendants at the confrontations themselves. Figuring out what a defense lawyer should do when appearing at a lineup made for some dicey legal dilemmas. Shortly after the Hines trial while the right was still new, I was the only one in the office late one evening when a detective friend from the robbery squad called. They were having a lineup and needed a lawyer. As I headed over, I considered my anomalous position. Supposedly representing a client I had never met, I was about to help the police make a case against him by seeing that they cobbled together a fair confrontation.

But this time, they had arranged a lineup of five uniformed police officers of medium height with their jackets removed and one six-foot-six man in a purple jumpsuit. Since the robber had worn such a garment, I gently suggested that this lineup was, in the words of the Supreme Court, "fraught with the dangers of suggestion."† But the officers had their witnesses on hand and no other clothing to fit the tall arrestee. They added that the witnesses knew him anyway because it was his own neighborhood liquor store that he had robbed.

Later, when I was called to testify at the hearing on the motion to suppress the identification, the judge startled me by barking, "Why didn't you stop the lineup if you thought it was so unfair? I know you—you would have made a scene." Actually, since he had seen me only in court trying cases, he did not know that I feared and avoided unstructured confrontations. That experience, my only one as a witness, made me realize how frightening it is to swear to tell the truth and try to do it. After that, I was more sympathetic to the witnesses I subpoenaed.

The right to a lawyer at pretrial confrontations was jettisoned in 1972, marking the passing of the Warren Court. The Burger Court held that a

---

* 384 U.S. 436 (1966).

† *Wade*, 388 U.S. at 234 (citation omitted).

lawyer was required only for post-indictment lineups,* which are rare compared to those that happen shortly after arrest. Before the Warren Court's lineup rulings were swept away, however, they had a lasting effect on fairness in many places. In D.C. the police and their counsel worked out regular procedures for pretrial confrontations, including filming them so they could be reconstructed at trial.

A second result of the five-year agitation over lineups was that it cast a useful light on problems inherent in eyewitness identification. In my experience, the ability to recall the face of a stranger seen under harrowing conditions varies widely among individuals. A few people are actually good at it; the face does seem emblazoned on their brains. But most people are not adept at remembering features, though usually they do not realize this about themselves. Cross-racial identifications are especially problematic— and this is true beyond the common stereotype that white people think blacks look alike. I found quite a few black people, for instance, who could not distinguish among Caucasians, as well as Asians who had difficulty identifying both blacks and whites.

At trial it is the defense lawyer's job to attack weaknesses in eyewitness identification—delicate work because the attorney can appear to be hassling victims and citizens doing their civic duty by testifying. On the other side, prosecutors seek to draw out and dramatize the testimony, even sometimes directing the witness to touch the shoulder of the person she is accusing. To cut short such a stunt, some defense lawyers ask their clients to stand at the first mention of their names in order to showcase the obviousness of in-court identification.

I did not use that tactic because of an incident early in my trial career in a case involving an assault with many onlookers who had identified my client. The witnesses were all kids high on drugs and booze, hanging out on a Saturday afternoon as they usually did. They had no sense of time or much ability to describe what they had seen. When the first teenager took the stand, the prosecutor started his identification ritual, culminating in, "Do you see the person in the courtroom today who committed the assault?" The witness stared at my client, the only black man within the bar of the court. Then he looked out into the courtroom. "That's him in the last row," he said, pointing out a spectator who did not at all resemble my client apart from being African American. Alarmed, that man jumped up

---

* *Kirby v. Illinois*, 406 U.S. 682 (1972).

and fled the room. I rose and suggested that the judge issue an arrest warrant for him on the spot. The judge did not think it was funny, but the jury did. If a jury laughs *with* you or *at* the prosecutor, you are well on your way to winning the case.

Most of my stories about the public defender days have some touch of comedy. We defenders laugh at ourselves and our clients and the whole hapless human condition as revealed in the criminal process. One of my favorite stories was when a fresh young prosecutor, well-versed in the rule that one should not lead the witness on direct examination, but apparently less well instructed on how to prepare a witness to testify, said portentously:

Q. Now, Mr. G, what, if anything, unusual happened that night?

A. [after a puzzled stare] You mean before or after he put the baby in the stove?

Then there was the robbery suspect who insisted on representing himself at the preliminary hearing. With a flourish, he asked a witness, "How did you know it was me when I had a nylon stocking over my head?"

Our laughter balanced somewhat the aggravation that is also a large part of the work—nowhere more than in plea bargaining. All defenders must plea bargain. Gary Bellow said we should do it even for clients we thought were innocent so as not to signal to prosecutors that some clients were guiltier than others. As I never litigated against a female prosecutor, my experience plea-bargaining was exclusively with male prosecutors who often assumed when I tried to bring up my client's positive points that I had been taken in because of my soft female heart. And I wasn't comfortable joking over drinks about my client's bad character and general scumminess. At the same time, I had some advantages as a woman, which I did not hesitate to deploy; if a little flirtation or a lot of flattery could save years in prison, I was willing.

Also on the bleak side of plea bargaining, a prosecutor comes to mind, his face and name emblazoned on *my* brain, who spun out a gratuitous scenario wherein I would be robbed and raped like the victim in the case we were negotiating. I sat there stunned—seeing that he thought this was an acceptable joke. I didn't acknowledge or participate in his twisted banter, but I managed somehow not to curse him and flee his office. We got a good plea offer, which my client gratefully accepted.

Plea bargaining was a dark side of defending for me, but the darkest was the obligation to defend cases where I was truly horrified by something I was quite sure my client had done. Examples were cases involving the rape of a child or an elderly woman. Because public defenders cannot choose their clients, I represented men who did those things. Though I believed that a lawyer might withdraw if she was too repulsed by the crime to be an effective advocate, I never turned away a client on that ground. I did not want it said that women were not tough enough to handle public defending. And if I didn't take these cases, someone else at the Agency would have to, and the facts would be abhorrent to anyone.

I remember one client, for instance, who was accused of participating in the gang rape of an airline stewardess, new to D.C., who did not realize that she had moved into a dangerous neighborhood. One night coming home late from work she was dragged into a basement and raped by many men. Over the next few days, she identified a number of men as her attackers, mainly from driving around the streets with the police. All the men she picked out were, like my client, large and dark. He had no felony record, but that was about all he had going for him. Ignorant and inarticulate, he was not a good witness, and he was terrified by the crime's notoriety and the hostility the police and the courts had trained on him. I went to the Court of Appeals to gain his release on his own recognizance.[*]

He met all the elaborate bond conditions, including checking in with me and others regularly and getting a job, but by the day of trial, he had absconded. Though I was embarrassed to face the court after fighting to obtain his release, I was also relieved that I would not have to cross-examine the victim. Several years later, he returned from North Carolina where he had fled and was promptly arrested. The victim had made a new life and refused to testify. At my side, he pled guilty to the much lesser charge of jumping bail.

The worst case I ever tried, one that gave me recurrent nightmares for years, was that of James L. Cockerham. He was a Caucasian alcoholic who lived a marginal life without family, friends, or regular employment, though he had worked as a plumber and a butcher. He lived in a boarding house where an attractive young woman with an eight-year-old daughter also lived. Cockerham befriended the little girl in an effort to attract the mother. She let him babysit while she went out with other men—

---

[*] *Earl Ball, Jr. v. United States*, 402 F.2d 206, 207 (D.C. Cir 1968).

apparently never acknowledging and perhaps not even realizing his interest in her.

One night while she was out, he slashed the child's throat and sodomized her dead body—insane acts—and insanity was the defense. Cockerham was in complete psychological collapse at the time of his arrest and was admitted to St. Elizabeth's, the public mental hospital. He wrote a chilling confession and received a diagnosis of paranoid schizophrenia, as well as anti-psychotic medication that eventually rendered him competent to stand trial.

In almost ten years of criminal defense, I had no other client or case that so repelled me. I could not even read the police report without crying. Though I truly believed him to be completely insane, I could not sufficiently separate the actor from the act. Fortunately, my co-counsel Bill Taylor, who was to become one of the star criminal defense lawyers trained at PDS, found it possible to pity him enough to take over client relations in the case. Together Bill and I mounted a strong insanity defense, with three medical witnesses and the wanton horror of the crimes on our side.

We went to trial before a judge who reputedly, and from this case pretty clearly, had no use for the insanity defense. In my closing argument, I entreated the jurors to see that Cockerham's crimes could only be the products of a sick mind. Never have I faced such cold stares from a jury. They took little time to return guilty verdicts.

At sentencing, Cockerham, against my advice but fully within his rights, said a few words for himself which he thought were mitigating: that the jury of elderly people had been unable to follow the evidence. This infuriated the judge who screamed at Cockerham, and some of that vitriol rained down on me as I stood beside him. On appeal, a good lawyer from our office argued various judicial errors in the management of the insanity trial, but the appeals court affirmed the conviction[*] with the addendum, "We sympathize with all parties involved in the trial of such a case as this. . . ."[†] Within months of the affirmance, Cockerham committed suicide in prison. I would bet that no one tried very hard to stop him.

Though remembering Cockerham and his ghastly act has been painful, his case accurately represents the hardest part of defending. The work was

---

[*] *United States v. James Cockerham*, 476 F.2d 542, 543 (D.C. Cir.1973).

[†] *Id.* at 545 (citations omitted).

hardly all good jokes, not-guilty verdicts, and appreciative clients. Aside from the worst part, the horror of the little girl's murder, the case also represents the disrespect toward defenders sometimes shown by courts. The trial judge's open disgust with the defense had a caustic and un-professional personal edge to it. Though I had never before tried a case in his court, I had gone to bat for one of our attorneys, Mat Zwerling, in a row with the same judge shortly before the Cockerham trial.

Mat's case was a one-victim robbery. Soon after the client's arrest our investigator had talked to the victim and reported that he was personable and had had a good vantage for seeing the robber. On the eve of trial almost a year later, the investigator went to re-interview him and found that he had moved but located him through a forwarding address from the post office. The witness was as persuasive as ever. Our client insisted on his innocence, however, and Mat, as he prepared for trial, thought they had a chance of winning.

On the day of trial, the government announced not ready because the victim had disappeared. The prosecutor asked for twenty-four hours to locate him and promised to drop the case if they could not do so. Mat objected to the continuance "for the record," but did not say anything else. The next day the prosecutor reported that not only had they found the victim but Mat had known all along where he was. The judge exploded, removed Mat from the case, and barred him from ever appearing in that courtroom again. He forced the second chair, a lawyer in training, to take over the trial.

Despite my efforts as PDS director to explain and to mollify the judge—backed by my deputy Norm Lefstein and a letter from the distinguished lawyers on our board—he remained obdurate. Our argument that Mat's disclosing the victim's location would have violated his duty to his client only made the judge angrier. Like most other judges on the District Court, he had never been a defense attorney, and saw no problem with the scenario in which a client hears that the case might be dropped, but then his own lawyer jumps up and saves the prosecution.

The issues with this judge made me doubt the wisdom of continuing to try cases while being director. I justified it by saying I should be in the trenches with my people, that my cases could serve as training vehicles, and that I needed a break from administrative burdens. Yet all rationales aside, what I loved most about criminal defense was talking to juries, and I could not bring myself to give it up. But there was a risk: a spirited defense could anger a judge who believed the PDS lawyer should help move the case along, and then the director needed to smooth things over—impossible when the director was the one who had enraged the judge.

The judge's animosity made Cockerham's case not only hard to try but impossible to win because, bad facts aside, jurors want to please the powerful patriarch in the black robe. They watch him closely for signals about his view of the case. I once heard a juror in the courthouse elevator tell another that he was sure they had done what the judge wanted in every case that month. Judges have many ways to influence the jury by devices as simple (and as blatant) as thanking them when they return guilty verdicts but not when they acquit or cannot reach a verdict.

Some defense lawyers are naturally combative and enjoy opposing the court's authority. But I wanted approval, or at least respect, from the towering figure on the high bench. Once, when I first started at the Agency, I tried two cases in a row before a great old judge who looked like God. I won the first one, an armed robbery and the judge complimented me and the jury. It was so early in my career that I did not appreciate the rarity of that event. During a break in the case, the prosecutor for the next one had stopped by and asked whether I would make "the usual stipulation" in our pending stolen auto case: that the owner had not given permission for my client to drive the car. Without much thought, I said OK.

But that night, I realized that I should not have agreed unless I was sure the government could produce the witness. The next day when I sought to withdraw the stipulation, the judge was apoplectic. He yelled that I had given my word, that a lawyer does not renege, and that I had no honor. As I stood there being bawled out by the man who looked like God, I felt tears building. If I were to cry, word would travel through the courthouse in a flash; I would be ruined as a trial lawyer, and everyone would say girls aren't tough enough for the job.

I clung to thoughts about my duty to compel the government to meet its full burden of proof, and, less abstractly, to the suspicion that the prosecutor did not have the witness—else why would he tattle to the judge about my withdrawing the stipulation. The case was continued and when the government could not locate the complainant, the charge was reduced to a minor misdemeanor with no jail time. Touched and appreciative that I stood up for him, the client gratefully pled guilty.

Other times I was insulted in court not so much for doing my job as for doing it too ardently, for being an all-out advocate. One crusty old judge who was in chronic pain from arthritis was especially cantankerous, and I happened to try a number of cases in his courtroom. Oddly enough, though he interfered with my efforts, I won most of the cases anyway. Juries may have picked up on his mistreatment and sided with me instead of trying to please him. He engaged in cheap tricks like declaring a recess just when I was about to spring a trap on cross-examination. Once he told me never again to make an argument about reasonable doubt that he (wrongly) considered improper. Another time when I argued a *habeas corpus* petition, he commented that since it was April 1, he thought I was making a foolish joke.

Professional ethics classes traditionally treat the work of criminal defense as fraught with conflicting duties and difficult moral decisions. Actually the prosecutor has the more complicated set of obligations: to the court, to due process for the defendant, to crime victims, and to the community at large. The defense has only one client, who is owed a duty of zealous representation. The clarity of the role was one reason I liked the job.

Despite that lucidity, the privilege of representing the underdog, and the special pleasures of winning against the odds, burnout often afflicts public defenders. Usually the cause is overwork, but even at PDS where caseloads were reasonable, the huge responsibilities of the job, the lack of public understanding of defense counsel's role, and the relatively low pay sometimes wore down even the most idealistic lawyers. I left before experiencing burnout, although maybe I sensed it coming after six years of intense practice and administration. A few months before leaving the Agency, I won my last case—a second-degree murder—and enjoyed it as much as, and maybe more than, my first trial.

A chance to enter academia at a top school opened in 1972 (as told in the next chapter). I saw that it was a small window of opportunity and sensed it would not be open very long for a white woman defender. I flew into a new life as law professor—a job with stresses very different from practice. Although teaching has been interesting, and even sometimes exciting, I'm not sure I could have left when I did had I realized that I would never argue to a jury again.

Recently, I returned to D.C. (which I call "my native city") for a wonderfully conceived meeting—PDS in the Legal Academy. From the 130 or so of us who have become full-time teachers, 60 or 70 were able to come to the meeting. We talked about the history of our little agency, second only to Supreme Court clerkships in supplying future professors. As I looked into the faces of the old and new defenders, I was overwhelmed by pride and familial feeling.

The rooms were full of people I had hired when I was director, and those I had taught as students. References to my mentorship stirred me. Many of the current PDS lawyers were also there. PDS has at last achieved the racial mixture of lawyers we had so long sought. Also, women are still in leadership positions, even though administering the Agency has become a more prestigious position in the law than it used to be.

I walked around the courthouse neighborhood, much improved over the Bowery/Tenderloin days of my youth. Though the federal court house on Constitution Avenue is as brutal and formidable as ever, it is much softened by an annex nearby named after my hero, William B. Bryant, before whom I tried my first case and in whose chambers I found sympathy and solace. A display of photographs from Judge Bryant's career had one of me in a receiving line. It's unlabeled, but I love the record that shows I knew him.

I was on a plenary panel with Norm Lefstein, my deputy and subsequent dean at Indiana; Kim Taylor-Thompson, also a director of PDS and later a professor at Stanford, now at NYU Law School; and Barbara Bergman, my student of many years ago, a professor at New Mexico. Addressing questions of the impact of PDS on our teaching and scholarship, the program aroused powerful memories such as the pleasure of occasionally feeling the attention and absorption of the class in a way close to that of a jury. I thought too of all the students I have encouraged to be defenders, and in later years, prosecutors as well, and whatever their practices, to take responsibility for the criminal justice system.

Sometimes I was uneasy when a student who seemed less than aggressive or tough wanted to follow in my footsteps. But then I remembered that in my youth I had been shy and scared also. Moreover, I've learned that there are many ways of being a good trial lawyer, many personalities that will work. The important things are to prepare to the hilt and to care about the client. These qualities were present at the creation when the founder of our movement, Clara Foltz, spoke on public defense at the 1893 World's Fair. (See chapter 14.)

I have written a biography of Foltz, and found great pleasure in bringing my heroine, Clara, to my people, defenders of all ages.

9

FALLING INTO FEMINISM

No one of my generation was raised as a feminist or took a women's studies course in college. Most people came to the movement through individual personal experience. With many it was simply reading Simone de Beauvoir's *Second Sex* or Betty Friedan's *Feminine Mystique*, or other works that changed the way they saw the world. I never had even that kind of low-key conversion experience; rather I fell somewhat accidentally into feminism, which then bloomed out to be, like public defense, a central moving force in my life.

My introduction to feminism came in 1970, while I was director of the Public Defender in D.C. Some Georgetown law students, who had been volunteering as investigators, were excited about an NYU Law School syllabus they had from friends for a new course titled Women and the Law. They had been unable to persuade anyone on the regular faculty to take it on, and wanted me to teach it.

Initially I begged off because I didn't know anything about the subject and had not even reflected very much on my own experience of being a woman lawyer. But they pressed hard, assuring me that this would be a great way to learn. I gave in, mainly because I felt some obligation to this particular bunch for their dogged, unpaid contributions to our public defender cases.

This was one of the first times a course like this had been offered at any law school, and it attracted considerable media attention.* A story in the

---

* There is as yet no history of the addition of women's studies to the law school curricu-

local tabloid described me as "hardly the classic women's lib type. She is feminine, soft-spoken and seemed to be wearing all her underwear."[*] (The latter was a reference to the bras that were supposedly burned by "women's libbers" at the 1968 Miss America pageant in Atlantic City.[†]) In another interview, I said to Judith Martin (later the famous Miss Manners), "This is going to be a meat and potatoes course, with an emphasis on remedies. Otherwise a small seminar like this could easily deteriorate into talk about how we were forced to play with dolls as little girls and how it spoiled our lives."[‡] I assume I did say that, but where did I get it? I had never taken a course even remotely resembling the one I was to teach—or played with dolls much either.

Feminism did not come easily at first. I had been trying for years to avoid attention to my sex, except in the rare instances when it might help me or my client. For me, being female was simply an obstacle and not as insurmountable as those many others faced. I did not like thinking of myself as a victim of injustice and initially felt uncomfortable pushing for my own advancement. Soon, however, I came to realize that the movement extended beyond equal opportunity for privileged professionals, and that it could change and improve all of human society.

Even as I moved to this more expansive vision, my main commitment was still to the criminally accused—who roused no rallies on their behalf.

---

lum, though contemporary articles, news stories, and now biographies tell something of the beginning of the courses. The *Yale Law Report* (the law school's magazine) published an article in 1971 about the course that I taught there. See Yale L. Rep., Spring 1971, at 8-9. It said that "comparable" courses were "presently being offered at the law schools at Georgetown, New York University, George Washington, Rutgers, Pennsylvania, Buffalo, and California." *Id.* Professor Herma Hill Kay, in writing a biographical chapter about Ruth Bader Ginsburg, tells how she and Ruth Ginsburg were both attracted to the course by students who were eager to learn it. See Herma Hill Kay, "Ruth Bader Ginsburg: Law Professor Extraordinaire," in Scott Dodson, ed., *The Legacy of Ruth Bader Ginsburg*, 12, 17-18 (Cambridge, Eng.: Cambridge University Press, 2015).

[*] Louise Lague, "Lady Lawyer to Teach Lib via Law," *Washington Daily News*, July 7, 1970.

[†] In fact, police would not allow protesters to set fire to a trash can containing accoutrements of womanhood, so nothing burned, but vocal feminists including Germaine Greer railed against strictures decreeing that we "cram our breasts into bras constructed like mini-Vesuviuses, two stitched white cantilevered cones which bore no resemblance to the female anatomy." Stephanie Merritt, "Danger Mouth," *The Guardian*, October 5, 2003.

[‡] Judith Martin, "Teaching the Womanly Art of Law," *Washington Post*, May 17, 1970 (announcing my appointment to teach in the fall).

But I did enjoy studying the history of the first-wave feminists' fight (1850-1920) for equality and the vote. As an American Studies major at Penn, I had learned almost nothing about this great liberation movement. Most textbooks devoted, at most, half a page to woman suffrage, with perhaps a picture of a parade in New York or of Susan B. Anthony and Elizabeth Cady Stanton, or of women protestors chained to the White House fence in the Wilson administration.

Just as I began teaching about women and the law, the Supreme Court decided *Reed v. Reed*, the first case to rule (and unanimously!) that the Fourteenth Amendment equal protection clause invalidated a classification based on sex.* Like so many of the first movement cases, *Reed's* facts made it appear less important than it actually was. An Idaho court had applied a statute that preferred men over women as executors of estates. The deceased was a young boy, the adopted son of an estranged husband and wife, and the estate totaled a thousand dollars.

A number of cases followed closely on *Reed*, mostly applying equal protection doctrine. But the Supreme Court stopped short of holding that gender discrimination, like race and ethnicity classifications required "strict scrutiny" (a strong presumption of unconstitutionality) by a reviewing court. Also percolating through the courts were cases on the right to abortion, which culminated in 1973 in the Supreme Court's *Roe v. Wade* decision, finding in the Fourteenth Amendment a woman's right to privacy and to an abortion.†

Even though I agreed that reproductive choice was central to improving women's lives, I would not have started there because it would arouse passionate resistance. Indeed the abortion cases were not part of the litigation campaign designed by the leaders of the legal branch of the women's movement. Rather, individuals including health care professionals fought for rights they deemed essential, without consideration for what might be strategically best over the long run.

In retrospect, I see that as much backlash as *Roe* stirred, the victory for choice signaled that the second wave of the women's movement was a serious force. Years later, I saw a similar struggle within the gay liberation

---

* 404 U.S. 71, 76-77 (1971).

† 410 U.S. 113 (1973). *Doe v. Bolton*, decided the same day, said that a woman could have an abortion after fetal viability if needed to protect her "health," which included "physical, emotional, psychological, [and] familial" factors as well as her age.

movement when some leaders thought employment and housing rights easier to achieve than immediate access to marriage, and worried that fighting for that would lead to defeat and ultimately hurt the cause. I agreed, and turned out wrong on that score too.

Another feminist legal effort was the push for an Equal Rights Amendment to the U.S. Constitution. In 1972, Congress adopted it easily, even triumphantly, but the ratification fight fell three states short of the thirty-eight required by the June 1982 deadline. A conservative woman Republican, Phyllis Schlafly, forcefully led the opposition, raising such prospective horrors as women being forced into military combat, and compulsory unisex bathrooms.

As to the amendment, I was once more an ideological laggard. I believed that continuing to plug for full inclusion of women under the already existing Fourteenth Amendment Equal Protection Clause was a better way to go. Silently, I lamented the tremendous amount of effort and energy expended, but the amendment came closer to adoption than I expected.

Without agreeing with all the strategies, I was impressed by the boldness and breadth of the political movement, and the early progress in the courts. We had lots of cases to incorporate into our class. In addition to the fast shifting constitutional doctrine, Title VII of the Civil Rights Act of 1964 prohibited employment discrimination by most organizations of any size, and included "sex" among the prohibited grounds for denying equal opportunity in the workplace.*

Title VII spawned many interesting cases—and somewhat to my surprise, as a dedicated criminal defense lawyer, I found that I enjoyed reading and thinking about them as teaching vehicles for the course. Being in the forefront of a new field was fun, and the engaged, enthusiastic students were a relief from some of the daily combat of public defense. After only a few months, I began to identify with the movement and to think of myself as a potential full-time law professor.

I offered the seminar at Georgetown in the fall of 1970, and in the spring of 1971, I taught it at Yale, flying to New Haven on Thursday afternoon and returning early on Friday morning. It had been seven years since I graduated and waves of nostalgia washed over me when I passed

---

* Civil Rights Act of 1964, tit. VII, Pub. L. No. 88-352, §§ 701(b), 702, 78 Stat. 253, 253-54, 255 (codified as amended at 42 U.S.C. §§ 2000e, 2000e-1 (2013)).

my favorite carrel in the library. Though physically unchanged, the building felt very different.

The cathedral-like main corridor lacked its former hush, and combative posters were taped to the stone pillars, announcing rallies and protests, denouncing leaders and policies. Since the late '60s the school had been in turmoil over civil rights, and over the Vietnam War, and a decided enmity had developed between much of the faculty and the students. One 1972 graduate described the various protests she joined, culminating in picketing the baccalaureate to support the strike of the janitorial workers. Some of the activists also refused to wear regalia at the graduation, hummed "we shall overcome," and upon receiving their diplomas shouted a few slogans into the microphone.[*]

Most striking to me at first was that the noisy halls were full of women; in my day one could go for hours without seeing another female. Now they were everywhere. Not only had Yale undergraduate school accepted women (in 1969), the nationwide proportion of female law students went almost overnight from three to twenty percent. After the initial rush, the numbers continued a steady climb, spurred partly by a decline in applications from men, who could not obtain draft deferments for law school during the Vietnam War.

These new women were unlike any in the past, including my generation from the early sixties. They did not accept the profession's hierarchies as we had done and did not try to assimilate to what they regarded as male "standards." Rather, emboldened by liberation ideology, they called for female law professors, attention to women's professional advancement, and coverage of gender issues in every area of the curriculum.

In his Yale Law School oral history, Abe Goldstein tells of how as newly appointed dean, he was "waited on" by a committee of "militant" women.[†] One of their goals was to have their own course in women and the law, and they had a list of hiring possibilities. Abe countered by suggesting me, saying "she's terribly well qualified and was an officer of the Journal here." They had never heard of me, and being "qualified" by establishment

---

[*] "A Conversation with Ann E. Freedman," interviewed by Mary Clark, New Jersey, Feb. 25, 2000.

[†] Interview by Bonnie Collier with Abraham S. Goldstein, Former Dean, Yale Law Sch. (Oct. 23, 1996), in "A Conversation with Abraham S. Goldstein," 30, 39-43 (2012), *available at* http://digitalcommons.law.yale.edu/cgi/viewcontent.cgi?article=1003 &context=ylsohs

credentials was more likely to worry than to excite them. Actually, I had not been chosen to be an officer of the law journal, due I think to my gender; if the women students had known that, they might have been more keen on me—but if Abe had accurately remembered that I was not an officer, would he have suggested me?

In any event, the students responded by asking that the school pay their way to D.C. to interview me. Abe remembers that he said no to that, but at least one of the women recalls that he did pay for the trip. I apparently assuaged their fears, and Abe reports their saying that I was "wonderful" and "how right you were." He added: "It was predictable because she was one of the best we had and the sort that we hoped they would shortly become, if they would just let themselves relax a little bit." Across the years I smile at this and think how the Yale and Georgetown students influenced who I became more than the other way around.

Just as I started teaching about sex discrimination, law schools all around the country came under enormous pressure from the increasing female enrollments to hire women professors; most had never had even one. As the director of the D.C. Public Defender Service, *and* a teacher of Women and the Law at Georgetown and Yale, I was a sought-after commodity; I received dozens of inquiries and offers to interview for full-time teaching positions. Without intending or earning it, I found that I was considered, by hiring committees at least, to be a significant legal feminist. And I had respectable (if not overwhelming) conventional credentials for appointment to a law faculty—Court of Appeals clerk (but not Supreme Court), very good grades, law review at a top school (not first or second in the class, or an officer.)

A little window of affirmative action for women (well, at least *one* woman per school) had opened, and I sensed that it would not be open for long. Though I was stressed at work and emotionally wrung out by my divorce, I decided I had better interview while I could. Looking back after decades in academia, I marvel at my naïveté about the process. People tried to help me; Ellen Peters, the only woman on Yale's law faculty, suggested that I plan a little presentation on the contents of potential courses and textbooks. Excellent advice, but I didn't have time for such preparation, and I hoped that my unparalleled experience, wit, and charm would carry me through!

I learned that those were not necessarily marketable qualities in academia, where some suspected that too much practice in the real world, especially of the rough adversarial kind I had done, narrowed the mind and disabled it for groundbreaking scholarship. Leading a large agency and trying cases to juries were not considered to be relevant. There was also a whiff of zealotry about me—not on behalf of women's rights but for the defense side in criminal cases.

At my first interview—at Yale—my former civil procedure professor tried to dissuade me: "You are doing influential and exciting work," he noted. "Why would you want to spend your time alone writing things that nobody—certainly not your colleagues—reads?" Next came what was surely a detrimental exchange. When another former professor asked about my scholarly agenda, I said my main interest was in criminal procedure. He countered, "Well, where would you turn for inspiration when you run out of tales from your practice?" I smiled and replied, "By then I would have tenure like the rest of you and could relax." Too late I saw that my somewhat tasteless little joke had fallen flat. For whatever reason, I did not receive an offer from my own law school.

Penn, my undergraduate alma mater, was more accepting. I was fond of the law school there, having often studied in its library, and I had benefited from law students' debate coaching. Philadelphia, where I still had friends, was close to D.C. on a fast train. Penn made me an enthusiastic early offer. The Dean called and visited a number of times; once he even observed me in court. It happened to be the day of James Cockerham's sentencing for child rape and murder when the judge lost his composure and screamed at the defendant.* I later received a copy of the Dean's letter to the judge criticizing his courtroom demeanor—an unusual, but welcome, recruiting device.

By the time I got to Harvard, I was tired of interviewing and could not imagine being the only woman on the faculty of such a large and intimidating institution. Yet Harvard's mystique—so ancient and so eminent—drew me in. I could hear Judge Edgerton's reverent tone when he spoke of "The" Harvard Law School. My friends Alan Dershowitz and John Ely were on the faculty there. So was Phil Heymann, the Legal Aid Agency's first visiting professor, and I consulted Phil in planning the Harvard foray, which he may have had a hand in arranging.

I asked him if instead of a talk, which I didn't have time to prepare, I could teach a class that people could attend. He said that would be fine,

---

* See *United States v. Cockerham*, 476 F.2d 542 (D.C. Cir. 1973), noted in Chapter Eight.

but I would still have to do individual interviews. The demonstration class went well, and the interviews were passable, but I concluded that I did not want to go there. The feeling was apparently mutual because I heard nothing further from Harvard.

For my fourth interview, I chose Stanford, where another public defending professor, Mike Wald, was teaching. In late 1969 when Mike returned to Stanford after being with us at PDS, he had said I should let him know if I ever wanted to teach. I promised I would but thought it would be a long time before I was ready to leave the active practice of law.

Over the next few years, however, I discerned that law school professorships are not sinecures for retired trial lawyers, which I had somehow been assuming. In fact, I saw that I was already late starting an academic career. I called Mike and within a week was invited to interview at Stanford. I did not recognize then what a feat it was to organize a law faculty for action on such short notice.

Before the interview, I had been to California only once, with my then-husband to a convention in San Francisco. Like most people, I had fallen for the city and was hugely disappointed to learn when Mike picked me up at the airport that Stanford was elsewhere. But after my initial shock, I was delighted with the campus in Palo Alto. It was October and the sky was an intense blue; deep purple cyanotis bloomed next to the golden sandstone buildings, and two lines of palm trees opened to an oval lawn and to the law school in one of the university's original late-nineteenth century buildings.

Dean Tom Ehrlich said that their faculty was small enough so that I could meet everyone, which, over two days and evenings, I did. I liked the laid-back atmosphere and the lack of pretension even though I suspected (correctly) that it was somewhat studied. But it was refreshing that not one of the men who interviewed me found it necessary to demonstrate how learned he was. One of them—an attractive, bespectacled guy sporting a sand-colored beard and love beads—even rolled himself a smoke right in the middle of a group interview. I imagined it was marijuana, having just heard the university motto: *Let the winds of freedom blow.* "Indeed!" I thought. (I learned later of course that it was tobacco.)

The smoker was Tom Grey, my future husband, who recollects that we had had an earlier first meeting. His friends Mike Wald and Mat Zwerling from Yale had encouraged him to apply to the Public Defender. Matt had urged me to hire Tom, arguing that his brilliance would add luster to our representation, and Mat thought he would make a splendid trial lawyer. At the interview, I learned that Tom's wife had been admitted to Stanford Medical School and he would be looking for a teaching job in the Bay Area after a single year with us.

Meanwhile, I had been trying to enforce the three-year commitment we had instituted at PDS, which was causing us to lose some promising applicants, especially minorities. (For the first time, they had prestigious, high-paying legal opportunities.) I felt I could not make an exception for a white Yale graduate. According to Tom, I was pleasant but definite about the three-year requirement, which meant he could not take the job; I don't remember the interview. With our marriage well into its fourth decade, I wonder now if we would have been so drawn to each other had we started out as boss and staff.

The outcome of my academic job search was that Stanford and Penn made me offers with comparable salary and benefits. I would be the first woman at Stanford and the third at Penn. The choice set off a seesaw of competing possibilities. Though I felt more at home in the East, California was romantic and adventurous and Stanford a paradise, especially compared to dingy old Philadelphia of the early seventies. My parents were rooting for Penn, but my friend and housemate Gail had promised to join me in the West within the year if I went that way. I also could have stayed in D.C. to teach at Georgetown and even could have spent another year as PDS director. I decided on Stanford.

By the time I joined the law faculty in 1972, I felt that I was a card-carrying member of the women's movement, though I had yet to belong to any organization with an actual card. The university welcomed me mainly for my gender, and I embraced the reception. Myra Strober, the first woman in the business school; Lily Young, the first in engineering; and I— all hired that year—appeared at many press and alumni events. The law school hired its first African American, Bill Gould, that same year, and he often joined the diversity-on-parade road show.

I taught the course in Women and the Law that I had begun to develop at Georgetown and Yale, and found the Stanford students eager for the class, still a rarity. They sympathized with my being the only woman on the faculty. Stephanie Wildman, one of those students and now a law professor herself, asked with wonder in her voice how I could tolerate faculty meetings "with all those white men." The question startled me because I had spent most of my legal career in rooms full of white men without realizing that it did not have to be that way.

Besides having the course in my pocket, I had arrived in academia with a casebook in progress on women and the law. Historian Linda Kerber has written a stirring account of the birth of the texts in the new field, which started with "syllabi circulated in samizdat."[*] A collection of these was clipped together and distributed at a conference at Yale in 1971. I had been a conference convener and was lead author of the packet (under the name of Barbara Bowman).

The conference was the brainchild of Ann Freedman, one of the student instigators of the Yale course. She envisioned bringing together all those involved in the still nascent field of sex discrimination, and inspiring them to produce a "Cases and Materials" book on the subject. Ann convinced me that women's legal studies could not succeed as a field without a textbook in a traditional format, designed for use in law school classrooms, and that she was the one to produce it, with my help.

At least, that is the way I remember that it happened. In her oral history, given for an organization of Yale women alums, Ann recalled that I was the one who enlisted her for the effort.[†] Either version could be true, though I am almost sure she had the idea originally. I can't believe that I would have launched the project while still directing the Public Defender, trying cases and interviewing for a permanent job in academia.

My idea for adding casebook writing to my schedule was ambitious in conception and impossible of execution; I proposed to get a grant to pay Ann for a year and that Eleanor Holmes Norton and I would edit Ann's work. Eleanor was then human rights commissioner in New York City and one of the first black civil rights leaders to connect with other liberation movements. Needless to say, her job, like mine, was more than full-time.

Acquiring a salary for Ann had been relatively easy. I called on my law school friend, Eli Evans, a professional philanthropist then at the Carnegie Foundation and later president of the Revson Foundation. He had recently

---

[*] Linda K. Kerber, "Writing Our Own Rare Books," 14 *Yale Journal of Law and Feminism* 429 (2002). See also Herma Hill Kay, "Claiming a Space in the Law School Curriculum: A Casebook on Sex-Based Discrimination," 25 *Columbia Journal of Gender and Law* 55 (2013).

[†] "A Conversation with Ann E. Freedman," interviewed by Mary Clark, New Jersey, Feb. 25, 2000.

spearheaded a new dedication of the foundation to women's rights. Our book was only the first of a number of projects Eli supported both at Carnegie and Revson, including the Women's Law and Policy Fellowship at Georgetown, and Equal Rights Advocates, a public-interest law firm in San Francisco. He also aided us in putting through a grant to fund the Yale conference.

Ann Freedman's vision and purpose in planning the conference was that it would bring together potential individual contributors to a single unified sex discrimination book. But it turned out others had already started on texts, and a number of different Women and the Law Cases and Materials were in the works by 1971 or soon after. First out in 1974 was one by Ruth Bader Ginsburg, Herma Hill Kay, and Kenneth Davidson.[*] Ours came the following year, with authors Ann, Eleanor, Susan Ross, and me; Susan had been an originator of the NYU course, and was a government litigator, specializing in sex discrimination.

We were disappointed not to be first ourselves, but we knew that two volumes from prominent publishers added legitimacy to the new field. Our book was titled *Sex Discrimination and the Law: Causes and Remedies*. Both books were tomes, quelling any concern about the thinness of the course material. Many other fine texts and casebooks followed as the course itself broke into subsets with titles like Feminist Theory and Gender & Public Policy.

At the Yale conference, I had met three young women from Berkeley Law School (then called Boalt Hall) who were to become close associates in California. Like the women in my seminars, Nancy Davis, Mary Dunlap, and Wendy Williams were a new breed: demanding, insistent, filled with confidence in themselves and their cause. They had not known each other well in law school but at the conference talked about forming a feminist law firm together. I had barely arrived at Stanford when Nancy was in my office to offer and enlist aid in teaching, textbook writing, and law firm organization. I can see her now, brown hair flowing down her back, flawless complexion, apple cheeks, and eyes dancing with energy and enthusiasm.

Just as Ann had (I believe) lured me into textbook writing, Nancy recruited my help for the embryonic Davis, Dunlap & Williams, conceived

---

[*] *Texts, Cases, and Materials on Sex-Based Discrimination* (St. Paul: West Publ. Co., 1974).

as a teaching law firm, which became Equal Rights Advocates. The three lawyers joined me at Stanford in a law clinic and class rather grandly titled Litigative Strategies against Sex Discrimination. Again, Eli Evans, still at the Carnegie Foundation, funded our efforts, which paid the salaries and overhead of the lawyers.

We wanted the Litigative Strategies course to provide a model for clinical teaching in which students worked on actual cases with real clients while also exploring the academic underpinnings of the subject. The class simulated the major phases of a civil law suit from initial client interview through summary judgment. We videoed and critiqued each student doing the oral assignments, and their written work and tactical thoughts were woven into the real case. The students also worked directly on the actual cases at the firm on Turk Street in San Francisco. Finally, we conducted a regular classroom seminar using the book-in-progress.

It was a costly enterprise not only in terms of the time of four practicing lawyers (Joan Graff had joined Equal Rights Advocates) but for the students as well. They were brave to give a semester to an experimental course, whose substantive material was unlikely to be on the bar examination. Yet we were usually oversubscribed, and even attracted a number of male feminists. Over the years, many graduates have confirmed that the course cemented their commitment to women's rights and prepared them for practice like nothing else they had done in law school.

A student-made photo book shows what a good time we had. I remember especially "the dress," a one-size-fits-all garment we kept in the office closet in case someone was suddenly required to go to court. Though pants were already the uniform of many professional women, especially the young ones, such garb was still not generally allowed in the courtroom or other official legal venues. The dress reminded me of the clothes we kept on hand at PDS so that our clients could appear respectable before the jury.

That Stanford would offer a course connected to a feminist law firm was proof of the growing acceptance of women's rights within the academy. Yet in the most important area, hiring female professors, the pace was glacial. In my first five years at Stanford, no women were even invited to interview, though a few were discussed. It became apparent that a majority of the faculty wanted to make sure I worked out before they continued the bold experiment.

Paul Brest, a chief faculty ally, told me that when he had come to Stanford several years before I did, there had been open debate about whether women could ever succeed in legal academia. Though admitted as students in most law schools for almost a hundred years, only a handful of women had been law professors. The doubters pointed out that no women had the qualifications of the best male candidates, failing to see that discrimination and the entrenched male academic network prevented the women from gaining the usual credentials. An influx of unqualified white women was the open fear of traditional academia in the early seventies. But the deeper unspoken dread was that once the barrier was down, people of color, male and female, would come next, demanding jobs without meeting the usual qualifications.

Not until I left for a few years to serve in the Carter administration did Stanford hire a second woman, Carol Rose, but she had come and gone before I returned. I think Carol found that being a single woman in Palo Alto and the only one at Stanford Law was too solitary. She went to Berkeley, then to Northwestern, and on to Yale where she spent the rest of her distinguished career. After Carol left, Deborah Rhode was hired and was on board by the time I returned to Stanford in 1979.

At last I had a colleague in the struggle to hire women, although, fresh from clerkships on the Second Circuit and the U.S. Supreme Court, she was even newer to academia and much younger than I. Not until 1982—a decade after I started at Stanford—did we appoint a third woman. I was head of the appointments committee when Ellen Borgersen, one of the first female Supreme Court law clerks (for Potter Stewart) and a partner at a top law firm, joined the faculty.

For me, the lack of urgency about hiring more women became an ever more grating irritant. Even some of my friends thought that if we could ignore the militant, mounting demands, women with credentials more like the men's would come along. They were right, and that is mostly what has happened. Meanwhile, as we waited, several generations of estimable women were passed over, and years went by in which I was the sole female on the faculty or one of two or three. Thinking about that still makes me angry and a little sad.

It was futile to try to get some of the men to understand the need for more women—why they, good hearted and brilliant, were not sufficient to our purposes, whatever they were. Around that time, I was writing a note on women jurors for the sex discrimination book and was drawn to Justice

William O. Douglas's explanation for a Supreme Court decision reversing a conviction where women had been excluded from jury service. "[T]he two sexes are not fungible; a community made up exclusively of one is different from a community composed of both; the subtle interplay of influence one on the other is among the imponderables. . . . [A] flavor, a distinct quality, is lost if either sex is excluded."*

Deborah Rhode and I wrote a memo to the whole faculty, asking them to imagine themselves as one of two men surrounded by a host of female colleagues. As far as I know, no one was moved by the hypothetical to change his position. In my later years at Stanford Law, our faculty full of female stars gave me a taste of what I had missed. Having the company of other women mattered, I realized, because I felt known and understood in a new and gratifying way.

Fortunately, even in the early lonely days of teaching at the law school, I found companionship among a small group of feminists scattered in different departments throughout the university but sharing the common experience of being women in the heavily male and politely hostile world of Stanford academia. I remember especially Diane Middlebrook in the English department (who died in 2007), gender and kinship researcher Sylvia Yanigasako and Michelle Zimbalist Rosaldo in anthropology (Sylvia is now department chair; Shelly was killed in 1981 in an accidental fall while doing fieldwork in the Philippines), and Myra Strober, a labor economist in the business school (and later in the education school).

In my April 21, 1982, diary entry, I wrote of "a gathering of the feminists to talk about our meeting with [Stanford's president Donald] Kennedy over Estelle Freedman—really such a fine little band." Estelle had been denied tenure by the university's Advisory Board (on which no woman had ever served), reversing a positive vote by the history department. We knew that the fact that her work was about women influenced the denial, and suspected that her open lesbianism might also have been a factor.

The women mounted a terrific campaign of rallies, petitions, meetings and classes. My role was to handle public and legal relations; I claimed that we were certain that the university would ultimately do the right thing, and I enlisted a first-rate lawyer to make sure it happened. That was Marcia Berzon, now a judge on the U.S. Court of Appeals for the Ninth

---

* *Ballard v. United States*, 329 U.S. 187, 193-94 (1946).

Circuit. Diane Middlebrook and I arranged lunch with Al Hastorf, the provost, to lobby him about Estelle. I followed the lead of Diane, who as always was lucid, gracious, sincere, sweet—and effectively a bit flirtatious. The exercise reminded me of the jury arguments in which I had subtly conveyed that I would be personally pained by a guilty verdict.

Hastorf decided to appoint a well-respected professor from psychology to investigate the case. The professor recommended reversing the Advisory Board's decision and awarding tenure to Estelle, which the provost did. We rejoiced in our first feminist victory at Stanford. I always thought of us as the "little band" (as Proust describes Albertine and her friends in Balbec). Especially during the years when I had few female companions in the law school, the "little band" provided much needed psychological support.

In 1974, led by Myra Strober, we founded Stanford's Center for Research on Women (CROW), which became the Institute for Research on Women and Gender, and ultimately today the Clayman Institute for Gender Research. I remember a lunch with Myra when she told me about the idea. She said some students had come to her about the need for such a center. It reminded me of how the Georgetown students had drawn me into teaching.

I was both impressed by the idea and doubtful about doing it. Here we were, two untenured first women; it did not seem a good position for launching an institute or center, or whatever it would be. Myra had two young children and was just settling into the West. But she gathered the little band and started the program, which today is a vibrant research and intellectual institution at Stanford, attracting students and scholars from all over the world. I do not want to imply that I had a large role in the success, only to say I was there at the creation and have tried to help over the years.

As my identification with feminism grew, it occasionally rested uneasily with my other calling: defense of the criminally accused. So-called rape-shield laws, which restricted the use at trial of the victim's prior sexual history, captured my quandary. In the early seventies, such statutes were passed in forty-nine states, and the Federal Rules of Evidence were amended to provide for exclusion of such testimony—an amazingly speedy result for the women's movement in the first years of the second wave.

A defender at heart, I was torn about limiting the evidence available to the accused. I knew firsthand that victims were often humiliated on cross-examination and that the prospect of public dissection of their sex lives made rape the most underreported of felonies. But I had also seen harshly punitive sentences, even the death penalty in some states, imposed on men convicted of rape, especially when the victim was white and the defendant black. I suspected that the reason feminists had won rape-shield statutes so swiftly had less to do with justice and more with the absence of any interest group advocating for the criminally accused.

The conflict came to a head for me in 1974 when I was asked with a colleague, Tony Amsterdam, to write a memorandum developing the local ACLU's stance on proposed rape-shield statutes. We thought that the accused should be protected in any legislation and suggested allowing the use of the victim's prior sexual history only when it tended to show certain specified circumstances such as prior consensual intercourse with the defendant or that he knew about the victim's history. Our scheme provided for a closed *voir dire* hearing to establish whether the evidence met one of the conditions. A number of feminists objected to what they termed our concern for "rapists' rights," but some form of closed hearing before excluding such evidence was widely adopted.[*]

Generally, I think the accused gets an extralegal boost in defending against all violent crimes when he has a woman lawyer; applying ancient sex stereotypes, juries may assume a woman would not represent a man who was guilty of such a vicious crime—especially if the charge is rape. As a public defender, I figured any such positive bump from my femaleness balanced some of the negatives from gender prejudice against me.

Public defenders cannot choose their clients according to the charge. Yet today, when I read a transcript of my cross-examination of the accuser in a 1969 rape case, I feel queasy about something I once viewed with pride. The two young people knew each other socially. There was no doubt that they had sexual intercourse, or that he was rough, hitting her and tearing her clothes. The question was her initial consent. Looking at her closely, I started my cross: "Do you know what it means to lead a man on?" There is no right answer, of course, but she said "yes," and then I went through my client's story of the sequence of events, pausing to repeat: "Don't you call that leading a man on?"

---

[*] Estelle Freedman, *Redefining Rape: Sexual Violence in the Era of Suffrage and Segregation*, 280-81 (2013); Leigh Ann Wheeler, *How Sex Became a Civil Liberty*, 182-83 (2013) (describing our memorandum for the ACLU).

In the end, when the jury believed the woman and found my client guilty, I was, on some deep level where a defender should not dwell, relieved, while still believing I had done my job well in the cross examination. Though I think defenders must do it if assigned, I realize now that it is hard going for a feminist to defend a rape case, especially when there is a claim of consent.

My women's rights activities—teaching the course and writing the book—opened academia to me. I'm sure that gender figured positively into my promotion as well. Detractors had to bow to the imprudence of firing the first woman the law school had ever hired. Moreover, I came to enjoy being part of the movement. The slogans, especially "the personal is political" and "sisterhood is powerful," spoke to me.

In the eighties and nineties, the women's movement was growing and diversifying. New leaders and thinkers were emerging, ranging from radical lesbian separatists to staid constitutional lawyers. And as with many progressive political movements, the more we succeeded, the more real the schisms became. I was bothered by some of the internecine struggles which to my practical mind dealt with unimportant matters of doctrine and nomenclature. Very soon, my liberal, equality-minded version of feminism seemed out of style. But I have never given up on the cause or on proselytizing for it.

What do I mean these days when I claim feminism as a central part of my identification? Not that I am a leading thinker or theorist in the field — though some of my best friends are. Even on the strictly legal side, I have not constructed arguments or written briefs. The actual "stuff" of the discourse never really interested me—intermediate scrutiny versus strict scrutiny, whether pregnancy is a normal condition or a disability to be compensated, sexual harassment as a form of discrimination. These are just examples of complicated legal issues that I could have but did not formally engage.

I feel also that I am a somewhat incomplete role model because I have not borne children. Interviewers sometimes ask about the absence of any biological offspring; perhaps I'm being overly sensitive, but I pick up the implication that I am therefore unfinished, which pushes me to try to explain. My standard story has been that my first husband did not want children and that by the time I remarried, I felt that I was too old, or that there were enough children to care for and love in my life. And there is some truth in that account.

On the whole, I believe that I just went merrily along assuming that when the time was right I would have two (the right number) children. But I never had a powerful drive to procreate; I had spent seven years raising my brother Starr, and though I found children fascinating creatures, especially after infancy, I preferred adults and books. Moreover, my friends had offspring they were willing to share: Gail's daughter Hannah; the Rabin girls Karen, Donna and Nina; Ann and Mark's boys Jake and Nick; and the Bankman-Fried sons Sam and Gabe, among others.

Though I have not been a thinker-feminist, or modeled having it all by successfully combining motherhood with a high-powered career, I have paid my dues in other ways. Feminism for me has meant putting concerns for women at the center of my thoughts and actions. Whatever I do, I consider its effect on women. I believe deeply and passionately that if we could achieve gender equality in all areas of life, the world would be better for everyone, including the indigent accused.

Barbara Babcock and Tom Grey, early-1970s Stanford Law School
newspaper photos, courtesy of the Stanford Law Library archives

Stanford Law School faculty, fall 1975

10

BECOMING A CALIFORNIAN (1972-1976)

Mother was unhappy about my decision in 1972 to move West, and I tried to console her with a trip to Europe, her first. I hoped that Dad would come with us too, but foreign travel held no charms for him and he said he would be fine staying home alone. He had been sober for some time and had been making good money in his law practice, as he always did between binges. We worried that he was likely to start drinking once we left, but then sooner or later we knew he would start anyway.

I also felt that we needed to move soon to realize Mother's life dream of a European trip. She had been diagnosed with multiple sclerosis in 1964 after bouts of paralysis that doctors originally attributed to nerves and depression. (Her attacks usually coincided with dad's drinking.) At that time, an MS diagnosis required eliminating all other possible causes for the symptoms. I took her to a specialist who was somewhat unorthodox in believing that MS could be slow-developing and non-lethal. But he proved correct in Mother's case. It took many years for the disease to finally put her in a wheel chair, and she died of a stroke.

When we went to Europe, she was still walking without a cane, though she tired easily and had given up her swimming and lifesaving classes. I wanted Starr to come with us for his company, but also because we needed his physical strength to help Mother when she flagged. There was some poetic justice in his supplying the muscle. Mother complained for years about the time Starr spent working out, pointedly asking why he did not lift the vacuum cleaner instead—an oft-repeated dig that drove him crazy. But when he picked her up in his arms and carried her on the run to barely beat closing time at the Sistine chapel, she came to appreciate his fitness routines.

The trip ran from April 28 to May 19, 1972. We started in Rome, then went to Florence and Paris, and ended in London. Italy was a great introduction to Europe for mom because it was truly foreign but also very friendly. We arrived at night and the next morning opened the shuttered windows to see a street blocked off from automobile traffic by huge baskets full of blooms.

I had been to Rome once a decade earlier with Eddie Cohen and I remembered the pleasure of traveling with an expert on everything we saw. At the Forum and also the Pantheon, he delivered spontaneous historical lectures, meant just for me, but good enough that they drew onlookers. I couldn't do as much for Mom and Starr, but discovered the uses of a first-rate guide book, and the joys of being planner-in-chief.

Mother had dropped out of college after two years because of the Depression, but before the MS hit, she had enrolled in art history and painting classes at the University of Maryland. For years, she took her children plus Patsy to the National Gallery on most Sunday afternoons for a lecture in the auditorium and pecan pie in the cafeteria. Patsy and I remember these outings fondly but David had a different view. Between compulsory attendance at the Presbyterian Church in the morning and the church of culture in the afternoon, Sunday was completely ruined for him. All he wanted was to be outside with his buddies or working on a car. As Freud says, every child has a quite different experience of the same family.

We spent a lot of time in the great galleries of Europe, ate wonderful food, made discoveries of gardens and churches. Though Starr and Mother did not usually have fun together, they both threw themselves into the once-in-a-lifetime adventure. Mom summed up our trip when we passed a couple in the street that also had an old lady in tow, and were all scowling. "See," she said happily, "those people traveling with their mother are having a worse time than we are."

There were a few downs to go with all the ups, of course. In Paris, where Addie and I had honeymooned, memories of our early happiness made me sad. In Italy and France my lack of any aptitude for languages was frustrating. Starr, who was in his second year at Georgetown Law School, began to worry about his upcoming exams. Our plans for my aiding him in regular study did not prove very practical.

But all in all, the trip was a success. We both felt we had done an important thing for Mother, and we had enjoyed our travel adventures. Back home, I started packing for California amidst a round of going away parties, feeling elated and depressed in about equal degrees. A separation agreement between Addie and me, drawn by Dad, promised that "each of the parties may hereafter conduct their lives . . . without interference in any way from the other, to the same extent as if this marriage had not been celebrated." The common law formula seemed peculiarly poignant and final.

The agreement also divided our earthly goods. He took the little sail boat, the white Maverick car, and his family heirloom desk, while I kept an oil painting Addie and I had bought together on impulse for $1800, a great extravagance at the time. I cherish it to this day, for itself, and as a memento of youthful exuberance. It is by Robert Burkert and has the bright lights of a city in the background of a lush park in which there is a small ambiguous figure, the subject of many stoned meditations on its gender and whether it was coming or going.

I arrived at Stanford in June, 1972, and immediately felt at loose ends; the students were gone and my new colleagues had mostly withdrawn into the solitary business of research and writing. Though people were welcoming, not many were around. Everything about my D.C. life seemed remote including a view from my office of a liquor store where the regulars drank Thunderbird from paper cups and passed out on the heat vents. Now there was a lemon tree outside my window, filled with sweet smelling blossoms.

I felt three time zones distant from real life. For a while, I subscribed to the *Washington Post* by mail but the news was too stale. Today with the internet the move might be easier. Life slowed down; instead of dozens of friends and more social events than I could attend, I knew only Mike and Johanna Wald, a cousin and her family in the East Bay, and Janice Cooper, one of my students from Yale. Janice showed me a beautiful secret beach accessed by going through a flower farm and climbing down a steep cliff. There was nothing like that in Washington D.C.

Gail Saliterman was planning to come soon and wanted to live in San Francisco, which sounded good to me. Meanwhile I took an apartment with a little deck overlooking a garden on College Avenue in Palo Alto, and rode my bike to the law school. In the days that stretched before me without appointments or appearances, I read *Middlemarch* and other nineteenth century novels and took tennis lessons from a patient woman who had once coached the Stanford girls.

Gail and Fred had given me a tennis racket, though Gail had doubted that I would actually play. "Have you ever seen her run?" she asked. Though I was slow, I developed a steady serve and a decent net game, so that Tom and I later made a competitive doubles team, with him covering most of the court.

I had entered academia with the intention of teaching and writing about criminal procedure, which is what I knew; I wanted to inspire students to practice in this field, not the career aspiration of many at leading law schools. But my plans ran up against the presence of the extraordinary Tony Amsterdam, a charismatic teacher who dominated criminal law classrooms at Stanford. Colleagues warned me that no one would take a class offered by an unknown when he was teaching the same subject.

The school needed a Civil Procedure professor. I decided to do that because it was a first semester course and I wanted to teach the students at their most open and eager. As has often happened to me, what looked like bad luck—not getting to teach my specialty—turned out to be a positive thing. I became an expert in procedure generally—not only the criminal side—and this put me in position for a high appointment in the Justice Department a few years later. If I had been solely a criminal procedure teacher with a public defender background, I could have faced some head-winds from law-and-order forces in the confirmation hearings.

From the beginning, I liked teaching Civil Procedure, involved as it is with legal history, the ideal of due process, and professional ethics, all of which interested me. And then there is the fun of teaching against expectations: the students had all heard the subject matter was technical and dull, so that any amusing or interesting point became much magnified in their minds

Only a few years into teaching the subject, I became co-editor of a textbook on Civil Procedure. The collaboration grew out of a casual con-versation at a law professors' convention, where I met Paul Carrington, then Dean of Michigan Law School. He asked me what text I was using and I told him, adding that I was dissatisfied with all of them except his, but that his was "too idiosyncratic to be readily teachable." Paul promptly invited me to join him in a major revision of the book on the next edition, which I did.

We went through two or three editions before he turned to other interests. Today, the book is into its fifth edition as Babcock, Massaro, and Spaulding. My current co-editors are both dear friends: Toni Massaro of the University of Arizona, and Norman Spaulding, my former student and now Stanford colleague. Teaching one's own book brings with it the advantage of always knowing the purpose of the questions posed and the answers to them. Further, the name on the book creates authority in the minds of students. And there is always the hope, forlorn in my case, of making good money if the book is widely adopted.

I expected to be a great teacher whatever the subject because I thought my courtroom skills were immediately transferable to the classroom: wrong on the whole. Though law professors proceed by asking questions rather than lecturing, and I am good at designing the questions, there is more to teaching than that. At first, I tried to exhibit originality and brilliance, and worried that I would bore students by emphasizing and repeating basic points. As a result, my classes were initially somewhat obscure. After a few years, I developed my mantra, which I have passed on to many junior colleagues starting out: Repetition is the soul of pedagogy.

My worst mistake in my first class was revealing that I was not an authority in the subject and would be learning it along with them. This had been an asset in teaching Women and the Law, a new subject where students knew that everyone was coming in on the ground floor. But for a basic course like Civil Procedure students expected to be taught by an expert, especially while paying a Stanford tuition.

Despite such missteps, I liked classroom teaching right away and told the student newspaper that it was much "more exhilarating than I expected. You're listening to everything so carefully that it's reverberating in all your nerves. . . . You're locked in with the students and trying to make them understand, and then, when people say really good things, it turns me on." On the best days, the atmosphere was charged and I could feel the students getting it. It was almost as good as a jury trial.

With photographs and a seating chart, I would quickly learn the names and faces of all the students (usually about 60), and sought to encourage them to participate. But I soon found that only the most confident, including few women and minorities, spoke up voluntarily. And since the answers of the confident speakers were usually good, the others left the talking to them and just took notes.

For a while, I turned to the system prevalent when I was in school, cold calling by name, without any prior warning. But this had the drawback that some students were obviously terrified and their tongue-tied performance embarrassed not only them, but me and indeed the whole class. Yet speaking in stressful conditions is a fundamental skill for lawyers, so I sought some other method to help them learn.

I eventually developed a middle path between all-volunteer and cold calling, a panel system, in which four students were assigned a single day's assignment in advance, and so knew they would be the first called on when we reached it. They were to think about the notes and questions, and prepare in depth. I would spend the first half of the class with the panel, taking care to give each person at least one really challenging question. Then the rest of the class could join the discussion on a volunteer basis, perhaps returning to the panel experts if we were stuck. I found that those who had broken the ice by speaking on panel were more likely to volunteer in later classes.

Thinking back on my own experience in law school, where I never volunteered for fear of being wrong and disgracing my sex, I tried to make participation costless; no one risked anything by giving it a try. But soon I realized that for the sake of the rest of the class I needed to signal when someone was far off base. The effect of trying to support a participant while clearly signaling a mistake could be comical, as Jay Wexler, now a law professor himself, pointed out in telling about an impression of me he does for his own Civil Procedure classes.

> I start with channeling the wildly affirming Babcock that we all loved and took great comfort in ("yes, Sean" "right, right, right, good, Laura, yes" etc.) but then the kicker is to give a taste of the horrified Babcock that only came out once in a while, most memorably in response to something this guy named Todd said, which caused you to break out in "NO, NO, NOOOO, Todd, wrong, no, no, absolutely not, NO." It turns out that when these two glimpses of you are combined, the effect is inevitably class-room delirium. (e-mail, Nov. 22, 2011)

It was somewhat unsettling to move from D.C., which had become a largely black city when I left, to the striking whiteness of Stanford. The law school had its first black graduate in 1968. That same year, Thelton Henderson had established a legal aid office in the minority community of East Palo Alto, which had never had a lawyer. EPA was a short hop across the freeway but a long way in social distance from the affluent suburban college town.

When Thelton read of the first black law graduate, he proposed to the Dean that he come to work at Stanford to recruit minority students, to facilitate their applications, and support them when here. He believed he could establish a successful affirmative action program that would make the embarrassingly monochrome school attractive to black, Latino, and Native American students. Though it required some years to accomplish it, Thelton turned out to be right. Along the way, he took on the title of Assistant Dean and taught some classes as well.

Thelton was one of the first people I met in California and we became friends immediately. Later after his success establishing a strong minority presence at Stanford, he started a firm in San Francisco with two other civil rights attorneys, Sandy Rosen and Joe Remcho. Then during the Carter administration he was appointed to the Northern District of California, and established a nationwide reputation as an exceptional trial judge. We are still close, and if a friend can also be a personal hero, as I think he can, Thelton is one of mine.

In the first years at Stanford, I felt in transition between D.C. and California, and between my hectic and public existence as a defender and the relatively cloistered life of academia. While learning how to teach law students and beginning to do research and write law review articles, I carried on the cause of criminal defense, serving on various national boards and committees, and giving a speech about the inadequacies of our system of representation to eight hundred people on a platform with Ramsey Clark, the former U.S. Attorney General. In addition to teaching civil procedure, I started an elaborate and time-consuming clinical course on sex discrimination law, and co-authored texts in both subjects.

Overall, I was working as hard as I had in D.C. but the life felt different. Partly it was the respect accorded a Stanford law professor in contrast to the embattled position of a defender. I was also much taken by the pleasures of Palo Alto life, the friendliness of people, the ease of daily interactions, and the perfect weather: temperate year-round, little humidity, the changes of season marked by the different flowers in bloom.

As in D.C. the main form of social interaction at Stanford was the dinner party, at that time usually soup-to-nuts productions by faculty wives who did not work outside the home. As best I could tell, the custom was for every faculty couple to have every other faculty couple to one of these dinners at least once a year.

And it was all couples; as a single woman, I did not fit readily into this routine, and since I was known as a feminist the wives were not sure whether to invite a dinner partner for me. Most did, and often it was the same guy, a single man from another department. It got so we almost expected to be paired in this way. I wondered why, since he seemed unattached, he was not more flirtatious. It turned out that he was gay, of course.

At the time I moved to California, all I knew about gay men was from *Tea and Sympathy*, which I read as a play and saw in the mid-fifties as a movie with Deborah Kerr, when it was considered extremely daring. Set in a New England boarding school for boys and treating homosexuality as an affliction, the play deals with the efforts of a housemaster's wife to help a gay student overcome his inclinations by offering herself to him, with the deathless words: "When you speak of this, and you will, be kind." (When I asked Tom Grey if he had read or seen the play, he said indeed he had because the play's author had gone to Exeter, where he also went. "We all were looking for a faculty wife like that.")

My student Jay Spears was the first openly gay friend I made. He was a star, president of the law review, and my research assistant. I recommended him for a law clerkship to Judge Bazelon, which could be (and was for Jay) a stepping stone to a much-coveted Supreme Court clerkship. The judge had never had an openly gay clerk, and I did not think he was ready for one in the abstract. But I knew that Jay would do a brilliant job, and would get along well with the famously difficult judge. So I didn't mention his sexual preference and advised Jay to leave evidence of it off his resume. In the first months of the clerkship, the judge said he was a great success, and then added: "you didn't tell me he was so . . . social." I just smiled.

One party I remember especially well, again early in my California life, was in San Francisco at the apartment of another new friend, Diane Middlebrook. She and I were the only women among wonderfully groomed, handsome men clad in soft fabrics and leather, and talking about poetry. In the kitchen, I said, "What is going on? I've never been at a party where there was no sexual tension." Diane laughed—"oh, there's plenty of that but they are all gay, so they're interested in each other." Another San Francisco lesson.

Diane was an English professor, the second good friend, after Thelton, that I made in California. We continued to be close, even when living far apart, from the summer of 1972 until her death in 2007. At a memorial service, I told the story of our friendship; here are my notes for the talk.

A staff member of the law school lived in the city, and commuted on a Stanford bus with Diane. She realized that I might be lonely, and said, "I know someone you would like to meet. She is a woman, like you. Why don't we all have lunch and I will introduce you."

I said yes of course, but I rather dreaded it—an English professor—think Beowulf and Grendel's mother, think dowdy, think dull. And then—think Diane—long honey blonde hair, aviator glasses, beautiful hooded eyes, incredible elevated talk. Most of all, I felt her genuine interest and warmth.

After lunch with our introducer we went off together and talked until it was time for the bus to return. In her last book Diane inscribed in her lovely distinctive hand—"For Barbara—during our long journey—the best of friends that could ever be."

My story—of meeting Diane and finding an instant deep and lasting connection—is not unusual. She had a genius for friendship. At a retirement party and working on this memorial, I was struck by the number of people who felt that their friendship with her had a special, even a unique, quality.

Diane taught us a lot about living fully in the present—and if there was ever any fun to be had, she found it. She was also wonderfully talented at searching out the best part, the beauty in small as well as great things: Look at the constellations in the sky, look at this brave little primrose blooming in the cold, look at this lovely dried fruit I'm serving on this silver platter.

People speaking of Diane summon up an afternoon, a walk, a time in class—hundreds of vivid moments and stories through which she lives in all our memories—

I'll tell you one of my favorites—it stretches back to the early seventies when the second women's movement was getting under way—We were walking through campus, the law professor and the English professor—striding along talking away as usual. We passed a construction site—whistles, cat calls—mostly directed at her—She was wearing her leather suit.

Although the correct feminist position was something between annoyance and outrage, Diane laughed and made some elevated remark about the difference between perception and reality. I thought: I want to be a feminist like her—a sexy feminist.

Late in my first year at Stanford, I met a woman at a party who was director of the Architectural Heritage Foundation, which had recently received the donation of the Haas-Lilienthal House at the corner of Franklin and Jackson streets in San Francisco. The foundation wanted the house lived in while they planned its use—with no caretaker duties and rent free. I accepted at once and lived in very grand style for over a year, celebrating my 35th birthday there.

The mansion was built in 1886, about the same time as my childhood home in Hyattsville, though of course it was much more imposing. Its architecture was in what the books always call the "flamboyant" Queen Anne revival style because the outward bays and turrets are unrelated to the floor plan. The dining room had leather tooled wall paper, there were Persian carpets and crystal chandeliers, two staircases, a ballroom, and perhaps my favorite feature, a sheltered kitchen garden tucked in the back where no one would guess its presence from the street.

The tempo of extracurricular life picked up when I moved into the mansion because Diane lived right around the corner on Larkin Street. Though she was in the midst of a painful divorce and had much of the care of her seven year old, Leah, Diane was full of social energy. We cooked and entertained and commuted together and her circle became mine as well. Vern Magee, who had grown up with Diane in Spokane, was a special friend and Arturo Islas, the first Hispanic in the English Department, was another. His partner was Jay Spears.

When I think of those first years in California, I recall the time that Diane and I went to an early showing of *Last Tango in Paris*, the Bertolucci film starring Marlon Brando that was explicit and erotic. In the nearly empty theater, we felt like we were at a private screening, as we sipped from a thermos of Gordon's gin and sank into the pleasure of the afternoon. The theater was among the many attractions of Polk Street, which was within easy walking distance of the mansion, and was becoming a center of gay and youth culture. I remember especially our meals at Tadich's grill, where we ate sand dabs while sitting on stools at a circular counter.

That first summer, Starr came out with the Oldsmobile Toronado Gail's father had found for me, a tank-like vehicle the students called the Queen Mary. I would need a car like that for regular freeway driving once I moved into the city. I had learned to drive relatively late in life and wasn't comfortable with the high speeds and merging lanes on the freeway, though it got better when the scenic and less traveled Highway 280 was completed several years after my arrival. To cut down on freeway trips, I fell into a pattern of living in the city, and spending a night or two in Palo Alto, staying over with colleagues and their families, Mike and Johanna Wald, Paul and Iris Brest, Bob and Yemima Rabin. I liked getting to know their children and making friends in a way that the formal dinner party setting did not afford.

Starr loved San Francisco at first sight and decided to move as soon as he finished law school. By the time he came for good, I was living in the mansion and glad to have him join me because it could be a little scary alone there, even with Diane nearby. Unlike Starr, I needed a few years to become a dedicated Californian; I had been so embedded in the East, coming into my own in college and law school, the excitement of my career as a trial lawyer in the nation's capital, that even in the civilized paradise provided by Stanford and the Bay Area, I still felt that I was living far from home. For one thing, I was often cold because of the temperature shifts during the day, and between Palo Alto and San Francisco. Also my first winter was the rainiest season for many years. Yet the storms were followed routinely by big-sky rainbows, such as seldom seen in the East.

While I was getting settled and exploring northern California, Gail was finishing up her Ph.D. dissertation, and looking for work that would bring her West. Finally, she decided to go to law school, an alternative she had long considered and enrolled at Berkeley Law (then Boalt Hall). We shared several apartments in San Francisco over the next few years, with her commuting to the East Bay and I to Palo Alto. I continued staying over with Stanford friends at least once a week.

Our first place was in a building on Nob Hill, the very center of the city. Each floor was a single flat, with the elevator opening into it. The living room and kitchen had spectacular views of the bay and city. I had never lived in a place with panoramas, and seeing the activity on the water in all kinds of weather and seasons was awesome. With her usual spirit, Gail joined the project of re-creating our D.C. social whirl. We started a poker game with Thelton and Starr and other public interest lawyers, and we carried on playing tennis, cooking and partying.

After we had spent a few years on Nob Hill, the owner wanted to sell the condo. We made a mistake in not buying it. But at that point in our lives, neither of us had ever owned real estate, or gone seriously into debt. And we were not sure what the future held for us together. We talked of remaining single and creating an extended family of friends, former and current lovers, and a rich life that included travel, and good work in the public interest. But neither of us was ready to commit to that concept. (As things turned out, we each married a younger academic named Tom.)

Instead of buying the condo, we moved to an apartment in a lovely old building, less than a block from the Haas-Lilienthal mansion at the corner of Franklin and Jackson streets. That area on the edge of Pacific Heights was my neighborhood in the city. Up the hill off Gough was a pretty park with a well-maintained tennis court, and shopping was a few blocks east on Polk. Except for the strain of commuting, I began to feel at home in California.

It was 1976, and it had taken me five years to settle in, but just as I began to relax into my new surroundings, the women's movement swept through again with possibilities I could not resist. Jimmy Carter had promised to appoint women to high level posts in his administration. When he was elected that November, I became an immediate beneficiary of that promise.

Photograph of the author by Howard Schatz, for the 1992 book *Gifted Woman*

Swearing-in as Assistant Attorney General, Civil Division, Department of Justice, March 1977; Henry Babcock holds the Bible while Judge David Bazelon administers the oath

11

"GENERAL BABCOCK" (1977-1979)

In March 1977, I was sworn in as Assistant Attorney General of the Civil
Division in the Department of Justice, with my friend and mentor Judge
David Bazelon administering the oath. My father held the Bible and said it
was the proudest day of his life. Just five years earlier, I had, with mixed
hope and sadness, left behind my native city and the Public Defender
Service I had helped to create. Now I was returning as a tenured law
professor to one of the most prestigious legal jobs in the country, presiding
over the work of hundreds of attorneys representing the United States in
court.

I learned that my official form of address was "General Babcock"—
though I think I was called that only once, by Justice Rehnquist when I
argued in the Supreme Court. He had been an Assistant Attorney General
himself and perhaps had enjoyed the military title. I liked the sound of it
too, even if it made me feel a little like a character in a Gilbert and Sullivan
operetta.

"How did *you* get the job?" The question came from doubters and the
curious; even friends and supporters wondered. Being a respected lawyer
was rarely all it took to win an assistant attorney generalship. A major
campaign contribution or some kind of political clout was usually part of
the equation. I clearly did not have money; a White House staffer who saw
my financial disclosure told me that no one in the entire administration
had fewer assets.

But it turned out I did have a new kind of political clout: the support of
the women's movement. Jimmy Carter was the first Democratic president
elected after the rebirth of feminism, and he was very conscious of this

141

constituency. In the transition period, he set up a committee tasked with identifying women who were qualified to fill some of the many federal openings at the disposal of the new administration. I was told that my name was suggested often, especially by the younger members of the transition team. Sometime in December or early January, I flew to D.C. to interview at the Departments of Justice, Defense, and Health, Education, and Welfare (soon to become Health and Human Services) for lofty legal positions, some of them never before held by women.

The chance that I would be moving back to D.C. threw my already-disorganized life into chaos. In the spring of 1976, I had been a visiting professor at the University of Hawaii Law School, then in only its second year of existence. It was not a prestigious post, and some Stanford friends advised against visiting there in the year I was up for tenure. But I did not want to be around while my colleagues discussed whether I met standards I did not fully grasp. I also liked the idea of living on a tropical island, and teaching students who were grateful to have their first local law school. After Hawaii, I absented myself for the following summer as well, teaching at Michigan Law School and working with Paul Carrington on the civil procedure text we were putting together.

Back at Stanford in the fall of 1976, with the faculty's vote on my tenure imminent and success looking likely, I should have been preparing my spring 1977 courses. Instead, after the November election I was on the phone with women's groups, members of the Carter transition team, and reporters pursuing rumors about where I might fit into the new administration. My heart's desire was to be Solicitor General, the government's chief lawyer before the Supreme Court—to my way of thinking, the best legal job in the world.

The Solicitor General's office was small enough to present few administrative challenges, and it allowed the person in charge to practice law at the highest level, shaping the government's legal policy and arguing to the Supreme Court. No woman had ever been SG. I imagined myself leading a brilliant little posse, always taking the side of the angels. Though I pursued other positions that seemed in play, I had my sights set on SG.

When I interviewed with Griffin Bell, the new Attorney General, he said he had already decided on Wade McCree, a black judge on the Sixth Circuit, for SG. What else did I want? My next pick was head of the Civil Rights Division, but it, too, had been filled. So I fell back on my third choice, the Civil Division. Judge Bell (as he was still called, though he had left the Fifth Circuit to rejoin a powerful Atlanta firm) was surprised at that. Wouldn't I rather head the Criminal Division, given my background?

I did not volunteer the whole truth, which was that I have the soul of a defender and really could not be a prosecutor or administrator of prosecutors. Instead I told him my interest in civil litigation had developed while teaching at Stanford. He countered with head of the Law Enforcement Assistance Administration, which I immediately rejected. Best known for supplying police with helicopters and tanks, LEAA had been troubled from its inception in 1968 and would be abolished in 1982.

Judge Bell did not offer me the Civil Division or say when he might decide. I went on to interview with Secretary of Defense-designate Harold Brown for the general counsel job there. My only previous visit to the Pentagon had been marching on it at a protest in 1967. When I made a light comment about that, I perceived a distinct cooling of the atmosphere, which was just as well. I would not have wanted to spend my days in that forbidding place. Finally, I met with Joe Califano, slated to be Secretary of Health, Education, and Welfare. We did not click, nor apparently did the job in question involve the management of litigation, which I thought I could do and would enjoy.

I returned to California, not knowing whether an offer would be forthcoming. Judge Bell had been encouraging, but that could have just been his natural courtliness. He had not given me a number to call if I needed a decision before I heard from him. The beginning of classes was closing in. And I had recently embarked on what was to be my last love affair.

Tom Grey had joined the Stanford faculty a year before I did. His office had been near mine in the old building, and was near again when we moved in 1975. We had become friends, and I showed him a draft of an article on *voir dire* examination of prospective jurors, one of my first scholarly efforts. Common advice counseled against sharing a rough copy with colleagues pre-tenure because of the danger of creating an irreversible bad impression. But I trusted Tom, and he made some helpful suggestions. I socialized with him and his wife, Cathy, in the same way that I did with the other young married couples, though perhaps less often because she was busy with medical school.

One day I saw Tom in the hall looking terribly sad and asked him what was wrong. We ducked into his office where he told me that he and Cathy were divorcing after fourteen years together. He was especially concerned about the effect of the split on their eight-year-old daughter. In my best "Miss Fix-it" manner, I offered him furniture I had in storage, food, and companionship. Within a month after he had moved into his new apartment, we were embarked on a full-scale romance.

From the first, I had been enormously attracted to Tom because brain power was the chief male attraction for me. One sunny afternoon I sat enthralled in the secret garden of my San Francisco mansion, reading his review of John Rawls's *A Theory of Justice*,* the book of the hour. I was struck by the brilliant clarity, jargon-free style, and lack of pretension of Tom's writing—he said his aim in the review was to enable cocktail-party conversations about the book among lawyers and law professors. That was the moment that prepared me for falling in love with Tom Grey. He also was fit and athletic, a bit taller than I, and when I later refocused on him as a single man, I realized that we were well matched in temperament and personality.

Staying on at Stanford instead of setting out for D.C. grew more appealing. In late fall, my colleagues had voted to keep me for life, heightening my comfort level there. Indeed, I felt an unexpected burst of confidence in myself and loyalty toward the school, and had no doubt that my next five years in academia would be less stressful than the first five had been.

Of course, I could have it all by taking a leave from Stanford to work in Washington for a couple of years, and then returning to life in teaching. But I feared losing Tom if I left. He assured me he would last a while as a bachelor, and in his reasonable (if un-romantic) way, he also pointed out that we had not been together long enough to be certain where we were headed. He was emphatic that I should be an Assistant Attorney General of the United States if I could.

So after some days passed with no word from Washington, I picked up the phone, called the main Justice number, and asked for the Attorney General. I got right through and told Judge Bell that I did not mean to nag but spring semester was starting and I needed to let Stanford know my plans. He made another pitch for LEAA. I repeated that I didn't want it. Somewhat dejectedly, he said, "OK then, come on and head the Civil Division."

---

* *A Theory of Justice* (Cambridge, Mass.: The Belknap Press, 1971). Tom's review is Grey, "The First Virtue," 25 *Stanford Law Review* 286-327 (1973).

I doubt he would have chosen me if I hadn't called him. Looking back I can hardly believe that I was so assertive. The women's movement at my back and my own desire to be part of the first administration in history to include many of us drove me on. I expected to like the work and thought that a prominent government position would further dilute my public defender past, leaving me better situated for future opportunities—maybe even that dream job, Solicitor General.

I had made the call toward the end of January; my first day of work was February 14. During the month before my March formal swearing-in, FBI agents interviewed dozens of friends and professional associates, teachers and deans, former neighbors and landlords. They did not go all the way back to Route 1 in Hope, Arkansas, but they hit every other place I had lived or worked.

Later the agent in charge of the investigation told me, "Everyone you have ever met has only the best to say about you." And when I obtained my FBI records years later, I had fun reading all the favorable opinions, including, most satisfying, that I had been considered by many to be the best trial lawyer in D.C. I was amused that one of my law school professors had called me "dignified," as if to offset any radical feminist image that may have lurked (no bra-burner she!).

After 233 pages, my FBI file concluded with a notation that a final item was being withheld, adding that I could appeal the redaction. I haven't pursued those three pages because I'm sure I know what they say. I had been Assistant Attorney General for a year when unfavorable publicity erupted about my friendship with D.C. gambler Joe Nesline, my favorite client from the Williams firm. (See Chapter Five.) Jack Anderson had kicked off the negative commentary in syndicated columns and on "Good Morning America."*

He said the Mafia had always wanted to cultivate a friendly connection inside the Justice Department, so far to no avail. Things might be about to change, he implied, reporting his discovery of a "strange relationship between a top Justice Department official," me, "and a notorious racketeer." He called Nesline, "the gambling king of Washington" who was currently under investigation, "a strange social companion for an Assistant Attorney General." Anderson noted that I had "insisted there was nothing wrong with the friendship."

---

* ABC's "Good Morning America," February 1, 1978.

Jack Anderson's staff had called me a few days earlier to ask about my relationship with Nesline, and I had alerted Judge Bell and the Deputy Attorney General about the potential bad press. Both responded supportively that my social life was my own business. Judge Bell said that all he needed to hear was that Nesline was a former client. Yet knowing Washington, I realized that if this snowballed, I could end up resigning in disgrace. It all depended on whether the press would keep the story going.

Although I had managed the media and enjoyed favorable press as director of PDS, nothing in my experience prepared me to handle this kind of accusation. My first statement was weak, relying too much on the facts that Joe had never been convicted of any organized-crime offenses and should be presumed innocent. When the *Washington Post* called, I said that as head of the Civil Division, I had no power over criminal matters, and anyway, Nesline had not been accused of a crime. I asked why this was news. "Because," the reporter replied, "my editor assigned me to it." I muttered something about "the Nuremburg defense," which may have hit home. To my relief, the *Post* did not pursue the story.

My brother Starr wisely advised me to stop talking. He was so right, though it was hard not to respond. I did put out a decorous second statement to the effect that I would give up my friendship with Nesline in order to avoid any possible appearance of impropriety. In fact I had seen him only once or twice since my return to D.C. because the job simply left no time for a social life. The local tabloid headlined: "Must Drop Mobster as Pal, Justice Dept Fem Concedes."[*] Within ten days, the story died from lack of oxygen.

Luckily the brief scandal did not affect my relations with division lawyers or staff, or my ability to function. My loyal father even suggested that the incident had made me a more colorful figure. But the negative press attention had unsettled me. Also, I was unnerved that someone disliked me enough to call Jack Anderson, even though the entirety of the tip was that my phone number had surfaced in Joe's address book, which had been seized in a raid on his house. Yet it was naïve of me, maybe even ethically obtuse, to think that in a job as visible as mine, I could maintain a social friendship with someone reputed to be connected with organized crime.

---

[*] *Daily News*, February 10, 1978.

My mistake, as I look back on it, was to assume that others would see my fundamental honesty and good intentions and interpret my actions accordingly. I also had something of a communications problem, at least at first. In a little talk to Civil Division lawyers at my swearing-in, for instance, I mentioned being a "feminist," in the same shorthand way I might say I was a liberal, a workaholic, a litigator, a procedure buff. Only a month later at a reception did I learn that this one word had generated all kinds of alarm. Some had concluded I would promote only women or would not defend sex discrimination suits against the government. My informant, who had had a few too many drinks, attempted to reassure me by adding, "I told them not to worry—the dizzy bitch will never get anything done."

In addition to communication issues in the Division, I soon realized that my boss Judge Bell also spoke a different language, almost literally. He called my hotline one evening while I was in a meeting and asked, in his deep Georgia accent, "Bawbra, does the Civil Division hawndle eeelegal taffs?"

I looked around the room and repeated the question, to puzzled headshakes. "Could you say that again, Judge Bell, and spell it?"

"Taffs," he said. "T-a-r-i-f-f-s."

It turned out that we did handle those, or could.

Judge Bell and I represented the reach of the Democratic Party from rather conservative to freewheeling liberal. At the time, several journalists were curious about how we managed in a day-to-day way. Though I did not say so openly, I felt that the AG and I had quickly reached an unspoken agreement—that I would try not to bother him and he would not trouble me unless it was absolutely necessary.

I was not asked to join Judge Bell's daily breakfast for the top officials in the department where current issues and overall policy were discussed. When I learned of the meetings, I did not press to attend because I knew my views would rarely prevail. Rather than trying to be part of policy making, I turned to administering the Civil Division and hoped to influence justice in that way.

Patricia Wald, who was Assistant Attorney General for Legislative Affairs, necessarily interacted much more with Bell than I did. We were friends, and I greatly admired her, especially as a role model for young women lawyers. A 1951 Yale Law graduate, she had been one of the first women to clerk for a federal judge and a famous judge at that: Jerome

Frank on the Second Circuit. Pat had married a classmate, and they eventually had five children. Until they were all in school, she confined her legal work to part-time volunteering for good causes, and then she plunged into full-time practice and became a successful and influential public interest lawyer.

As AAG, she helped develop the administration's position on Justice-related proposals and worked on the Department's legislative initiatives. Though our responsibilities seldom overlapped, it was comforting to know Pat was there. For once, I was not the only woman at my level of authority. Some of our colleagues—including, occasionally, Judge Bell—tended to confuse us, though I'm six inches taller and ten years younger. Our hair *was* once the same shade of brown.

The one thing Pat and I did together got us into trouble with Judge Bell. We had been at Justice for six months when the President's advisor on women's affairs summoned high-level female appointees to a meeting at the White House. President Carter had agreed to listen to our objections to his recent statements opposing public funding for abortions unless the life of the mother was threatened or the pregnancy had resulted from rape or incest. Neither Pat nor I thought twice about going—and we rode over in a DOJ limousine.

Arriving at the White House, we saw many other women alighting from big black cars in the portico. My delight at the scene diminished when I realized that the meeting was in effect a pro-choice rally with the press in attendance. It was reported as a revolt of women in the executive branch against the President who had appointed them. One news story quoted Bell as saying that he had told his "two top women aides" to "get out" if they could not agree with administration policy.* Neither Pat nor I had heard him say anything like that, and it didn't sound like Judge Bell, who was a true Southern gentleman. But he did make his displeasure known, and the presidential advisor who had set up the meeting was soon out of a job.

Judge Bell tried on several other occasions to rebuke me or tell me to change course on some matter. But my gender and his upbringing made it hard for him to do either. And we both knew that if my authority was seriously challenged, I was always ready to return to Stanford. On the

---

* "Carter Warns Cabinet 'Back Me on Abortion,'" *New York Post*, July 25, 1977.

other hand, if he could keep me there, he realized I might be a useful buffer between the administration and demands from women's groups.

In administering the Civil Division, I developed two major projects. One was partly inspired by a congratulatory letter from a friend when my appointment was announced. He added some advice: "I hope that when you and your minions interpose the doctrine of sovereign immunity, the statute of limitations, failure to sue the right party, and similar technical defenses to every lawsuit brought against the government, you will remember from your old PDS days that some suits should eventually be decided on the merits."[*]

The friend was Harold Greene, chief judge of the District of Columbia Superior Court. A remarkable man, born Heinz Grünhaus in Germany, he had fled the Nazis, served as an intelligence officer in the American army during the war, attended night law school at George Washington, and worked in the Justice Department, helping to frame much of the path-breaking civil rights legislation of the sixties. As chief judge, he had done a great deal to make the local courts more responsive—most memorably for me, when he opened them at midnight to hear our *habeas petition* to release antiwar May Day demonstrators in 1971. (See Chapter Seven.) I told that story when I spoke at his investiture as a federal judge in 1978.

Judge Greene was not the only one to suggest to me that Civil Division lawyers were overly inclined to raise technical defenses to meritorious claims and to wear down deserving litigants with delaying tactics. One early interviewer asked if I planned to tackle the Division's unsavory reputation. I said my aim was to make the government a model litigator but that "there are 270 lawyers here handling 40,000 cases a year," and changing how they approached their day-to-day work would be a challenge.[†]

And so it proved to be. A decade after returning to Stanford, I wrote a little piece about my efforts called "Defending the Government" (its title a take-off from "Defending the Guilty," my article about being a public defender). Concluding that defending the government is sometimes more difficult than defending the guilty, I wrote: "The criminal defense lawyer owes unswerving duty to a single client whose interests are crystalline.

---

[*] The Honorable Harold Greene. Letter to me, February 17, 1977.

[†] Larry Baskir, "A Look at Barbara Allen Babcock," *District Lawyer*, 24 (Summer 1977).

Within the balance of advocacy and ethics, the client's best interest dictates all choices."[*]

By contrast, the government lawyer must play multiple roles and serve
many interests. She has an actual client who often expects the same total
devotion as the criminally accused. In a broader sense than expressed by a
single agency, she also represents the interests of the United States and
should take explicit account of the public good in her litigation practices
and policies.

It is complicated to play many roles and represent multiple interests;
all-out aggressive lawyering focused on the client's goals is easier and
perhaps more satisfying professionally. My efforts to modify the adversary
culture in the Division were, I think, largely unsuccessful. My second
administrative initiative for the civil division was more popular among
those I soon came to think of as "my lawyers."

I threw myself into improving the physical resources of the place. My
first indication of a problem was when I asked for a typewriter. I preferred
drafting mechanically rather than dictating or handwriting. It took several
weeks before a machine could be found deemed good enough for the front
office. I also had the feeling that some thought it inappropriate for the boss
to type, in public at least.

The resource issues went well beyond equipment needs, however.
Upon arrival I had made inspection visits to all eighteen Civil Division
sections and sub-sections, which were scattered throughout several
buildings. What I saw alarmed me. The lawyers and support staff often
toiled in worse conditions than our public defenders had. Two or three
lawyers might share a small, poorly ventilated room with one secretary on
an old typewriter—accommodations vastly inferior to those of lawyers in
the big firms who represented our opponents.

Before I could embark on my goals for improving the Civil Division, I
needed to put together a front-office staff. I hired Bill Schaffer, a friend
and former public defender, as one of my three deputies. When he learned
of it, Judge Bell was both irritated and plaintive: "You can't just hire your
own deputies. We won an election and have lots of debts to pay." I had
interviewed some of the lawyers on the administration's list, and while

---

[*] "Defending the Government: Justice and the Civil Division," 23 *John Marshall Law
Review* 181, 185 (1990); see "Defending the Guilty," 32 *Cleveland State Law Review* 175
(1983).

they seemed capable enough, I wanted people who were either familiar with the Civil Division or who I was sure were hard and effective workers and loyal to me.

Bill charmed and impressed Judge Bell, so nothing further was said about how I should choose my deputies. I had already decided on two career attorneys, Irwin Goldbloom and Irving Jaffe, who were both well respected in the Division. No one, however well connected politically, could be as effective internally as they could. As a special assistant, I hired Roanne (Ronni) Mann, my former student who was clerking for the D.C. Circuit. My old friend Judge Bazelon was still chief judge and agreed to release her early from her year's commitment. And Janis Sposato, another career DOJ lawyer, also joined us as a special assistant.

They turned out to be a great team of old and new hands, excellent lawyers all, and we got along well. When Irwin left for private practice (with Carla Hills, who had been AAG for a brief period in the Nixon administration), he recommended Tom Martin to replace him. Tom had been a special assistant to my predecessor, Rex Lee, and was currently in the SG's office; he fit right in with the others. For a year after the Carter administration ended, he was the acting AAG.

Bill and Ronni already knew how I work and the others quickly took up the easy, open, and informal relationship I needed with my closest advisors. Despite occasional glitches, I felt that after the first six months I had achieved reasonable control over the Civil Division and that its work was going pretty smoothly. A syndicated news item headlined, "Grumbles, Bitterness over 2 Female Assistant Attorneys General Easing." It complimented Pat Wald and me and closed with: "[Both women] say they have no problems in directing male subordinates [but both also] suggest they might be the last to know about gripes."[*]

Though I felt that I had a grip on the daily administrative work, I could not see how to go about significantly upgrading our resources, and making us model litigators. One day at lunch, Irwin unveiled a proposal he thought would help us do both. He had in mind a major reorganization of this old and tradition-encrusted institution.

Established in 1868 to handle claims against the government, Civil was the first of the litigating divisions in the Department of Justice. It had no

---

[*] *Arkansas Gazette*, October 27, 1978, 15A.

legal specialty like Tax or Lands and Natural Resources and no designated policy area, like Antitrust or Civil Rights. Rather, it had just grown piecemeal as statutes were passed that required the government to sue or defend in court. Funding for a special section to handle the new work would be sought from Congress and would then become a budget line item, never growing, never shrinking.

Over time, through this haphazard process, the Division had come to have fourteen major sections and several mini-subdivisions, each with its own hierarchy, management style, and reputation. There was much unproductive competition among sections—even, or especially, those doing similar work—and unwillingness to share resources and expertise. Success was typically defined simply as satisfying the client agency, which easily translated as "win at any cost"—hence our unflattering nickname "Widows and Orphans Division," referring to the victims of our litigation tactics.

Irwin proposed reorganizing the division into three large functional branches, merging the sections that did complementary work. It was a simple idea that in time would make the division more efficient, more responsive to policy leadership, and a better place to work. From my first introduction to the plan, I was enthusiastic, and I thought it would not only enable us to do better work but also to argue more persuasively for adequate resources.

As usual, I failed to anticipate that not everyone would see things my way. Of course there was vehement opposition from people who feared or disliked change or who anticipated the loss of valued turf. They complained to Judge Bell, who called me in to remonstrate: "You can't just do whatever you want without getting approval." I smiled pleasantly and replied that I would love to explain the reorganization to him right then and there. Nodding wearily, he surrendered: "No, no, go ahead then." I think a respectful twinkle in his eye credited me with a shrewd political stroke, when I was actually just forging ahead in my fashion, oblivious to the naysayers.

Some good effects of our reorganization of the Civil Division manifested right away. We were able to marshal resources for important cases and to stave off the efforts of certain client agencies to wrest their own litigating authority away from us. Fighting to be the ones to represent the United States in court was (and probably still is) a constant burden for the Civil Division's chief. It was obvious to me that the government should take consistent positions in all the various courts where it practices, and the statutes clearly state that the Attorney General should represent the United States.

But I soon learned that executive branch agencies would often prefer to litigate for themselves; a few already did, having been created with the authority or winning it later from Congress. Sometimes the Justice Department made formal arrangements with agencies to allocate litigation responsibility; in my experience, these deals tended to exacerbate turf battles rather than settle them. In the struggle over litigation authority, I came down without reservation on the side of my division.

I believed that Justice Department litigators were more likely to take an independent view, and to analyze the state of the law objectively. Where agencies had technical or specialized matters under their jurisdiction, I thought skilled generalist litigators like ours were usually best at translating and conveying these complexities to judges and juries. And the Justice Department lawyer was better positioned to consider the litigation positions and needs of other agencies. Because I was convinced that the Justice Department was overall better suited to litigate for the executive branch, and that our battles with agencies over litigation authority weren't just bureaucratic turf struggles, I was able to fight with conviction and quite successfully.

One of the best examples of the need for central litigation authority was in defending cases brought under the Freedom of Information Act (FOIA). Regardless of what a fair reading of FOIA required, most agencies wanted their lawyers to fight the release of potentially embarrassing material. Instead I wanted to implement a presumption in favor of disclosure, in keeping with the spirit of FOIA, which had been strengthened in the wake of the Watergate scandal to help expose government cover-ups.

I first would try to persuade an agency to disgorge the information. Many times I met with our clients to urge that in a particular case, a release actually would make the agency look good, showing, for instance, that it had considered arguments against the action it eventually took. But instincts to stonewall were profound and pervasive, and the agencies' tenacity tended to exhaust overworked Civil Division lawyers.

Ultimately I ordered that all refusals to release information in response to FOIA requests had to be cleared with me. General orders like that were one way I tried to control litigation decisions in our far-flung operations. Though most division lawyers worked in Washington, they litigated everywhere, and each U.S. Attorney's office, one or more in every state, had a civil section that, at least in theory, was under my direction.

Another item on my agenda was to improve working relations with the Civil Rights Division; tensions had developed over interpreting federal antidiscrimination law. They sued businesses and state and local governments alleging discriminatory practices while we defended the federal government against similar claims. Representing defendants, Civil Division attorneys pressed for much narrower interpretations of the statutes than the Civil Rights Division urged on the plaintiffs' side.

Drew Days, the head of Civil Rights—the first Assistant Attorney General for that Division who was African American—and I drafted an order from Judge Bell directing our divisions to take consistent positions in bringing and defending discrimination cases. But given our conflicting litigation interests, this commonsense goal was not always easy to achieve. Endless meetings were necessary to harmonize our approaches and even when we reached agreement at the top, implementing the decisions was often hard going.

An example was the struggle over "moving for costs" when the government prevailed in a discrimination suit. Civil Rights declared that the government should never move for the losing plaintiff to reimburse costs because the risk would discourage people with good claims from litigating them. Finally, after many meetings and memoranda, I issued an order to all general counsels and United States attorneys limiting motions for costs to litigation that was patently groundless, pursued in a vexatious or harassing manner, or brought in bad faith. In effect, the order created a fairly strong presumption against moving for costs.

I don't recall hearing much more about that order—until 1985 when back at Stanford, I learned that the new head of the Civil Division in the Reagan administration had revoked it: "the United States like any other litigant is entitled to recover the costs of litigation,"* the new order read. Of course, my version was based on the belief that the United States was not like other litigants—that it should be more concerned with fairness than with victory.

Endless meetings and reams of paperwork—nothing was accomplished in Justice without both. As a devotee of due process, I could hardly object, but it got tedious. Sometimes I would jot down my goals for a meeting and

---

* Quoted in "Defending the Government," 23 *John Marshall Law Review* at 193-95.

the likely objections and give myself points when I won one, or subtract if I lost. The concept of winning or losing a meeting helped me get through the hours spent in them.

My life fell into a rhythm of twelve- or fourteen-hour days that started with an early bus ride to work. I was often the first arrival at the Civil Division and I relished an hour or so alone in my beautiful office in the grand old building on Pennsylvania Avenue. Then the meetings started, and as I sat in closed rooms, hassling and being hassled, I grew a little jealous of our trial lawyers in courts all over the country. Couldn't I handle a few cases myself, as I had when I ran the Public Defender? But I soon realized that even if I could justify spending time to prepare a single case, I could no longer simply appear in court without causing a stir. An Assistant Attorney General's presence signaled a matter's importance and would magnify any loss.

After almost a year on the job, I managed to argue a case in a federal appellate court. Bill Schaffer, who understood my hankering, found it for me. I was thrilled to have clients again, to marshal legal arguments, and to regain my expertise at finding plain words to describe the situation. The case involved a recurring situation in which Civil Division lawyers represented both a government agency and individual employees, all sued together.

Plaintiffs were regularly moving to disqualify our lawyers from representing the individual defendants, claiming that there was a conflict of interest in representing them along with the agency. Their underlying motive, of course, was to divide the defense, and hope some of the defendants separately represented would turn on each other or the agency. In the case I argued, the individual defendants had chosen to go with the Civil Division lawyers, and the plaintiff had persuaded the trial judge to override this choice. We saw increasing numbers of plaintiffs' lawyers using this ploy, and too many judges falling for it, and so we took the unusual step of appealing a pretrial order in an effort to get a ruling that these disqualifications were disfavored.

I argued the case before the Fourth Circuit Court of Appeals in Richmond. The whole enterprise was a welcome break from my office routine, and I enjoyed the Southern graciousness when the judges descended from their high bench to shake hands with the litigants, a special tradition in that circuit. The court ruled in our favor, and when I recently reviewed the old typewritten (on a typewriter) notes I had used in the argument, I was pleased with my presentation.

Shortly after this victory, Judge Bell and I had our only serious open disagreement. It arose in the case of Frank Snepp, a former CIA agent who wrote a book alleging the United States government's extreme negligence in its disastrous evacuation of Saigon at the end of the Vietnam War.[*] Snepp had left the CIA, but his original employment contract required him, before publication, to clear anything he wrote about his time there, a clause meant to prevent even inadvertent disclosure of intelligence sources and methods.

The CIA wanted us to preemptively sue Snepp to prevent his publishing without "preclearance," but he repeatedly denied that he was even writing a book. Though I did not say so openly, I was relieved not to be part of a suit that would impose prior restraint on speech, which First Amendment doctrine permits in only the most exceptional circumstances. Within months of his denials, however, Snepp did publish his book and even promoted it by bragging that he had tricked the government out of censoring it.

The book became a cause célèbre and the fact of its publication made the CIA appear inept. The Agency wanted us to sue Snepp for breach of contract. Such a suit would not be a classic prior restraint in attempting to prevent publication, yet it was only one remove from it.

I still had misgivings about challenging Snepp's right to free speech and doubted that a lawsuit was really necessary. It did not fit the spirit of President Carter's policies in favor of protecting whistleblowers and of promoting more open government. Moreover, I thought the book would soon be forgotten unless we drew further attention to it, and that proving damages would expose more secrets than the book itself revealed.

For a while I thought these arguments against bringing a lawsuit might prevail. But I never had a chance against Director of Central Intelligence Stansfield Turner's opinion that suing Snepp would have the long range effect of saving lives and protecting sources. Judge Bell was also worried about the effect our refusal would have on morale at the CIA, whose own lawyers lacked statutory authority to sue.

That was the only time Judge Bell got really angry at me (at least that I

---

[*] *Decent Interval: An Insider's Account of Saigon's Indecent End Told by the CIA's Chief Strategy Analyst in Vietnam* (New York: Vintage Books, 1978).

know about). In his memoir, he wrote that he "virtually had to order the Civil Division to file suit,"[*] which is how I recall it, too—perhaps without the "virtually." "You were a public defender," he told me. "You should not be afraid to go to court."

To be accused of timidity was a new one for me, and seemed inappropriate here where objecting to the suit in itself took some courage. I considered not signing the pleadings. On reflection, I rejected this course; if I really thought suing was wrong, I should resign. In the end, I decided that whether the First Amendment barred a suit against Snepp for damages was a point on which reasonable people could differ, not such a violation of principle that I had to leave the job.

In preparing the case, Civil Division lawyers designed an ingenious theory that helped overcome some of the practical problems I had raised about bringing suit. Since it was the proof of damages to the CIA that could reveal secrets, we did not sue Snepp for breach of contract but rather for breach of trust, that is, violating his fiduciary duty to his employer. The measure of damages for this action was not the amount of harm to the plaintiff, but the extent to which the defendant had unjustly enriched himself by his wrongdoing.

Besides endorsing the novel breach of trust theory, the Supreme Court approved our request for "a constructive trust for the Government's benefit on all profits that Snepp might earn from publishing the book in violation of his fiduciary obligations to the Agency." Forced to "disgorge the benefits of his faithlessness,"[†] Snepp lost all his royalties forever.

I was proud of the work the Civil Division lawyers had done.[‡] One of them recently reminded me that I had aided her in preparing to cross-examine Snepp. This kind of effort took me back to the pleasures of the public defender days, when we often helped each other with trial strategy. In the end, though I was never totally convinced that suing was right, I had very little sympathy for Snepp himself, which was not enlarged in 1999 when I read his self-pitying account of the litigation.[§]

---

[*] Griffin B. Bell, *Taking Care of the Law*, 128-29 (New York: Morrow, 1982).

[†] *Snepp v. United States*, 444 U.S. 507, 515 (1980).

[‡] For a discussion of the problems arising from the government's efforts to use civil litigation to deal with national security disclosures, see Tom Martin's article "National Security and the First Amendment," 68 *ABA Journal* 680 (1982).

[§] I like to think I'm not prejudiced by the fact that he described me as having "chipmunk features"! Frank Snepp, *Irreparable Harm: A Firsthand Account of How One Agent*

My last story of being the AAG is about my only argument in the Supreme Court, a perquisite of the job in matters that originated in the Civil Division. Some of my predecessors had appeared in the High Court many times, but I had trouble finding a case where I felt sufficiently enthusiastic about the government's arguments to put myself on the line for them. Finally, *Chrysler Corp. v. Brown* came along, a so-called "reverse Freedom of Information Act case," that is, one in which the government wanted to disclose and the non-governmental provider of the information sued to keep it secret.*

The provider was Chrysler, the defendant the Defense Department; the information was Chrysler's report on its affirmative action efforts, which it was required to submit in order to obtain lucrative government contracts. Those seeking the information were actual and potential plaintiffs in discrimination suits against Chrysler. The juicy issues and the high stakes made it an interesting case and one I could argue with conviction.

Appearing in the Supreme Court was as thrilling as I had always imagined it would be. Only once before had I been inside the low barrier (called the "bar") that separates the public from the lawyers and Justices. That was in 1966 when I was sworn in as a member of the Supreme Court bar, qualifying me to appear there as an attorney. I had wanted to join during the reign of the Warren Court, which was doing so much to protect the rights of the criminally accused. A lot of us D.C. public defenders made the short trek from our office up the hill to have the rite performed. My father moved my admission, so his name is on my certificate.

I joked then that I did not expect ever to argue in the Supreme Court: winning jury trials was my forte, so there would be no appeals and no petitions for a writ of *certiorari*. But there I was in 1978, arguing a case as Assistant Attorney General of the United States. Though I have not been back to the Court since that day, I can still visualize the marble pillars, the red drapery, and the nine variably sized justices, all men at that time, looming up as they filled their variably sized chairs. The space within which Justices and advocates conduct argument is surprisingly narrow, even intimate, compared to most appellate courtrooms.

Took on the CIA in an Epic Battle over Secrecy and Free Speech 231 (New York: Random House, 1999).

* *Chrysler Corp. v. Brown*, 441 U.S. 281 (1979).

Tom and my parents were in the audience that day, sitting right behind me during my half-hour argument, which was lively, with most of the Justices participating. The record shows me speaking clearly and smoothly, answering their questions while managing to make my main points. Yet reading it today I do not get that ego lift, as I sometimes do from old transcripts and say to myself, "Damn, I was good!"

Though people who watched the argument were complimentary enough, I was disappointed with my performance. I had skimped on preparation, failing to take the time to practice in a moot court, something I've constantly urged on lawyers who are arguing an appeal. At trial there are always surprises, but for an appellate argument it is possible to anticipate all the likely questions and to formulate answers. But I was hard-pressed on administrative work, and neglected that part of the preparation.

The Chrysler case was, moreover, tangled in technicalities about the meaning and interrelation of three statutes and two sets of regulations in addition to FOIA. Justice Rehnquist would comment in his opinion that the situation made the "alphabet soup" of New Deal legislation appear like "a clear broth."[*] At any rate, the case came out mainly in our favor in a long, dense, but unanimous opinion. In a letter to the Civil Division lawyers and the general counsels of all federal agencies, I explained the opinion and how to apply it.[†]

I consoled myself for being less than stellar with the thought that the argument was like the Assistant Attorney General's job itself—so complicated that no one could say for sure whether I had succeeded or failed. When I left the Justice Department in 1979 to return to Stanford, Judge Bell wrote a gracious letter thanking me for my contributions. I did have a hand in some good changes. One was to bring women and minority lawyers into the Civil Division and to campaign for more diversity in the overwhelmingly white and male Department of Justice.

Again, Drew Days and I worked together, beginning soon after we arrived at the Justice Department in 1977. Judge Bell assigned us to head a new Employment Review Committee, created with an eye to ensure that

---

[*] *Chrysler*, 441 U.S. at 285, 316.

[†] Assistant Attorney General Babcock, Letter to Agency General Counsels on Current and Future Litigation under Chrysler Corp. v. Brown, 441 U.S. 281 (1979), June 21, 1979.

hiring and promotion were done from a diverse group of candidates. Opponents of this effort warned that we were opening ourselves up to suits for race and sex discrimination by qualified white men passed over by this process, but no such "reverse discrimination" suits materialized. In an interview I was able to say, "Qualified white males are doing very well here, as they always have. I myself have hired and promoted many of them."[*]

Along similar lines, I was gratified when Judge Bell asked me to take primary responsibility in the Justice Department for pursuing the President's policy of increasing the number of women on the federal bench. Drew played the same role for members of racial minorities. In my part of the work, I found that identifying women who would make good federal judges was not a problem, but getting them nominated and confirmed was more difficult.

Democrats had been out of office for years, and because the legal profession had until recently been overwhelmingly male, there was a long line of qualified men who had worked hard for the party, each of whose life's ambition was to be a federal judge. To elevate a woman, often younger and with less party service and professional experience, would mean thwarting one of these identifiable, faithful, and deserving men.

Largely because of discrimination, women's résumés did not look like those of the men who typically were chosen. Persuasively setting out women candidates' experience to show that they were in fact qualified was a big part of my role. I met with support groups and politicians and candidates, and had many conversations with Margaret McKenna who was in the White House counsel's office.[†]

I did not keep records of all the contacts and efforts I made, mainly because I was not set up for it in these days before personal computers, and I've never become accustomed to dictating regularly to a secretary. Without records, I remember only two times when I felt I was actually instrumental in an appointment. One was Stephanie Seymour's appointment to the Tenth Circuit and the other was Ruth Bader Ginsburg's to the D.C. Circuit.

---

[*] "Grumbles, Bitterness over 2 Female Assistant Attorneys General Easing," *Arkansas Gazette*, October 27, 1978, 15A.

[†] Sally J. Kenney, *Gender and Justice: Why Women in the Judiciary Really Matter* 70-73 (New York: Routledge, 2013).

Though I did not know Seymour, she had articulate supporters in the women's movement and in private practice. Ruth was a friend from the world of law professors and feminists. A half decade ahead of me, she had attended Harvard and Columbia in the mid-fifties, among the first and few women in either school. I first met her when she was a law professor at Rutgers and then Columbia and chief architect of the constitutional litigation campaign for women's rights. I'm not sure exactly what I did for her appointment on the D.C. Circuit after a selection panel had rejected her for the Second Circuit. But Ruth herself has taken many opportunities to thank me for "the good job" I helped her obtain, so I surmise that I was effective.

When I first came to know Ruth I wondered where in the legal profession's hierarchy her concentration on women's rights cases, especially ones involving great principles and small stakes, would take her. Hers did not seem the path to the profession's best honors. Needless to say, I was proud and amazed when it took her to the highest court in the land. President Clinton appointed Ruth Ginsburg to the Supreme Court in 1993.

We got off to a slow start in diversifying the federal judiciary, but the Carter administration finished fast and the results were impressive. President Carter appointed five times more women and minorities than all previous presidents combined: forty-one women (15.7 percent of total Carter judicial appointees), thirty-seven African Americans (14.2 percent), and sixteen Hispanics (6.1 percent).

Judge Bell offered to support me as a nominee to the Ninth Circuit, the federal Court of Appeals in whose jurisdiction California falls. I was touched, but I preferred to go back to being a professor. It was not a difficult call; I loved the job of law professor because of the autonomy and the chance to influence future lawyers. Pat Wald, the other woman Assistant Attorney General from the Carter years, went to the D.C. Circuit where she had a distinguished career.

As much as I like trying to move and improve a large bureaucracy, it is tiring work, partly because so many of the problems and issues recur; nothing stays solved. Photos of me from this period show deep circles under weary eyes, belying an omnipresent bright smile. After two-and-a-half years of administering the Civil Division, reorganizing it, lobbying for greater resources, diversifying the staff, and seeking to establish the government as a model fair litigator, I felt myself losing steam.

While I was in Washington, Tom and I corresponded often on paper (e-mail had yet to arrive) and talked on the phone some, though that was not his medium. By writing regularly, we learned a lot about each other, which might have taken much longer if we had been together—so much goes without saying in daily life. We also rendezvoused every six weeks or so, in D.C., Palo Alto, or in between when one or both of us had a gig somewhere.

I remember especially one winter weekend when we met first in Chicago where I spoke, and we had a psychedelically enhanced view of that great town from the observatory on the 94th floor of the John Hancock Center; then we proceeded to Iowa City where Tom did a workshop on constitutional law. By June 1979, I was ready for a normal life. I went home to Stanford for love and marriage.

Appropriately enough, my last move as AAG was one that drew Judge Bell's usual protest: "You can't just choose your own successor!" But I had lined up Alice Daniel, general counsel of the Legal Services Corporation, to take over. I don't remember exactly how we accomplished it, but she remained head of the Civil Division for the rest of the Carter administration.

I brought home with me three medium-sized boxes containing piles of files that I thought would provide grist for articles I planned about the role of a government lawyer. But instead I started teaching and writing about criminal procedure.

A decade after returning, I finally opened the boxes in order to write "Defending the Government,"* the article described earlier in this chapter. Then I put the files away again, still thinking I would use them some day. Twenty more years passed before I took most of them to the curb in plastic garbage bags for recycling. None of the particulars of those struggles, over which I once brimmed with energy and passion, mattered anymore.

Remembering my time at Justice, I can still summon the early AM thrill of entering the stately building with its classic and art deco elements and elaborate decoration throughout, all much as it was when constructed in the 1930s. One need not be a history buff to sense the majesty of the place and of its aspirations, which seem to emanate from the very walls. I

---

* "Defending the Government: Justice and the Civil Division," 23 *John Marshall Law Review* 181 (1990).

came to be very fond of DOJ as an institution and impressed with its traditions.

Recently, Eric Holder announced his resignation as Attorney General. He was tearful in talking about the experience even though he hardly had an untroubled ride in the job. Some of the media made fun of his emotion, but I understood it completely. Despite the reams of paperwork, the endless meetings, and the resistance I encountered, it was intensely interesting and exciting to be a high government official.

Speaking at Stanford Law graduation, June 1998

12

LOVE AND FRIENDSHIP IN SCHOLARLAND
(1980-PRESENT)

Several months before I returned to Stanford from D.C., Tom and I started looking for a house together. He was a faculty advisor in one of the theme houses on campus—American Studies—and enjoyed living among the bright, hopeful young people. I could have joined him there but, though I liked Stanford undergraduates having observed and admired them for years, I wanted to save my counseling energies for the law students.

The northern California real estate boom had barely begun, and we could afford to buy in quite a few neighborhoods. We thought about someday living in "The City" (native-speak for San Francisco), but Tom had joint custody of his ten-year-old daughter, Becky, and needed to live near her mother in Palo Alto. Despite friends who decried the lack of privacy in faculty housing, we decided that living on campus, minutes from the law school, was worth some undefined inconvenience.

I was not crazy about the post-war Eichler-type house we found. It could not have diverged more from my ideal: the old Victorian in Hyattsville where I grew up. Our "California Modern" house, built on the side of a hill, does not have an upstairs, much less a basement. Its single floor and narrow hallways have a motel vibe, and the façade, with its lack of windows, is unprepossessing, to put it mildly.

Yet inside the front door, a floor-to-ceiling window looks out onto three beautiful Chinese elms and a yard teeming with flowers and birds in all seasons. I thought it would do as a starter home and that we would move on when Becky left for college. Instead, we have grown old on Mayfield Avenue, and now it is convenient not to have stairs to climb.

As for privacy, couples have moved in around us, raised families, and left the neighborhood without our even meeting them. At the same time, many of our law school colleagues are within walking distance. It has been especially pleasant having Bob and Susan Weisberg so nearby that we could hear their daughter doing her soprano scales through the open windows in the summertime. We have been next-door neighbors for many years now.

From more than two-and-a-half years of exchanging letters and rendezvousing with Tom while I was in D.C., I knew him well and deeply, and I was sure we would be happy together. I proposed marrying at once; he thought we should try living together for a while. Some friends also thought we should wait since we had gotten together when he was on the rebound, and we had never shared daily life. But for a reason that now sounds ridiculous, I wanted to get married right away.

I still harbored the ambition to be the first woman on the Supreme Court, and I had seen nominations founder on personal issues like "living in sin," to which women were (and to some degree still are) particularly vulnerable. The Supreme Court was the only judicial position that attracted me—not because I thought I would find the work more satisfying than law teaching, but rather because of the historical significance of being the first woman. As far-fetched as it may have been to hope for such a long shot, I wanted to be ready just in case Carter was re-elected, and Tom went along with the program.

In the event, the wedding was a lot of fun—an informal and champagne-permeated affair in the back yard of our new campus house on the afternoon of August 19, 1979, with a small group of family and friends in attendance. We had enlisted an Episcopal priest, one of the ministers of Memorial Church at Stanford, who was willing to preside over a secular ceremony using the non-religious parts I had culled from *The Book of Common Prayer*. But at a prenuptial conference in her office, she asked us if we wouldn't at least include the Lord's Prayer. Right after we refused, a small earthquake rattled the crosses above our heads. Nevertheless, we stuck to our plan.

We memorized our vows, planning to say them without the usual sentence-by-sentence prompting. I once had a photographic memory that projects words from a page onto a screen in my mind's eye. But on this momentous occasion, the screen went blank. I couldn't remember the words at all, though Tom had just said them. To this day I can't account for the lapse. Too much champagne before the wedding? Maybe I had not adequately visualized the words. Perhaps I was overwhelmed by existential fear about the gravity of this step. Everyone including Tom laughed, and our celebrant fed the lines to me in the traditional way, but I still feel bad about it.

I think some colleagues were a little surprised that I could attract and interest such a brilliant scholar as Tom Grey. Others, I'm sure, admired his courage in taking on life with an ardent feminist. A consummate academic and an activist outsider just seemed an odd couple to some people. Yet beyond the partial truth in the stereotypes, we are more alike than different, and well suited, as our happy marriage of many decades now attests.

Our tastes, from literature to popular culture, are similar. Both of us had been avid readers since childhood, and neither had an ear for music or could even carry a tune. Early on I addressed a letter to "my darling print-oriented man," which delighted him. One of our first projects as newlyweds was to read aloud *Remembrance of Things Past*. I recall sitting on a Mexican beach, weeping over the death of Marcel's grandmother.

We both love the outdoors and theater, movies and TV nature shows, museum art and travel. Each of us was the oldest of three and was comfortable being the favored first child, though Tom's mother at least tried to be impartial. I have brothers, he has sisters. Only one thing gave me pause about Tom; he seemed to have a sophomoric sense of humor. "We are off like a herd of turtles" he would say, more than once. On his side, the Babcock tendency to tease and then disclaim any hurtful intent bothered him. But these difficulties, if they were such, faded quickly, and we each somehow discovered that the other was truly witty; we laugh a lot together.

Tom's parents welcomed me into the family and were relieved that he was happier than he had been for some time. His first wife was an attractive, interesting Yale-educated lawyer who had later become a medical doctor, with a Stanford M.D. But they were not temperamentally well matched. Tom is slow to anger and even slower to express it because he sees the other side of almost every argument. I am more partisan on more issues, but I too avoid displaying my ire for fear of hurting someone. Over many years, we have had very few fights, and even those were pale

WASPY imitations of the real thing, in which something unforgivable might be blurted out.

Tom is a third-generation Californian whose parents met at Stanford at the end of the twenties. His father George was an athlete, throwing the discus and playing varsity football. When I told Aileen, Tom's mother, that it must have been exciting to be in love with a star athlete, she replied, "Yes, and listen to 70,000 people cheer while he is being carried off on a stretcher." She tended toward a dark view of most things.

Tom grew up in a large house owned by his maternal grandfather, in the upscale neighborhood of Pacific Heights in San Francisco. His grandfather was a successful surgeon who died when Tom was six. Thereafter the family lived in the house with his widow, Alice O'Connor, known as "Bombi." To Tom, she was as much fairy godmother as blood relation. When he was at school in the East, she flew out to take him to the Pierre in New York and to Broadway plays. In college the friends he brought home to her San Francisco flat were welcome to sleep over—even, very progressively for the times, with their girlfriends.

Another important figure in Tom's life was his maiden great aunt, Bombi's sister Olympia O'Hara, known as "Umpa." She was an elementary school teacher and later a principal in San Francisco—"of two schools," she always added. Umpa taught the Grey children to read and showered them with love and admiration. She always referred to Tom as her "Achilles heel." Umpa was a marvelous cook who conjured up cheese balls ("Tom loves cheese," she told me very seriously), cookies, and entire meals ready to be heated and served with no added work.

I envied Tom his picture-book childhood with the sound of Golden Gate fog horns outside his bedroom window, a wonderful private school where his superior education began, and summers and weekends at Bombi's apple farm in Sebastopol in the Russian River country, or earlier her house near the beach on Monterey Bay. He and his father were sports fans and outdoorsmen; they listened to baseball and football on the radio, attended many games together, and hunted and fished.

In Tom's last year at his elementary school, he heard a recruiter talk about Exeter, the private preparatory school for boys in New Hampshire, and set his heart on it though it was a long way from home especially in the days before jet travel. With the help of a scholarship, his parents sent him there. After Exeter, he came back to California for college at Stanford, won a Marshall Fellowship for study at Oxford, and attended Yale Law School (five years after I did).

It was a splendid education, and he took full advantage of it, developing a framework for his learning that serves him today. We used to play a parlor game called Deprivation, in which each person receives a token from everyone in the group who has had an experience he lacks. Tom won many tokens with the tongue-in-cheek "I never went to a public school," and I raked them in with "I didn't have shoes on my first day of school in Arkansas."

When I first heard Tom's biography, I envied not only his education but his carefree youth, untroubled by insoluble adult problems. But I came to realize that his family had issues, too, centering on Aileen's dissatisfaction with her life as a mother, homemaker, and volunteer in various organizations. Later, she enjoyed being a docent at the L.A. County Art Museum, but she did not have the career for which her intelligence and interests suited her. When Tom left home at fifteen for boarding school, never to return, he probably was fleeing the tensions generated by his mother's unhappiness, just as I had escaped my family's trauma by going away to college and law school.

Aileen always expected the worst, which Tom does too, though in his case it means he is rarely disappointed and often pleasantly surprised by the turn of events. His intellectual brand of pessimism compared to my ebullient optimism showed up as the only discordant sign in a personality inventory we took before marriage. This real point of difference between us has never caused any trouble, though we often laugh at our divergent expectations of upcoming events.

At first, my mother resisted my relationship with Tom; it meant my certain return to California after serving in the Justice Department. But she soon came to love and appreciate him. Dad would have liked anyone I chose, though a Westerner and a real scholar was a new type for him. He might have been a professor himself had the Depression and alcoholism not intervened. But his intellectual curiosity gradually atrophied in the many days he spent "blotto," as Mother described his general state while drinking.

After our wedding, Tom and I settled into a satisfying family life. Reading back over my diary entries, I'm struck mostly by the eventful pace of our days. Tom's daughter, Becky, spent half the time at our house, often with one or both of her friends Megan and Sarah, a fragile and sometimes explosive trio. Starr, who was practicing personal injury law in the city, was a frequent visitor. He was learning a lot and was fully engaged in the social life readily available in San Francisco to a handsome, amusing, straight man.

Tom's sisters and their families, Umpa, his parents, and Becky and Starr joined us for holidays and other occasions. My cousins Gail and Tom Colter, who lived in the Sierra Nevada mountains, sometimes visited for overnights with their two children and Gail's mother. This lovely woman was called "Mutt" all her life because her father said she had looked like one when she was born; Ardell was her given name, which Mother thought she should change to Adele. But she was Mutt Moses, and after marriage to her high school sweetheart, Wallace Cook, she became Mutt Cook. Mutt and Wallace lived most of their lives in Hope and Little Rock, Arkansas, though for their last years they moved to northern California.

Once when Mutt and the cousins were visiting, I called Mom in Hyattsville so the sisters could talk.

> Mutt: Barbara's house is beautiful, and her husband is wonderful.
>
> Mom: He's real smart, too.
>
> Mutt: That's what they say. I can't tell.

I memorialized a Christmas celebration at which we had a "core of 15 people" and others coming and going:

> I wrestled a 25-pound turkey into the oven (breast down for the first two hours of cooking: flipping a hot turkey is no joke, especially for a nervous man like Tom); made stuffing from Silver Palate cookbook (apricots simmered in Grand Marnier, cornbread, herb sausage, herbed bread crumbs and almonds); mashed potatoes for some people who have to have them; gravy with a beer base (great stuff); peas and pearl onions; and for dessert a persimmon pudding made by Umpa and a lemon cake sent by Tom's parents, plus sweet potato pie and chocolate candy. An American classic."

While I was away in Washington, the law school had hired several new faculty members, including its second female, Deborah Rhode. At last I had a comrade in the struggle for more women, though for many years Deborah and I together made very little progress on that front. Deborah is married to an environmental lawyer, Ralph Cavanagh; they met at Yale where she was an undergraduate in the first class to accept women. She is an ardent player of racket sports. We spent many hours at such games, especially tennis doubles, which, though they were better players, Tom and I usually won.

Mark Kelman was also new to the faculty. The younger men, Tom among them, were especially excited to have him. A Harvard graduate, he became a leader of the Critical Legal Studies movement, a radical successor to the Legal Realism of the 1930s and '40s. The "Crits" decry formalism and the belief that law can or should be scientific and certain. Mark's way of pursuing this view of law was called "trashing," which captures the exuberance and liveliness of the work. Most people who know Mark speak of his stunning intellect, but I love him for his warmth and wit.

Ann Richman, Mark's girlfriend, moved from the East with him, and though she is more than a decade younger than I, we quickly became close friends. They married a week after us in 1979, and we four have spent hundreds of evenings together in more than thirty years, usually over dinner and a movie. Ann, a clinical psychologist who works with Stanford women graduate students, is a deep empathizer and with her friends an artful practitioner of telephone therapy. We have lived through all kinds of highs and lows together.

They are like family to us.

I had been back in California and married for only three years when my father died, slowly and painfully, from esophageal cancer. His last years had been peaceful because his alcoholism had simply ceased. Apparently he finally was unable to drink at all. He practiced law a little and in pleasant weather sat on the front porch and read the paper. When he entered his final decline in the spring of 1982, I did not go to Hyattsville to say goodbye. I was in the midst of teaching a large class and I was still angry at him for not even trying to stop drinking earlier. Now I have mellowed about his faults, and wish that I had performed that final filial duty.

Dad died at 73, a ripe age for someone who had abused his body so badly. Aside from consuming immense quantities of bourbon, he had smoked three packs of cigarettes a day. I remember his looking in a mirror and saying wryly, "If I had known I would live so long, I would have taken better care of myself." Writing this in my late seventies, I'm sorry he did not live to see more of the comforts and joys of old age.

A large crowd of mostly lawyers and Mother's church friends came to the memorial service. My brother David delivered the eulogy for Henry Babcock, a country lawyer who had started out when Hyattsville was a sleepy small town. David recalled the people Dad had helped, that he had never turned anyone away for lack of money, and lamented that there were few country lawyers left. It was a moving speech and evoked the man without hinting at his dark secret.

Next, our cousin Walter Green, who had grown up with Dad in Batesville, Arkansas, described their boyhood in that bucolic village on the White River. He then said, "Henry had a weakness—everyone knows it." I was horrified by the public allusion, but of course everyone did know it.

My father's alcoholism was a central fact in my life; I was always trying to fight it, forget it, or escape its effects. Usually I also tried to hide it. Paradoxically, while being secretive and ashamed, I was convinced that no one could really understand me without knowing it. Nor could anyone appreciate the degree to which my achievements were my own, accomplished without paternal guidance or financial support. Sometimes people whose offspring had gotten into drugs or crime would ask Dad how he had raised such exemplary children. "By setting a terrible example," he would say.

I do not know what insight, if any, he finally gained into his life. In a rare moment of candor about his drinking, he said, "I just love likker—like a hog loves sunshine." That was as deep as I ever heard him go on the subject. David thinks it is the whole truth and that our father's life was pretty much what he wanted it to be. But that is far from the story mother raised us on, in which he was a brilliant, gifted man brought low by addiction, and her life also was ruined.

"I never wanted a career, like you," she told me, "but just to marry a great man and help him." At the same time, I think she did imagine fame, glamour, and material success. Evidence of her aspirations is in the portrait she had taken the year she was twenty-five and newly married. She went to Bachrach, the photographer of D.C. elite society. The picture is very beautiful. When I was twenty-five I went to Bachrach also and copied the pose and draping, but not to the same effect.

Mother loved Dad, though his lifetime of binges had to have undermined her affections. Somehow after each episode, she contrived to believe it would be the last—or at least to act as if she did. That made each lapse a fresh assault and her life an emotional roller coaster. I rode many of the ups and downs with her.

After Dad died, I prevailed on her to come and live near us, which she did for her final twenty years. At last, I thought, I could lavish on her some of the things she had largely missed: travel, fancy meals, shopping without anxiety over cost, a backyard swimming pool. I had not adequately weighed the down sides of the move for either of us. She left behind fifty years of friendships, her church, her bridge games, and the beautiful old house she had decorated and struggled to maintain. Tom and I lost our potential mobility; we could not take off to teach for a year on the East Coast or even decamp to San Francisco.

But Tom supported my daughterly devotion and did not begrudge the many hours I spent with her. (He never objects to having time to himself.) I folded her into my life, often taking her to class, to lunch with students, and to other school events. She came to our dinner parties, and we traveled together—most memorably, for a winter vacation to the Yucatan Peninsula in Mexico, where we joined David and his wife, Kathy.

For some years, the arrangement worked as I had hoped. I was proud of Mother for taking up her new life so readily, and pleased that she appreciated the beauty and ease of California. With the proceeds from selling the Hyattsville house, she bought a one-bedroom condominium in a high-rise near campus with a lovely swimming pool. She joined a large Presbyterian congregation in a nearby town.

My brothers and I tape-recorded some of her reminiscences. She recalled childhood on the farm in Hope, Arkansas, "where we were poor, but we did not know we were poor." She had an older brother, Perry, and two younger sisters, Ardell (Mutt) and Margery. Her childhood was idyllic, with never a cross word between her parents and long summer days in which she bicycled to the quarry where she was the only girl who swam in the deepest part.

Mom described the thrill of being the first in her family to go to college and the disappointment of having to drop out during the Great Depression to teach in a one-room country school near Hope. She lived to see a man from her little town become President of the United States. Bill Clinton reminded her of the boys she had grown up with, indeed Mutt's daughter Susan went to kindergarten with him; Mom spent many happy hours following his campaigns on TV. Unfortunately, she also heard all about

Monica Lewinsky and saw Clinton impeached, but she largely blamed his enemies and was able to forgive him at about the same time Hillary did.

Over the years, Mother's multiple sclerosis worsened, deadening the feeling in her left leg. Finally she had to use a wheelchair. At first, we still went on many outings, which were eased by the advantages of the handicapped-parking placard. The progress of the disease increased her nerve pain, and though Mom was stoical, especially around other people, she became increasingly depressed.

Even if her health had not declined, I'm not sure I could ever have given her as much as she wanted. Her lifetime of longing and disappointment could be assuaged it seemed, only by my exclusive attention. Though I saw her every day I was in town or explained why I couldn't, she regularly accused me of inattention and of "sandwiching" her in with other people.

Yet even as I came to feel burdened by her care, we still had many good times and to this day I try to emulate her socially, especially her skill at drawing people out and drawing them in. She died in May 2001, and so she missed the September 11 terrorist attack as well as her own 90th birthday, also in September. The morning after she died, I awoke crying with a grief deeper than I have ever known—partly over the loss of any further chance to bring happiness to my greatest admirer. Nobody loves you like your mother does, I realized.

Another central relationship in my life (one more BFF, if anyone is counting) is with Toni Massaro. It came about in the late eighties, a period in which concern grew among some of my younger male colleagues over the paucity of female faculty members and the implicit message that women were not up to these plum jobs. Mark Kelman surveyed the published scholarship of every young woman law professor in the country, which led to our inviting the most promising of them to visit for a semester, starting with Toni, who was then on the faculty at the University of Florida.

Mark introduced Toni and me soon after she arrived in fall 1989. I felt immediately at ease with her and launched into a comedy routine. She was funny right back, surprised but tickled by our exchange. Usually it takes me a while to warm to people, and I don't often start with jokes, but Toni and I connected instantly. Tom and she also liked each other immediately; she was the first friend we made together.

Toni's path to Stanford was not typical in that she had not attended Harvard or Yale, had not clerked for an important judge, did not have the backing of prominent scholars, and did not teach at a leading school. Mark had discovered her in the law reviews where she had written impressive doctrinal articles, notable for their recognition of all sides of an issue and their lack of pretension.

Like me, Toni enjoyed Civil Procedure, and we taught parallel sections of the course at the same time that autumn out of the Carrington-Babcock book, often using shared notes. She found our students to be an exciting bunch, and they reciprocated with adoration. To this day, I run into alumni who ask about her. Neither of us had ever had this kind of pedagogical companionship. Toni soon became a co-author of the Civil Procedure book. Seeing our names together on the spine still elates me as we are now in the sixth edition (with Norman Spaulding carrying the laboring oar).

After her year at Stanford, Toni joined her friend who became her life partner, Genevieve (Jerry) Leavitt, and took a job teaching at the University of Arizona Law School in Tucson, Jerry's home. We vowed to keep our friendship alive, and embarked on regular letter-writing (composed on the word processor, sent in the mail). I would talk about getting something into "the one o'clock post"—as creaky-sounding now as dropping it off at the Pony Express. We also had long talks on the telephone and got together as a foursome many times in California or Arizona. Toni and I dedicated the Civil Procedure book to "Tom and Jerry, neither cat nor mouse."

For a decade starting in 1999, Toni was dean of the law school at Arizona, where she did an extraordinary job. Her tenure impressed me anew with how hard it is to be dean: bearing the responsibility and blame without hiring or firing power. And every law school faculty has prima donnas, instinctual dean-haters, and obstructionists.

Because law professors tend to be skilled rhetoricians and are naturally contentious, running a faculty full of them is no small feat. I thought about trying for it myself as Stanford dean when I came back from D.C., but am glad now that I had little encouragement. Even if I had been able to get the job, I doubt that I would have been good at administering by persuasion and consensus rather than by use of unarticulated power such as I had wielded as head of the Public Defender and as Assistant Attorney General.

Toni's visit to Stanford coincided with the Loma Prieta earthquake in mid-October 1989: the "Big One" we had all been expecting. It was 6.9 on the Richter scale. Years earlier when I was contemplating moving to California, people had mentioned earthquakes as a reason not to go. That sounded ridiculous, though I did have a few nightmares after seeing a picture of a cow swallowed by a quake somewhere in Indonesia. Only its legs were left above ground.

At any rate, I easily survived the Big One. I was driving to pick up Mother to go grocery shopping when the radio signal abruptly vanished and I had the sensation that all four tires had gone flat. Then I saw other cars pull over and other drivers examine *their* tires and understood. Mother was still walking with the aid of a cane and had been waiting for me in front of her building when she was knocked down by what she thought was the backdraft from a train blasting through on the nearby tracks. I later learned that survivors often describe a sound like that of an on-rushing train right before the quaking starts.

As Mom struggled to regain her feet, a physical therapist happened by on a bike and helped her up. That was the kind of luck she had: not the kind that saved her from MS, or from falling in the quake. She still wanted to go to the store despite her fall because she had a hard time pinning me down for such shopping trips. But we made it only to the Safeway's front doors, which were wildly swinging open and shut. Inside, mountains of merchandise had tumbled into the aisles.

I urged Mother to come home with me, but she wanted to sleep in her own bed. We made our way back to her apartment building through streets unregulated by traffic lights. Though some utilities and the phones were still working in her building, the elevators were out, so we began trudging up seven flights, pausing to rest at each landing.

Cell phones were not yet in widespread use, and I had not spoken to Tom since the quake but assumed he was safe at home watching the World Series between the San Francisco Giants and the Oakland A's. (In fact, the game had been called off.) On the fifth-floor landing, we heard a man running up the stairs, panting and cursing softly. It was Tom, who, unable to reach Mom on her home phone, had feared she might be in danger. When he saw us sitting peacefully on the steps reading a magazine aloud, he was amused and relieved.

At home, the TV had fallen from our bedroom chest of drawers, the blender had crashed out of the kitchen cabinet, and books had flown off shelves to rest in heaps on the floor in every room. But everything else survived intact. I called Toni, who was shaken. Her dog and cat were even more upset than she, and she did not want to desert them for a calming drink with us.

That Big One has been the only natural disaster to impinge on my life so far. I don't count a couple of hurricanes that came close, one in D.C. and the other in Jamaica. I thought I was handling the quake experience with aplomb until the next day when Toni, Tom, and I went out for breakfast and tennis, and I suddenly felt infirm and frail, a case of shock that lasted for a few days. My friend Ann said of a colleague's reaction to the quake, "It turns out he is really worried about mortality." And we laughed: "Who isn't?"

Actually, the Big One did not stir thoughts of mortality for me, but five years later breast cancer did. I was fifty-two. Because there was a lot of cancer in my family, I had always been faithful about regular examinations. The cancer showed up at a very early stage in an annual mammogram.

"How will I handle this?" I wrote to Toni soon after the diagnosis. She had suffered breast cancer as a young woman, which was scarier than my situation. "Courageously, of course," I answered myself. "And cancer gives a lot of scope for being courageous. But people are always courageously battling cancer. I think I'll battle it cravenly.... Or I could just be cowardly and skip the battling .... But it's not fear exactly. Or maybe it is, and I just have never felt it at this level."

It turned out that if one must have breast cancer, I was lucky: I had the kind that fed on estrogen. After surgery, I took the hormone Tamoxifen, which blocked the production of estrogen to any cancer cells that may still have lurked or escaped. Within a year of the diagnosis, I was physically recovered, and after five years of Tamoxifen, my cancer risk had receded to that of other women my age.

I was fortunate to have had the dread disease in a very treatable form and even luckier to be surrounded by compassionate friends. Tom is the perfect companion in and out of stress, and at Stanford I had great medical care as well. I do not call myself a cancer survivor, as if to take credit, nor do I think I showed any unique bravery or virtue. I have always supposed that cancer will ultimately be my end. As my friend Diane said in her last days with a rare form of the disease, "Everyone has to die of something."

Gathering these recollections, I looked back on the cancer correspondence I have saved: hundreds of letters and cards and e-mails. My friend Eli Evans sent me a year of beautiful flowers, delivered each month. I wrote thanking him with a story. It's about being back in the classroom after almost dying (which is not what happened, but is what it felt like):

> The other day I gave my class a lecture about due process of law, and it was almost like talking to a jury. Started out by telling them that this lecture was not only to summarize a bit—but also to show them how much they had learned, that what I was about to say would have been incomprehensible to them just a few months ago, and now though there would be some ideas and connections not previously made, they would understand everything. This *really* got their attention. At the end, I repeated it, and sought their acknowledgment that in fact they had understood it all—and they burst into prolonged and spontaneous applause.
>
> I do think somehow that I have gotten more, shall we say spiritual, from my brush with cancer. Somehow I was inside their heads, looking through their eyes and willing them to understand.

Like the old days in D.C.

13

TEACHING AND TESTIFYING (1980-PRESENT)

When I returned to Stanford from my stint at the Justice Department, I took up teaching Civil Procedure again, now backed by the authority of a published text (Carrington and Babcock) and by having run the federal government's civil litigation department. My passion still was for the criminal side of procedure, which I had never taught because of the legendary Tony Amsterdam's prior claim on the class. But in 1980, soon after I got back, he announced his move to NYU.

Losing Tony was a blow to the school and a personal disappointment, but professionally I rejoiced at the chance to teach what I knew best. Many years followed in which I taught Civ Pro to first-year students in the fall and Crim Pro to second- and third-years in the spring. I had several students on their first and last days in law school classes.

The first year I taught Crim Pro, I won the John Bingham Hurlburt Award for Excellence in Teaching, given to the graduating class's choice of their best teacher. I had coveted the prize since it had been instituted in 1974, and I won it three more times, almost whenever I was eligible (every five years). The winner speaks at graduation, my favorite occasion for oratory because the audience is in a celebratory mood.

My Crim Pro classes usually numbered well over a hundred students, large for Stanford; teaching a class this size with many third-year students in it was a necessary condition for winning the Hurlburt. By teaching civil and criminal procedure, and later, a seminar in women's history, I came to know most of the 170-180 students in each of the law school's three classes. To a person, they were bright and accomplished. I told Mother, who often visited at school, how fortunate I felt to be teaching "the cream

179

of American academia"—to which she responded, "They are darling young people." We were both right, and I loved them.

I was especially close to the women students no matter what their politics, and wanted to help them succeed. Plenty of male students, especially those drawn to work in criminal justice or teaching law, also sought my advice, as did gay men. At the end of the seventies few lawyers were out, and there were no openly gay men or lesbians on the faculty or staff. Also, I came to know many, if not most, of our Latino and African American students, partly because they sensed I understood how strange and white Stanford seemed—and was.

Now in retrospect, I'm amazed at the decisiveness with which I dispensed personal and professional guidance. Alums tell me that I freely coached them to break off their love affairs or to make job choices in furtherance of romance. One reminded me that I consoled her about a recent divorce with a brusque "You'll be fine—you'll be over it in exactly one year"—and she was. Sometimes I stunned them by dismissing their existential doubts about studying law with "Cut your losses and go do something else. If you don't really enjoy the basic stuff of the law, it can be drudgery." But I always reminded them of the near-infinite of paths open to someone with a law degree.

Commiserating with Mary Minow, who came from a long line of attorneys (her sister, Martha, later became Dean of Harvard Law) and who felt guilty about finding law study dull, I told her of a similarly disappointed student who was a wine connoisseur and had made a successful legal career as a wine lawyer. I asked Mary about her enthusiasms and she said she had really loved her prior work as a librarian. "Well, become a library lawyer," I said, and she did, entering (and helping to establish) the field just as the digital revolution took off. She is now a widely published writer, founder of the Library Law blog, and manager of Stanford libraries' Copyright and Fair Use website.

One colleague sarcastically called my classes "love fests"—implying that my questions were not rigorous, and that I oversimplified the material. It may have appeared that way. But I had learned that even super-bright Stanford students needed to have the obvious stated, and several times repeated. My actual secret sauce, though, was not that my classes were easy but that I was good at devising compelling questions and then interlarded the Q & A with stories. My syllabi were built around the theme of a lawyer's duties—to the profession, to the community, and to moral principles. In Crim Pro, I entreated the students to become defenders or prosecutors, or at least members of the bar concerned with the sorry state of criminal justice.

I would tell them that Crim Pro is a subset of the (undeservedly) more prestigious subject of Constitutional Law, dealing not with the principles of government organization but with individual rights to be free of unreasonable searches and compelled confessions, to confront witnesses, to be tried by a jury, and so forth. It is the dark side of Con Law because those who carry the rights forward in court are usually the criminally accused, many of whom are in fact criminals. Most of all I wanted them to see that despite the noble guarantees of the Bill of Rights, the system is skewed against defendants, especially the poor and non-white.

In the early days of teaching Crim Pro, I would announce my defense bias on the first day of class and justify teaching from the underdog's perspective because our students were not likely to encounter it elsewhere at an elite law school. After a few years, I shifted to saying that I was pro-defense, but I would do my best to present the material neutrally and let them reach their own conclusions. As a result I would more often have a law-and-order oriented student burst out with the very attack on a particular unfairness that I would have made myself under my earlier regime. I could then remark, to much laughter, "I'm glad it's *you* who said that." It was a subtler way to proselytize.

Criminal Procedure was a perfect setting for trial stories from my days as a defender. Students remembered the tales long after the doctrines had faded. A distinguished intellectual property lawyer at an alumni event laughed again about my account of the very tall client who was arrested in the signature purple jumpsuit he had worn to rob the corner liquor store.

Another favorite story involved William "Blue" Miller. Ten years before I met him, a unanimous U.S. Supreme Court had reversed his conviction for drug offenses, holding that the soft-spoken words "Blue, it's the police" were insufficient to announce the cops' authority and purpose before they broke down his front door at 4:00 AM.[*] When I pressed Blue for a defense to his current charge, he flashed his charming smile and said, "Don't worry—the Supreme Court will take care of it." I never encountered a more touching faith in the system.

---

[*] *Miller v. United States*, 357 U.S. 301, 303, 304 n.2 (1958).

Around the dawn of the twenty-first century, students started bringing laptop computers to class, enabling them to take amazingly complete notes and do on-the-spot research. Teaching a big class started to feel like conducting an orchestra or directing a gospel choir, with my call and their keyboard-tapping response. Occasionally they would all fall silent when I thought I was saying something important, and I would exhort them— "Click! Click!"

Pedagogical objections to laptop note-taking arose immediately, partly because it enabled playing games, shopping, and following sports. Moreover, fast typers would transcribe virtually every word spoken, failing to develop the essential legal skill of sifting the wheat from the chaff. I found that the raised screens interfered with the eye contact I relied on, but I retired before I decided whether to ban them from the classroom. (Now I conclude that I would have joined my colleague Norm Spaulding in forbidding laptops for the first-year students.)

Teaching is only half of being a law professor and upon my return to Stanford, I was eager to fully engage the other fifty percent: scholarship. Though my head was teeming with topics from my time in the Department of Justice, I wanted to write about my first love, criminal procedure, a field where too little of the scholarship was informed by a close knowledge of how the system actually functioned (and malfunctioned). For many months I toiled over an article with the cumbersome title "Fair Play: Evidence Favorable to an Accused and Effective Assistance of Counsel."[*]

It started in 1963 with *Brady v. Maryland*,[†] which required the prosecution to provide the defense with exculpatory evidence in its possession. Decided the same year as the Supreme Court required lawyers for the indigent accused,[‡] *Brady* could have aided the appointed counsel in mounting an effective defense and ultimately revolutionized criminal practice. But it wasn't to be: practicing in the early years following *Brady*, I saw firsthand how strongly prosecutors and judges resisted its dictates. "Truth, justice, and the American way do not require the Government to discover and develop the defendant's entire defense,"[§] one court said in an oft-quoted line.

---

[*] 34 *Stanford Law Review* 1133 (1982).

[†] 373 U.S. 83 (1963).

[‡] 372 U.S. 335 (1963).

[§] *United States v. Brown*, 628 F.2d 471, 473 (5th Cir. 1980).

Duty-to-disclose issues could arise in almost every criminal case. They were litigated before and during trial, on appeal, and then repeatedly on habeas corpus review and appeals from those denials. Defense lawyers pushed for broad disclosure, and demanded reversal of convictions if the government failed to produce exculpatory evidence. Prosecutors fought back mainly by arguing that the undisclosed evidence was not significant enough to influence the outcome.

For more than a decade, lawyers struggled over the meaning of *Brady;* hundreds of conflicting decisions were handed down from state and federal courts, but it was not until 1976, thirteen years after the decision, that the Justices addressed the reach of the doctrine. In the case the Court finally took, *United States v. Agurs,*[*] the government had failed to disclose that the deceased in a murder case had a criminal record for knife assaults. Obviously this evidence would have supported the defendant's claim of self-defense, and the appellate court had reversed.

But the Supreme Court held that since the defense had not made a specific request for the deceased's record, the conviction should stand unless the defense could establish an overwhelming probability that the verdict would have been different if the record had been supplied.[†] In adopting that standard, the court largely ignored the pro-defense precedents that had built up around *Brady* in the previous thirteen years, thereby throwing the administration of the constitutional doctrine into chaos.

Dismayed, I undertook a critique of *Agurs*, and also discovered a silver lining to its specific request mandate. Probably without intending it, the opinion strongly implied that defense lawyers who did not make such requests were ineffective. *Gideon* had held that the indigent accused were entitled to counsel, but had said nothing about standards for their performance. A line of appeals even longer than that on *Brady* issues was forming to challenge convictions on the basis of ineffective assistance of appointed counsel, which many argued was equivalent to having no lawyer at all. *Agurs,* by spelling out what a lawyer must do to raise a *Brady* issue, strengthened the claims of defendants whose attorneys failed to seek exculpatory evidence.

---

[*] 427 U.S. 97, 99 (1976).

[†] *Id.* at 106.

In the days before search engines, I set out with the help of my top-notch student research assistants to find and analyze the hundreds of post-*Gideon* cases in which there might be lawyer error in failing to seek *Brady* material. Atop all the doctrine, I overlaid a metaphor comparing the ideals of fair play in sports with due process in criminal trials. There is a much-repeated admonition against "the sporting theory of justice,"[*] on the grounds that it demeans the process to compare it to a game. I agree of course that criminal justice is serious business, but the wholesale rejection of the sports metaphor of "fair play" as guidance was, I argued, misplaced. A level field, clear rules, unbiased officials, and equal treatment of participants seemed to be good aspirations for the criminal justice system, which could only improve if scrutinized with the intense passion for quality that we Americans lavish on sports.

I urged that the Supreme Court should set high standards for court-appointed defense attorneys and ratify reversals of convictions without requiring proof that the defendant had been prejudiced by his attorney's defective performance. Naïvely, I expected attention and praise for my contribution to the development of the law. Instead, when the Court finally took a case on ineffective assistance of counsel, the majority decided it contrary to my recommendations, presuming lawyer competence, requiring a strong showing of prejudice, and not mentioning my article.[†] (Later it would be cited in quite a few cases, but mostly in dissent.)

Even though my effort to make a practical difference (and even a splash) through criminal justice scholarship had largely failed, I felt good about returning to academia after the hectic years in Washington. I quickly settled into fulfilling routines, a transition made all the smoother by having tenure and being married to a star scholar. Stanford has always seemed to me especially congenial among law schools because of our non-confrontational culture: political and ideological enemies tend to politely ignore each other. Some might think that the life of the mind flourishes in a combative atmosphere, but I find that the best intellectual exchange happens among people not too far apart on fundamentals.

My favorite example of Stanford's *modus operandi*, as well as its *modus vivendi*, was our solution to affirmative action admissions after the Supreme Court's *Bakke* decision, which questioned preferential treatment

---

[*] *Brady*, 373 U.S. at 90.

[†] *Strickland v. Washington*, 466 U.S. 668 (1984).

for racial minorities.* A white student who had been denied admission to a University of California medical school sued, claiming his academic record was superior to that of any student of color admitted. Ordering Bakke's admission, a fractured court nevertheless upheld affirmative action that could be justified as an effort to gain the educational advantages of a more diverse student body, but not for the more deeply felt purposes of these programs, which were to overcome the effects of long-standing discrimination, and to promote integration of the upper echelons of the society.

Stanford's post-*Bakke* problem was that while our affirmative action program (begun by Thelton Henderson a decade earlier) was producing excellent applicants, undoubtedly some white students with better records on paper were rejected. Being a private school did not immunize us from lawsuits; our various forms of federal support (e.g., student loan programs) could be put in jeopardy. We decided to set up a diversity-oriented preferential admission program for white applicants while continuing our existing programs for students of color.

When we tried to settle on which non-racial qualities contributed to a desirable diversity, we quickly realized that we would never be able to agree by the application of reason. We hit on a uniquely Stanfordian scheme of having each faculty member who wanted to participate in the diversity program pick five candidates from among files of fifty Caucasian applicants who were close to qualifying but needed an extra push. There would be no agreed-upon definition of diversity; instead, we would each use our own standards.

We gave written reasons for each choice, and then the admissions director and a faculty committee made the final decisions. Whenever one of my "diversity admits" excelled, I was secretly thrilled—secretly because students were not supposed to know they had been specially chosen. Indeed, many students may have been unaware of the program, though I occasionally heard a first-year say he must be a diversity admit since everyone else seemed to be smarter.

Most of my diversity admits were female; many of them were feminists, and many had played varsity sports. The athletes' ability to maintain high grades while juggling practice and competition schedules exhibited discipline that impressed me. I'm not sure how long our formal diversity

---

* *Regents of the University of California v. Bakke*, 438 U.S. 265 (1978).

program lasted. Now it has been folded into the general admissions process where it originated. Because of the skills of Faye Deal, our admissions director, I doubt that we have lost anything on the diversity front.

I have spent nearly all of the last forty years at Stanford. My only experiences teaching elsewhere were the semester at Hawaii in 1976 when their law school was only a year old, a summer at Michigan, and several months in Japan. That invitation came about through my colleague, Lawrence Friedman. When I mentioned that I would like to dive into an Asian culture as more than a tourist, he started the wheels turning that led in 1995 to an invitation to teach a course on the American legal system at Toin University, a brand new school in Yokohama.

Luckily, at Toin I had the help of Satoshi Miyajima, who had studied law in the United States. He was my co-teacher (I lectured; he explained and graded), and we became friends. His English was impeccable, and he was eager to learn the latest idioms. Satoshi smoothed out the logistics involved with my being a visiting teacher at Toin, and his good company enabled Tom and me to understand what we saw in Japan better than we could ever have done on our own.

At that time in Japan, law was entirely an undergraduate course of study; professional training came afterward for specific legal occupations. (Now, Japanese legal education is more like ours.) To introduce a class of Japanese undergraduates to the American legal system, I drew on a recent tragedy in which a Japanese exchange student looking for directions to a Halloween party in Baton Rouge had been shot and killed by a homeowner who mistook him for an intruder. Sixteen-year-old Yoshihiro Hattori, dressed in a tuxedo as John Travolta from *Saturday Night Fever*, had not understood the command to "freeze."[*]

The homeowner was tried for manslaughter and acquitted, to worldwide headlines. In a wrongful-death suit, the boy's parents were awarded a large sum by a judge who sat without a jury and the judgment was upheld on appeal.[†] Including as it did both criminal and civil proceedings, the Hattori case seemed like an ideal tool for teaching about the American court system. I gathered legal opinions, analytical articles,

---

[*] *Hattori v. Peairs*, 662 So. 2d 509, 512 (La. App. 1st Cir. 1994); 666 So. 2d 322 (La. 1996).

[†] *Hattori*, 662 So. 2d at 517-18.

and news stories, and wrote explanatory notes, all of which Toin Press packaged in a handsome booklet which served as the text for the course.

But my case study was perhaps too sophisticated for undergraduates beginning the study of law, and the format was unfamiliar to the students. I might have done better to have used a standard text about the American legal system and filled in with illustrations from the Hattori case in lectures. I have a tendency to let my reach exceed my grasp.

Twice a week, I was driven from Tokyo to Yokohama for class, which I taught via simultaneous interpretation. It was unnerving to lecture to a roomful of strangely inert and intently staring young people with perfect posture who were not listening to my actual words. Sometimes I tried to joke, but there were no cracks in the carapace of their attention. I never knew whether they had understood anything I said, though Satoshi said they did well on the examination. It was the strangest and one of the least satisfying teaching experiences of my life.

By contrast, late in my visit, I had a memorable classroom experience, at Chuo University in Tokyo, one of the top law faculties in Japan. I was asked to illustrate to the students, and also to the faculty, the American mode of teaching law, with professor-student exchanges rather than straight lectures. An enthusiastic professor who was hoping to influence teaching at Chuo in the direction of the American system, Mr. Osini, interpreted for me paragraph by paragraph, perhaps adding his own insights. I used the due process game Toni Massaro had devised to open our Civil Procedure textbook.

The game starts with a problem: "You are a student at a university, and one day you come home to find a notice from the president on official letterhead. It reads, 'You have been accused of a serious breach of the rules. Please discontinue class attendance immediately and make arrangements to leave campus.' What further information would you want from the university? What procedures would you expect? What kind of hearing would you seek? What rights would you assume?"

The room was crowded, with students sitting close together on benches and in the aisles. I read the problem and asked the first question: "What would you want or expect from the university?" Mr. Osini interpreted. No one stirred. I repeated; he repeated. Silence. I knew that if I answered the question myself, the demonstration would end before it had started; no one would say a word for the rest of the class. So I waited. Eternities passed; eons. Then a young woman ventured her hand into the air and said in English, "I would want to tell my side." I can still hear her clear, soft voice.

And they were off. "I would want to know the charges." "I would want someone to present my case." "I would want to have witnesses." Some spoke in English, some in Japanese; Mr. Osini translated back and forth. The Chuo students built an elaborate procedural framework, not very different from the ones constructed by my American law students. After collecting their recommendations, we then discussed the cost in time and resources required for increasingly formal procedures, and what is lost when this isn't done. The ninety minute class sped by. Afterwards, Mr. Osini said I had taken them "like a shepherd, bringing them safely over rocky roads."

During our time in Japan, we were constantly enacting the cliché of the Westerner struck by the inscrutability of the local culture, but we couldn't help ourselves. Satoshi was always there to answer questions, but we had many more than we were willing to ask him. Sometimes we watched Japanese soap operas, and tried to decipher what was going on, with no confidence that our inventions bore any relation to what we were watching. We went to the Kabuki theatre, and even with English commentary coming through headphones, we could not fully grasp that we were seeing a man playing a woman who became a lion driven mad by butterflies—the famous lion dance. But we were moved by it!

We lived in a high-rise in a residential neighborhood on the banks of the Tama River along the southern border of Tokyo, and featuring the iconic view of Mount Fuji in the distance. I shopped at the corner grocery store where nothing was in English. Towering over everyone there and attracting many sidelong glances, I enjoyed puzzling out the contents of mysterious packages and examining the unfamiliar produce.

Twice a day, the fish vendor called out something in a hoarse voice, drawing shoppers to the shelf where he displayed his freshly filleted wares on ice. One day there was a great rush when he called; I joined in and spied chunks of glistening ahi tuna. I reached to snag one for Tom and one for me. But the vendor started yelling and crossed his arms in the hex sign while violently shaking his head. What could he possibly be saying? "No fish for foreigners" was all I could imagine.

When I started to put the fish back, he became even more agitated. Then an old woman came forward and said in English, "He says you can get three pieces for the price of two." Gratefully I took a third, and the fishmonger smiled and said what may have been the only two foreign words he knew: "Bonjour, mademoiselle." "Gracias, señor," I responded in kind. We all laughed, and afterward I heard the ladies telling their friends about the incident all over the store, the two Romance-language phrases popping up amidst outpourings of Japanese.

Back in the familiar setting of Stanford, I taught my classes, did committee work, counseled students, and wrote letters of recommendation. Law school faculty politics (swirling especially around hiring and dean changes) and life as an active campus feminist also occupied me. Though the various battles were absorbing at the time, they no longer seem so compelling, and I would be hard-pressed to recreate the fervor they once aroused. An exception was my role in opposing Robert Bork's nomination to the Supreme Court in 1987.

Bork had been a popular teacher at Yale when I was there in the early 1960s, but I had not taken his course because I had no interest in antitrust or law and economics. More than one classmate told me that I was missing out on one of the school's great teachers.

By the time he was nominated to the Supreme Court, Bork had branched out from antitrust to constitutional law, and had established himself as one of the intellectual leaders of the legal conservative movement. That had led to his appointment to the D.C. Circuit by President Reagan, and he had served on that "second highest court in the land" for more than five years. No one could doubt his ability, and he was an obvious choice to further the President's project of creating a solid conservative majority on the High Court. Women's rights activists were convinced that Bork's appointment would be the death of *Roe v. Wade*, which he had strongly denounced.

As one of the first teachers of a course we called "Women and the Law," I was asked by the Senate Judiciary committee to testify about the nomination. At first I said that I was deep into this important biography of Clara Foltz, the first woman lawyer in the West. I was behind on the project, and plenty of other good women were available. After refusing the invitation, my sleep was troubled. "What would Clara do?" rang in my head. To be asked for the woman's viewpoint on such an important nomination—why, Clara Foltz would have jumped on the next train even though it took five or six days to get from California to Washington, D.C. in the nineteenth century. I called back and said I would do it.

I was to appear on a panel of prominent feminists while Tom was invited to join a group of constitutional law scholars. We arrived in D.C. to find a city obsessed, as only D.C. can be, with a single political event. From the Ethiopian taxi driver to lawyers in all walks, from print and broadcast media to people on the street, all were focused on the televised spectacle.

We women met at the offices of a leading firm where partner Brooksley Born, a Stanford graduate who had clerked for Judge Edgerton after me, had organized a strategy session for us to plot on maximizing our impact. As probably the first panel of women lawyers ever to testify in a Supreme Court confirmation hearing, we wanted to make sure we did it right by covering all the bases, and avoiding repeating or contradicting each other.

On the women's panel were Shirley Hufstedler, a former Ninth Circuit judge and President Carter's Secretary of Education, and Sylvia Law and Wendy Williams, law professors at NYU and Georgetown, respectively. Women were on several panels in addition to the one devoted specifically to our issues; Judith Resnik from Yale, for instance, was on the constitutional law panel with Tom and three other male scholars. It was electrifying to gather in the corridors of power and feel that what we said might matter there.

Looking back now on that day in late September, 1987,[*] I am struck first by the directness of our attack, starting with my charge that "Judge Bork's rhetoric is a good fifteen years behind the times on women's rights, just as it was on civil rights for blacks before now." I tried to illustrate that Bork's views were to the right of other conservative appointees, Rehnquist and Scalia, and I said, "This is the first nomination that I've *ever* opposed because I feel that this is the most extreme."

I got into a debate with Senator Orrin Hatch (R-Utah) about the interpretation of a case in which sexual harassment at work was found to be a form of discrimination under Title VII. Senator Hatch tried to show that Judge Bork's opinion did not disagree with the Supreme Court's holding to that effect.[†] In exasperation, I said: "The woman *loses* with Judge Bork's reading, and she *wins* in the Supreme Court." I remember feeling satisfied with that exchange.

---

[*] http://www.c-span.org/video/?10176-1/bork-nomination-day-9-part-3; http://www.c-span.org/video/?10177-1/bork-nomination-day-9-part-4

[†] See *Meritor Savings Bank v. Vinson*, 477 U.S. 57 (1986).

Tom's panel came on late in the same day, when only six of the committee's eighteen members—two Democrats and four Republicans— remained in the room. Although the panelists' written statements would be in the record and were the most important contribution, the lack of drama was a little disappointing—until, that is, we saw the video. At the outset, the panelists were asked to pare their remarks to five minutes. The first to speak simply ignored the injunction and reading every phrase of his statement, took twenty minutes. Seated beside him and next to testify, Tom didn't know the camera was on him too and his eye-rolling and wriggling were very funny to watch later.

Before Tom spoke, committee chairman Joe Biden implored him to "try to keep it to the five minutes, OK?" Tom brought his remarks in at eight-and-a-half minutes.* Representing a group of liberal law professors, he focused particularly on Bork's extrajudicial writings and speeches, arguing that they revealed the man as far more radical than a run-of-the-mill conservative. Of course, as a lower-court judge he would not carry out the most far-reaching implications of his right wing approach.

In response, Bork's proponents had argued that the radical views were merely academic theorizing, "tentative, speculative, ranging shots." To refute this, Tom quoted from a recent speech in which Bork had savaged "nonoriginalists," a term Tom said described himself and all the other panelists. Bork had told his Federalist Society audience that though it may take years for conservative constitutional theorizing to crest, "crest it will, and it will sweep the elegant, erudite, pretentious, and toxic detritus of nonoriginalism out to sea!" Tom's sardonic parting shot was: "Tentative?" And I heard him mutter: "Ha."

The decades since the Senate defeated the Bork nomination, by a 58-42 vote, have seen much academic and popular discussion about whether our campaign helped or hurt the judicial system and the selection process. But there can be little doubt that it was important for preserving women's legal victories and critical for achieving future gains. Anthony Kennedy, a more moderate thinker and less forceful intellectual leader, was appointed instead of Bork, who resigned from the D.C. Circuit court the next year and spent much of the rest of his life railing against "'ultraliberals, radicals

---

* http://www.c-span.org/video/?10178-1/bork-nomination-day-9-part-5

and leftists."""[*] To come so close to the pinnacle and be brought down by people whose ideas he loathed embittered Robert Bork, as his subsequent writings documented.

The triumph of liberal and feminist believers in an evolving Constitution was bracing; it seemed a hopeful portent for future appointments that would at least hew to the middle of the road. But the Court today, with Justices appointed by Reagan and two Bushes, harks back to that of the 1930s in its conservatism and its disrespect for the legislative function. As one whose formative years in the law were spent under the influence of the Warren Court, it pains me to see the current situation.

Except there is the heartening and inspiring presence of three liberal women appointed by Democratic presidents: Ruth Ginsburg, Elena Kagan, and Sonia Sotomayor. My own far-outsider dream of being the first woman on the Supreme Court was dashed when Carter lost to Reagan, who in 1981 appointed Sandra Day O'Connor—a Stanford graduate, a Republican moderate, and a very smart woman.

A legal mega-event of similar weight to the Bork hearings dominated national headlines in 1994-1995: the jury trial of football hero O.J. Simpson for the murders of his former wife and her boyfriend. It dragged on for more than eleven months in the main criminal court of Los Angeles before an overly excited judge who allowed it to be televised. I agreed to write columns about the proceedings for the *Los Angeles Times* in order to compare the difference in the quality of justice available to the rich and famous contrasted with the indigent and unknown. My first column[†] followed the six-day preliminary hearing—already a marked contrast with a poor person's lightning-quick, perfunctory prelim (if he had one at all). "People v. Simpson has shown the public a defendant with the money to fully exercise every right provided to him under the Constitution," I wrote, noting that Simpson's defense team so far encompassed "half a dozen lawyers plus forensic pathologists, criminal investigators, analysts and paralegals" costing "millions of dollars."

I ended that column by predicting that the trial would not turn on "factual guilt so much as Simpson's mental state and whether a jury will be

---

[*] Al Kamen and Matt Schudel, "Robert H. Bork, Conservative Judicial Icon, Dies at 85," *Washington Post*, December 12, 2012.

[†] "Equal Justice—and a Defendant with the Money to Exercise Every Right," *Los Angeles Times*, July 10, 1994.

inclined to grant mercy to so famous and well-liked a defendant." If only! Instead the trial devolved into an extravaganza, nearly a farce, about race and racism, featuring a rush to judgment by the police and a myopic performance by prosecutors who seemed unaccustomed to tangling with skilled defense lawyers. Meanwhile, Judge Lance Ito, obscure before the trial, was enthralled to be at the center of the media world. Whenever a celebrity would enter the small courtroom, he would summon the person for a chat at the bench or in chambers, dismissing the jurors to their windowless room.

Simpson's lead counsel, Johnnie Cochran, a charismatic former prosecutor, had total control of the courtroom. For the mostly black jury, he created an atmosphere of "us against them," subtly and skillfully calling upon jurors to send a message (against racism and racist police practices) with their verdict. Eventually Simpson, a patently guilty man, was acquitted. Watching the return of the verdict on TV, I knew—the moment the jury walked in and smiled at the defense table—he had won.

My heart sank. As a deep believer in the jury system, I was appalled to see such a colossal error. Some of my pro-defense friends rejoiced at O.J.'s victory, reading it in part as progress when any black person is acquitted—especially if charged with crimes against whites. For years after the verdict, the case reverberated as subject and example in classes and in the media, often with conflicting morals drawn from the story.

Issues in the O.J. case were resurrected for me in 1997 when Dean Paul Brest proposed that I occupy a law school chair to be named for Judge John Crown, scion of a wealthy, philanthropic Chicago family. I had been the Ernest MacFarland Professor of Law since 1979, the first woman to hold an endowed chair at the law school. I have always trumpeted such firsts on my résumé, although since I was the first woman hired, the other honors followed in turn unless I somehow got fired along the way. Too late for that, today I am Stanford Law School's first professor emerita.

Judge Crown, who could have continued his remunerative career with a leading law firm, chose instead to be a judge on the baseline criminal courts of Chicago for more than twenty years. In honor of the judge's history and mine, Paul conceived of a mock trial. Not one to do anything by halves, he asked our alumni Supreme Court justices, William Rehnquist and Sandra Day O'Connor (both Class of '52), to preside, and they agreed. We searched for a good case to moot and came up with that of Lizzie Borden, who in 1893 was acquitted of ax-murdering her father and stepmother. It happened a century before the O.J. trial, but had many parallels to it.

Perhaps most striking was that Borden had great lawyers who had played "the lady card," calling on stereotypes about woman's delicate nature to argue that Borden was incapable of the dastardly acts. Her gender was as central to her defense in 1893 as Simpson's race was to his in 1995. In Borden's case, too, the defense lawyer's forensic and psychological insights far outran the prosecutor's ability. And Borden's acquittal, like Simpson's, was almost certainly a wrong result.

Usually I turned down invitations to participate in moot courts—they took up time better spent on a real case or a real class. But it would have been rude to refuse this one in my honor, and it turned out to be great fun. I was Borden's defense attorney; Charles Ogletree of Harvard did the considerable service of playing the prosecutor, even though his spirit, like mine, is always on the other side of the courtroom. Other professors were witnesses. Law students played roles, too: Julia Wilson, also a professional actress, played Lizzie, and Cara Robertson, who as a historian had written a study of the Borden case, was Lizzie's sister Emma. We had an audience of seven hundred in a large auditorium and an overflow crowd watching on closed-circuit TV.

I crafted my closing argument along the lines of ones I had given as a public defender, trying as always to make it entertaining. The large audience served as the jury. After explaining that Lizzie did not have to testify, I boomed, "*I* am the voice of Lizzie Borden in this courtroom!" Playing the lady card, I admonished the jury (i.e., the audience), "You *saw* Emma Borden testify under oath in this case. You *saw* that she is a lady to the *core*. And a *lady* does not *lie* under *oath!*"

That brought laughter, as did my peroration cautioning the jury against letting Lizzie be convicted "by a rhyme." I was referring to the in-criminating ditty that began, "Lizzie Borden took an ax and gave her mother forty whacks." Parading outrage, I declared: "In many ways what has happened to this young woman is peculiarly hurtful because she has been convicted by a *rhyme!* And *don't pretend* you haven't heard it! You've *all* heard it, the rhyme. *Now* it is time for reason: Without an ax or bloody dress, Lizzie's *not* a murderess!"

To whoops and wild applause, I continued: "Rather than the *criminal* type, she's a victim of media *hype!* So put aside the ugly *rhyme* that linked her name with brutal *crime! Give* us, without a doubt or worry, an *honest* verdict from an American *jury!*" Justice O'Connor gaveled the audience to order. The videotape of my closing argument* has been used as an exemplar in Stanford's trial advocacy program for years now.

When it came time for the audience to vote, I thought the prosecution might win because Charles had been so good. He started à la Johnnie Cochran, "I'm surprised that Miss Babcock did not say, 'If the glove don't fit, you must acquit'"—and then imitated the cadence of my doggerel: "It's one thing to spend time in rhyme; it's another thing to address the crime." But folks apparently remembered that they were there to honor me, and maybe they, like their historical counterparts, really did not want to believe in Borden's guilt. She was again acquitted. At the banquet when I accepted the professorship, I mentioned the help and support of my mother, who was there with me. It was great to have the chance to praise her before such an illustrious crowd. She loved it.

Another memorable oratorical occasion for me was my last graduation speech, in 2004, the year that I retired. I was pleased when the graduating students voted me the teaching award in my last year—a real chance to say goodbye and to tell them what they needed to know at a time when they were ready to hear it. Our law school ceremony that year was in an old auditorium on the main campus, which had a balcony and seated several thousand. When full, as it was on this occasion, there was a surprisingly intimate feel to the huge space.

The graduates were in the first few rows and I felt that I could see each individual. I started by suggesting that this class was different from all others because they had started their time together shortly before the events of September 11, 2001. "My Civil Procedure notes for September 12 show that I tried, feeling never more challenged in the classroom, to model calm and fortitude," I said and then entreated them to throw themselves into the tasks at hand, "the beautiful daily-ness of life and law study."

At their graduation, I suggested that living through September 11 together had made them as a class unusually tolerant and understanding, interested in and supportive of each other. Then I went on to urge them to join a movement, do public service, contribute to the criminal justice system, and all my other usual entreaties. But the concentrated waves of feeling they returned to me were different from any other speech I

---

* http://www.c-span.org/video/?91387-1/lizzie-borden-moot-court

remember. The quality of the attention of the large crowd felt almost like talking to a jury.

When I first entered academia in 1972, I had been unsettled by the absence of a job description for the law professor position. But plenty of people were willing to advise, and I soon found it liberating to design my own path. In the last stage of my career, I turned to something entirely new and different: I became a biographer.

Barbara Babcock and Tom Grey, 2003

Book talk at Politics and Prose bookstore, Washington, D.C., 2011;
photographs by law professor Angela Davis, American University

14

WRITING A LIFE:
RECOVERING AND MARKETING CLARA FOLTZ

For many years of my life in academia, I worked on a biography of Clara Foltz, the first woman lawyer in the West. Living with a biographical subject was like having some combination of mentor, mother, and sister always at hand. Her story and my own became intertwined: Clara and Me.

I learned about her when a public defender friend asked me to help him enlist a woman's history expert to write a piece celebrating the female founder of our movement for free justice. Astounded to learn about Clara Foltz, and wanting to know more, I told my friend I would produce the piece myself. It seems fitting that I discovered Clara by way of women's rights and public defense. These passions I shared with her also enabled me to see meaning and coherence in her career.

Though I was excited about writing the biography, it was a somewhat outlandish undertaking, which I can admit now that the book has been published. Not only was Clara Foltz "an unknown regional figure" (as one rejection letter put it, possibly referring to me as well), but her papers had not been collected anywhere, and little secondary material was readily available.

Public defense, her greatest achievement, has never been a subject of scholarly interest, and many academics disparage biographies as absorbing too much energy for the amount of light they shed. Friends warned against the project, pointing to the example of Gerald Gunther on our faculty, who had devoted many years to a monumental biography on Judge Learned Hand.

"Think of all the more influential articles on current constitutional issues he might have done instead," they said. At least Hand was a famous jurist, arguably worthy of years of scholarly devotion. The same was not exactly true of Clara Foltz. "Not yet," was what I said to myself, disregarding this and all other warnings and admonitions.

From the first I felt that I was meant for this venture and it for me. Determined and patient, I have a good temperament for the long haul, and though I regularly advise others to cut their losses by abandoning projects, I myself seldom give up anything I start. Moreover, I enjoy research and have the imagination and intuition to picture what might exist and pursue it beyond the usual reference points (or, some would say, beyond reason). My legal training enables me to appreciate what I find: for instance, in reading a brief Foltz wrote, I can understand not only her arguments but their origins in her experience.

I found Clara Foltz at a time when I was discouraged by the (lack of) reception of my kind of doctrinal writing about criminal justice. When I returned to Stanford in 1979 from serving in the Justice Department, I realized after one article that the sort of close reading of cases I liked was out of vogue. Worried that I might not be able to fulfill institutional expectations about the scholarly side of the law professor job, I briefly thought about returning to practice while my Assistant Attorney General-ship was still a valuable credential.

A new academic field of Gender Studies (formerly Women and the Law) was emerging and ardent young scholars were pouring into it. But even though I was a pioneer of the second-wave women's movement, I was not inspired to write about feminist legal doctrine or theory. Instead, I plunged into resurrecting Clara Foltz, and took on a new identity—biographer.

Initially, I learned that though celebrated in her day, Foltz was barely a footnote in history a hundred years later. In bringing her back to life, I had a pleasing sense of mission, enhanced by the realization that without my efforts she was likely to sink permanently into obscurity.

Through Clara Foltz's published writings, her letters in the papers of other people, press interviews, trial transcripts, and speeches, I came to recognize her as a true Western character: larger than life; prodigious in her enjoyment of the moment and in her ambitions for the future. Unwilling to relinquish any possibility, she was determined to be an inspiring movement leader, a successful lawyer and legal reformer, a glamorous socialite, an influential public thinker, and a good single mother to her five children.

The result of these often-conflicting roles was a life so frantic and scattered that it resisted shaping into a lucid narrative. Yet Foltz's determination to "have it all" made her biography particularly relevant in the twenty-first century. It is a tale both cautionary and heroic for women professionals and their male allies.

At about the time I started on the work, my friend the English Professor Diane Middlebrook (see chapter 10) was writing about the poet Anne Sexton. Though hers was a literary and mine a legal biography, our obsession with our subjects was the same, including alternating periods of abhorring and adoring Clara and Anne. Under the auspices of the Stanford Humanities Center, where we were each fellows for a year, Diane and I convened a Biographer's Seminar, which brought scholars in several fields together with non-academic writers. For three or four years, we met once a month for a presentation of a chapter by one of our group. Published biographies of Abigail Adams, Wallace Stevens, Miriam Von Waters, Alfred Tarski, Charlotte Solomon, as well as of Clara Foltz and Anne Sexton, owe something to our seminar.

Over the years, Clara became not only my companion but my guide and, in a way, my protector. When asked to help on various projects, I assessed whether my potential contribution would be worth taking time away from Clara. Usually the answer was no, though once, as related in the previous chapter about the Bork testimony, she had the opposite influence.

My initial book-writing plan was to publish a series of articles about the main events of Foltz's career and combine these into a single volume. After writing four such pieces, I realized that each involved getting all the characters back on stage and essentially repeating the previous story to lay the groundwork for the current one. Also, I came to fear that I would never finish the book if I wrote a separate treatment of each major event in an extremely eventful life, especially because an inner stylistic perfectionist emerged for the first time in my career.

I decided to stop writing articles and to eliminate most other projects, aside from teaching, and push the book to completion. That decision was fresh in mind in 1993 when the newly elected President Clinton was looking to appoint the first woman Attorney General. My friend and former student Cheryl Mills, who was Deputy General Counsel in the

White House, wanted to put my name forward. I was moved by Cheryl's support, and of course part of me wanted to go for it. The first woman spot on the Supreme Court, my lifelong ambition, had been taken in 1981, but the first woman Attorney General would also occupy an eminent place in legal history.

A proposed nominee faced several obstacles, however. The President's choice of any particular woman drew intense attention to her lifestyle. His first two candidates were tripped up by issues about hiring undocumented workers. I did not have that problem, but revelations about my free-wheeling younger years could have raised eyebrows. Also, in class and elsewhere, I had spoken out about the neglected rights of the criminally accused, the evils of prosecutorial misconduct, and the government lawyer's duty to see that justice is done even if that means losing a case—"soft on crime" accusations could have led to a difficult confirmation process.

I tried to explain my reservations, murmuring that "I've lived too hard and said too much," but Cheryl does not give up easily. My name was on a short list leaked one weekend in January. The calls began at 7:00 AM on Saturday and continued through Sunday night. The more I denied, the more the media were convinced that I was discreetly avoiding announcing my own appointment before the President did.

I was one of very few women who had actually served in a high Justice Department post. And someone dug up the coincidence that my mother's family had been pioneer settlers in Hope, Arkansas, Clinton's hometown. Being from Stanford and Silicon Valley also was a plus, and it was clear that I would have the backing of organized women.

Explaining to persistent reporters why, despite my qualifications, I was not really in the running proved somewhat difficult. I hit upon telling part of the truth: that I was too involved in my life's work, a biography of Clara Foltz, first woman lawyer in the West. At least, I thought, I'll get Clara's name in the national media. And as always when there was a chance for publicity, I hoped someone might come forward with her papers, which might even include a draft of her memoirs.

My reference to writing a biography instead of heading the Justice Department led *San Francisco Chronicle* columnist Jon Carroll to write: "What? Is this the New Commitment we hear so much about? Ask not what your country can do for you, or even what you can do for your country, but ask what you can do for Clara Shortridge Foltz?" In response to the column, Regina Gagnier, an English professor friend, offered to write the book for me if I would be her Attorney General.

Quite wrongly, I thought I was very near completion and feared putting the book aside and losing momentum for the finish. A savvy scholar might have stitched my already-published pieces into a single volume and declared herself done. But the format, diction, and heavy documentation in these law review articles were not ideal for bringing a biographical subject to life. I owed it to Clara to finish the book.

Foltz often spoke of writing her own memoir and claimed that a number of publishers were interested. But her only surviving autobiographical writings are twenty-eight columns in *The New American Woman*, a monthly magazine she edited and published from 1916 to 1918. She called them *The Struggles and Triumphs of a Woman Lawyer*, taking her title from the memoirs of circus impresario P. T. Barnum.

In the first installment, Foltz apologized "for the hurried style . . . as I throw from the table-book of memory a few of the incidents of a career . . . crowded with noteworthy incidents, and with startling points of contact with a world I seek to serve and a profession I hope to have adorned." That's Clara's voice: so nineteenth century; elevated, hyperbolic, and ornate. I grew very fond of it.

Clara denied that *Struggles* was a start on an autobiography, which, she explained, must "be written with care as to arrangement." Instead, her story begins *in media res*, and ends abruptly—a slapdash production composed of speech excerpts and oft-told tales largely out of chronological order, and omitting such essential episodes as her public defender crusade. Though she does not try to enhance the significance of her account by (in her words) putting "dimmers on the fourflushers, and [making] minnows talk like whales," the fact is that she barely mentions anyone else at all—whether minnows or whales.

Still, for all its defects, *Struggles* not only preserved Clara's voice; it also saved some of the stories she had told in speeches and interviews for more than fifty years. Like my own stories, hers were repeated in many settings, composed for oral delivery, altered and improved over time: "embroidered with flowers of my fancy," as Foltz wrote. Her account began when she was thirty years old and had decided to be a lawyer, with very few flashbacks to childhood.

Born Carrie Shortridge in Indiana in 1849, she was the only girl and the middle child between two older and two younger brothers. Her father,

Elias, had apprenticed as a lawyer with Oliver Morton, who subsequently was the Civil War-era governor of Indiana and an important Unionist. Elias Shortridge and Morton were early Lincoln supporters and stumped for him throughout the Midwest. One day Clara would model her own passionate political oratory on her father's.

Elias left the law when, according to one of *his* stories, he won an acquittal for a guilty murderer. He turned his oratorical gift to itinerant preaching in the Campbellite or Christian Church (known today as the Disciples of Christ). During the Civil War, he became head of its congregation in Mount Pleasant, Iowa. Though the town was small (population 3,500 in 1860), a good road connected it to Iowa Wesleyan University in Burlington, and a railroad station made it an agricultural and business center.

Young Clara thrived in the aptly named Mount Pleasant. She attended Howe's Academy there from 1860 to1863 and loved school. Years later her teachers remembered her as "a bright, ambitious, hard-toiling girl." Foltz recalled that she had mastered the first *two* books of Latin by the age of twelve (an achievement she continued to boast about into old age).

She wrote that her father had "delighted in his only daughter's talent for abstruse thinking" and had sighed, "Ah, if only you had been a boy, then I would have trained you for the law." Foltz remembered that her mother had warned him against telling the girl such things: "For one of these days she will take it into her head to study law, and if she does, nobody on earth can stop her." "Indeed that was prophecy!" Foltz would intone when telling that story.

That was the only vignette in *Struggles* about Clara's childhood, which ended abruptly when she went to teach at a country school near Keithsburg, Illinois. Perhaps at a nearby hospital for Civil War soldiers, she met Jeremiah Foltz, who had mustered out of the Army there because of severe lumbago. Without informing her parents Clara and Jeremiah married; she was fifteen and he was twenty-five.

I could understand that the romantic girl thought herself in the grip of a grand passion. But what was Clara doing in Illinois? Why had the Shortridges left the prosperous and progressive Iowa community where they had been happy and successful? I could not find a clue or come up with a theory. Then an idea hit me: church history. In the archives of the Disciples of Christ I found an unpublished manuscript that briefly described Elias Shortridge's expulsion from the Mount Pleasant church for heresy in 1864, the year Clara married.

Shortridge had begun preaching the doctrine of "soul sleep," which holds that after death the spirit has no conscious existence until the resurrection of the body at the Last Judgment. Considered heterodox by Protestants and Catholics alike, the doctrine was especially contested during the Civil War, when people wanted to believe that the souls of dead soldiers went straight to heaven and did not linger in their maimed, decapitated, or even incinerated bodies for the Second Coming of Christ, however imminent that might be.

Elias Shortridge was expelled as pastor because he was "a preacher of much more than ordinary ability [and] numbers were carried away by the strange doctrine," according to the church history. It appears that the whole family moved to Illinois, where Elias resumed the camp meeting and revival preaching he had done before heading the flagship con-gregation in Mount Pleasant. That was when Clara left the student life she loved and became a teacher herself.

For the first five years of her marriage, she helped Jeremiah run a farm in Iowa and bore a child almost yearly. Looking into the lives of Iowa farm wives in the mid-nineteenth century, I was taken aback by the rigors of women's work. Child care, housekeeping, and help with farm labor were only the beginning. Other tasks included feeding large numbers of extra men at planting and harvest time; washing and ironing, making clothes and mending for the whole family; canning and preserving. All this fell to Clara at the age of fifteen. Her large, well-muscled hands and her extraordinary physical energy would be points of comment for the rest of her life.

In *Struggles*, Clara told very little about her marriage. She did write that her husband had praised her cooking as "better than that of his dear old German mother." And she claimed that her children were unusually beautiful and healthy: "better babies." Perhaps to avoid the common charge that women activists like her would destroy domestic life, she claimed to be "a worshipper of home and all that pertains to that institution. . . . I love to wash dishes and clean house and cook and sew and all the rest of it." Maybe she did, but probably not as much as she loved starring in a dramatic trial or receiving the applause of thousands for a political speech.

When Clara was pregnant for the fourth time, Jeremiah took off for

Portland, Oregon. From subsequent events, it seems likely he was trying to leave for good. Clara tracked him down, however, and they all settled in Oregon for a few years before moving to San Jose, California. Shortly after the birth of their fifth child, Jeremiah again abandoned the family, this time successfully, and moved back to Portland. Clara Foltz listed herself as a widow in the City Directory, which she continued to do after their divorce, though Jeremiah was alive and had remarried as soon as the decree was entered.

Foltz's false presentation of herself as a widow reveals several aspects of her character. As a romantic, she believed that desertion symbolized the death of love enabling her to claim the widow's weeds. As a movement woman, she feared that her divorce would support the argument that suffragists were out to destroy the home and engage in free love. Also, Foltz was deeply pragmatic. She well knew that a widow with five children to support was more acceptable to the men whose help she needed than a divorcee could possibly be.

Clara Foltz's life was enmeshed with the political events and social movements of her time. In her phrase, she was "present to history." Much of what I know about her I have learned from studying the story of California, which joined the union in 1850, a year after she was born, and a year after the Gold Rush that tremendously increased its population, wealth, and prominence on the national scene.

When she came to the state in the mid-1870s, with a wandering husband and four little children, Clara Foltz was an obscure housewife who supplemented the family income by taking in boarders, fashioning hats, and sewing dresses. By the end of the decade, she was California's famous lady lawyer, the first in the West. She also played a major role in the passage of two amendments to the 1879 California Constitution that guaranteed women access to employment and to public education.

In one of those portents beloved by biographers, I ran across Clara's constitutional clauses many years before I met her. It was 1971 and I was teaching Women and the Law at Yale when I read a California case striking down a law that had prevented most women from bartending.* The case was brand new and bold in applying the Fourteenth Amendment of the U.S. Constitution and finding that would-be female bartenders were denied equal protection of the law.

---

* *Sail'er Inn v. Kirby*, 5 Cal. 3d 1, 485 P.2d 529 (1971).

But the result rested also on an old clause from the California Constitution: "No person shall on account of sex be disqualified from entering upon or pursuing any lawful business, vocation, or profession." Arguably, the directly applicable state clause rendered the federal constitutional discussion superfluous. And the clause itself appeared to be an anomaly unlikely to be found in other state constitutions.

I wondered how the clause had originated and tried to find out more when I moved to California, but nobody knew anything about it or its companion measure guaranteeing female admission to public schools. When I became Clara's biographer, I read in *Struggles* that *she* was partly responsible for both clauses, which she called the "first streak of dawn" guiding California women into "larger fields of opportunity."

Tracking the efforts of Foltz and other suffragists, I came to see that the two clauses were in fact the milestones they thought: the first guarantees of equal rights for women in the public arena ever to appear in any American constitution. I discovered also that, contrary to general belief, suffragists had had a significant role in the political history of the young state of California. Taking off from the feminist slogan, "The personal is political," I wrote an article under the epigram, "The personal is historical." It told of discovering the clauses' origins, so obscure until seen through a biographer's lens.

But it's not all glorious epiphanies for the biographer. Early on in my research, I confronted the racism of the first women's movement, though Clara was far from the worst. Indeed, she supported the liberation of black Americans and never spoke publicly, as many suffragists did, against allowing "ignorant freedmen" to vote while denying "respectable white women."

Yet Foltz also failed to distance herself from the virulent anti-Asian sentiment that was a major feature of California politics at the end of the nineteenth century. In my article titled "Clara Shortridge Foltz: Constitution Maker,"* I explain that the passage of the women's clauses depended on the support of the populist Workingmen's Party of California, who were a third of the delegates at the convention, and rabidly anti-Chinese. The WPC believed that the immigrants were an alien and undesirable race, who refused to assimilate and who took their jobs.

---

* 66 *Indiana Law Journal* 849 (1991).

As far as I've been able to discover, Foltz never used anti-Chinese rhetoric herself, but neither did she do or say anything at any point that recognized the common humanity of the Chinese laborers, or their oppression. In addition to her intolerant attitudes, I also confronted my subject's more personal flaws. While Clara had plenty of courage and charisma, I saw also her vanity, self-promotion, and poor judgment. The combination led me to joke that women's biography requires mixing the hag with the hagiography.

Foltz often told of being converted to feminism at age fourteen by hearing Lucy Stone speak in Elias Shortridge's church in Mount Pleasant. Stone lamented the subjugation of women and enslavement of Africans, using the same biblical passages to urge the abolition of both. From Clara's first published interviews until one given the year before her death, she spoke of the women's movement and usually told her Lucy Stone story. "I have written, talked and toiled" for the cause, she said, emphasizing that in all she had done, as lawyer, orator, thinker, and organizer, she had put women first.

From the beginning of her public career, Foltz's personal cause was joined with women's progress. It started when Jeremiah deserted her, and she determined to be a lawyer to support her five children. The California Code provided that only "white men of good character" need apply to the bar. In the caboose of a cattle car where she rode for free, Clara journeyed regularly from San Jose to Sacramento to lobby for a woman lawyers bill, which she drafted herself, and which allowed "all persons" to be attorneys. The battle that followed hardly mentioned the potential it created for a multi-racial bar; the whole fight was about women out of their sphere.

On the strength of her statute and having passed an unusually rigorous oral examination, Foltz joined the California Bar in 1878. She was the first woman lawyer in the state, maybe the first in the West and one of the first in the country. (The 1880 national census showed a total of 75 women lawyers in the United States.) In 1879 California's first law school opened its doors, the Hastings College of the Law in San Francisco. Clara thought it would be appropriate for the first woman lawyer to attend the first law school. Her only education had been a few years at Howe's Academy in Iowa and reading law in her father's office.

She paid her tuition and attended one lecture, but then the trustees decided not to admit women, ostensibly because the rustling of their skirts bothered the other scholars. Foltz and her friend Laura Gordon, on the way to be the second woman lawyer in California, sued the school. After a remarkable court argument, before a large audience of "lawyers and women" according to the papers, they won decisively. But in the end Clara's victory was pyrrhic because Hastings appealed, and by the time she won in the Supreme Court, it was too late to attend, and the scholarship her friends had provided was exhausted.

Foltz threw herself into law practice and soon made a reputation as a jury lawyer. I was able to follow many of her cases through the newspapers—San Francisco boasted twenty-one dailies, often with several editions, and most of them reported her exploits. She seems to have won more than she lost, and she took appeals for the losers. And to the delight of the lawyer biographer, the record on appeal might include at least partial transcripts of the trials.

The news stories and the transcripts provide evidence that Foltz was a skilled trial lawyer, just as her published writing shows her brilliance and originality. Both stories and transcripts are something of a relief to me, because we biographers of obscure figures often fear that they might be unknown for good reason.

Foltz's greatest achievement was as founder of the public defender movement. Discovering what she did—speak, write articles, draft a statute, and see to its introduction in a dozen states, was a matter of straightforward legal research, though no one had done it before. But my sources offered few clues to answering the big "how" question: How had an undereducated woman lawyer, far from the centers of advanced legal thought, come up with an original theory about the practice of law and the duty of the government to the criminally accused?

Part of the answer is that she was highly intelligent, intensely curious, and amazingly energetic, and thus able to educate herself. Also, she was inspired by her own experience as a woman lawyer. Especially in her early days, many of her clients, perhaps most, were poor people accused of crimes. They came to her in desperation when no male lawyer would take their cases, or sometimes a judge would see her in the courtroom and appoint her to represent them. When she went to court, she was usually the only woman within the physical bar separating courtroom personnel from onlookers, and she was sometimes the only woman in the entire courthouse.

A well-paid, comparatively well-trained adversary represented the government as prosecutor. In the past, Foltz wrote, he had been "a minister of

public justice," responsible for seeing that the verdict was fair, even producing evidence favorable to the accused. But now, she claimed, many
prosecutors had succumbed to "the vanity of winning cases" and "the lust
for gold."

In 1895, long before there was computer research, Foltz published an
article in a national law review detailing some two hundred cases of
prosecutorial misconduct from thirty-four jurisdictions. Her examples
included very serious lapses such as soliciting or condoning perjured
testimony, and seeking to place inadmissible evidence before the jury.
Deterring such conduct was one function Foltz imagined for her Public
Defender.

Foltz brought her creation forth, whole and freestanding, as a complete
solution to most of the problems with the criminal justice system. Her
Public Defender would be a powerful and resourceful figure: the prosecutor's equal, even in some ways superior because she was representing
the innocent. Drawing no distinction between the presumed and the
factually innocent, Foltz made the highly original argument that the
presumption of innocence created an individual right to counsel for the
accused.

At the same time she spoke of justice for defendants, Foltz's subtext
was equal treatment for women lawyers in the courtroom. Too often she
had found *herself* on trial along with her client for doing the dirty,
unfeminine work of representing criminals. Prosecutors also reacted
harshly to what they saw as her unsporting advantage with all-male juries.
Somewhat irrationally (since they thought she had an edge) they
experienced losing to a woman as a peculiar humiliation.

While suffering personal attacks as plain Mrs. Foltz, she imagined a
well-paid government official—herself perhaps—with the inspiring title,
Public Defender. Such an official would elevate representation of the
criminally accused so that all lawyers, especially women, could do the
work without risk to reputation. The Foltzian defender would investigate
every case for favorable evidence and would summon witnesses, seek
expert testimony, and prepare to cross-examine.

She had no models for this ideal. No government-paid defender like
the one she envisioned had ever existed. As a personal achievement,
Foltz's invention of public defense ranks with her opening the legal
profession to women and winning the state constitutional clauses.

From my first days with Clara Foltz, I started a cottage industry of students, fellow women historians, and law professors devoted to Clara and other early women lawyers. Most important were the law librarians, who are a scholar's best friends. Paul Lomio, Erika Wayne, and Alba Holgada were central to a seminar and a website around Women's Legal History.* Some students served as my research assistants, and I tried to thank them all in the book's acknowledgments, but even more than one hundred names did not fully capture the far-flung Clara community we created.

The seminar students rapidly metamorphosed into biographers, starting with their choice of subjects as they searched for someone like themselves: someone they wanted to rescue, explain, and defend, someone who spoke to them across generations. Occasionally the romance did not take. I remember the student from Kansas who picked the first woman lawyer from that state (Mary Ellen Lease), only to find that "Yellin' Mary" was not at all to her liking. "She was crazy, not in a good way" is how the student put it.

As the years churned by and still I wrote on, my pleasure in the project dimmed in response to the mounting queries about when it would be done. To people who asked how long I had been working on Clara, I developed the stock answer, "I do not recall." And I sometimes added, from my criminal defense days, "They can't charge perjury when you say that!"

I was beginning to feel ridiculous and that my scholarly life was in a shambles, when a truly inspirational occasion lifted me from despair. In a ceremony worthy of her and of Los Angeles, the main criminal courthouse was named after Clara Foltz. It was a rare honor; very few courthouses in the entire country are named for women.

Before it became the Clara Shortridge Foltz Criminal Justice Center, the large, rather brutal structure bore no person's name, and was simply known as CCB, Criminal Courts Building.

As I heard the story (and I wish I had written down the particulars), members of the local women's bar realized that though there were quite a few monuments to male attorneys throughout the city, especially near the courthouse, there was in all of Los Angeles no public recognition of even a single woman lawyer. The women consulted with Judge Arthur Alarcon

---

* http://wlh.stanford.edu

about it; though he was a federal judge, he had been on the state judiciary, and before that, was a noted local prosecutor. He encouraged them to identify someone to recognize and to mount a campaign and helped them do it.

Here is where I come into the story. The women lawyers found my articles and website entries on Clara and called me. They saw how appropriate she would be for the honor. Clara had not only invented the public defender, but had been the first female deputy D.A. in Los Angeles. My favorite connection is that she practiced in the old red sandstone building, an imposing Victorian heap that preceded the current courthouse on the same site.

Admiringly I watched the L.A. women lawyers make all kinds of arrangements—for a splendid souvenir program, for a ceremony in which Sandra Day O'Connor spoke, and to expand the celebration to cover eleven distinguished "first" Los Angeles women in addition to Foltz.* I made a short speech, and as I looked out at the large and distinguished audience, I felt Clara's presence, and sensed her pride in how far women lawyers have come. This kind of embodiment in my subject, or perhaps vice versa, has been one of the thrills of writing a biography.

The courthouse dedication, February 8, 2002, was a moment when I felt the joinder most immediately. And that was not all—a few years later, an artistic installation was unveiled which tells in tapestries and text Foltz's life story. I gave another speech at that ceremony, while wondering what the hundreds of thousands of people passing through the Los Angeles criminal courts would make of the tale in the lobby. Now I occasionally hear from former students and women lawyers that they saw justice done in the Clara Foltz courthouse.

Renewed by the courthouse dedication, I kept on writing, trying to reach the end. Finishing was hard, in part because Foltz's old age was distressing. Her reputation had dwindled as she grandiosely declaimed about her own achievements, downplayed the roles of others (contrary to her generosity when she was in her prime), and resented the lack of recognition among women activists and from the bar.

---

* Other first women honored: Yvonne Brathwaite Burke, Shirley Hufstedler, Joan Dempsey Klein, Mildred Lillie, Consuelo B. Marshall, Margaret Morrow, Andrea Ordin, Patricia Phillips, Maria E. Stratton, and Venetta Tassopoulos.

Certain incidents, such as sending a chain letter to the Attorney General and appearing in court in crimson "Portia" robes of her own design, suggested dementia. Certainly she was not in full possession of the mental acuity that had marked her best days. And there was grim personal tragedy: four of her five children predeceased her.

I decided to conclude her story well before her death in 1934, thus easing what had become a heavy load. The book closes with women winning the vote in California in 1911 and with a 63-year-old Clara Foltz casting a legal ballot in the national election of 1912. In that year also, with women voting, a measure passed in Los Angeles that created the first public defender office in the country (or as Clara said, "the world").

Perhaps the best year of Clara writing was one when Tom was also deep into essentially biographical work: producing *The Wallace Stevens Case: Law and the Practice of Poetry.*[*] It was a magical time, with both of us on sabbatical in our separate studies; crossing paths in the kitchen, the garden, the bedroom; experiencing together the presence of Wallace and Clara and the unblocked flow of ideas and prose.

We helped each other on our biographical projects. Tom thanked me: "Over many hours taken from work on her book, Barbara Babcock touched nearly every line of this one with her ruthlessly loving editorial pencil. Beyond that, her person is in every word of it: an example, a comfort, a delight."

He dedicated the book to me, and I reciprocated in my book: "For Tom Grey, bird photographer"—a little joke since he is most notably a distinguished legal scholar. But among his various creative avocations, including writing about poetry, bird photography seemed to have subsumed all the others by the close of his teaching career, and it may last to the end.

In addition to the dedication, I thanked him for being a "faithful editor even when it required adverse criticism—a hard thing for him to do." And I added, "He has brought his cool intelligence and warm encouragement to the struggles and triumphs involved in writing and living this life."

The book ends with an interview Clara Foltz gave in 1912, the year California women first voted in a national election. Echoing her lifetime themes, Foltz told of "all the first woman things" she had done, while also

---

[*] Thomas Grey, *The Wallace Stevens Case: Law and the Practice of Poetry* (Cambridge, Mass.: Harvard University Press, 1991).

"blowing the horn and waving the flag for the laggard suffrage army." Then I wrote: "That was and is the end of the story, except to say that the interviewer writing it down was herself an attorney, one of a long line not yet ended—Clara Foltz's daughters in the law."

Finally in 2011, I released the text from my care, still making improvements in the last minutes before final submission. I decided to devote a year to selling the book and made over seventy appearances: multiple times each in San Francisco, Los Angeles, and Washington, D.C.; numerous local gigs in Palo Alto and at Stanford campus venues; also in Baltimore, Chicago, Durham, Iowa City, New York, Portland, St. Louis, and Seattle. Clara Foltz made her international debut at the London School of Economics, Legal Biography Center. In addition, many clubs, leagues, and associations were celebrating the 100th year of woman suffrage in California. I spoke on Clara's work for women in Sacramento, Davis, Morgan Hill, Half Moon Bay, Monterey, Oakland, Long Beach, Berkeley, San Luis Obispo, Santa Barbara, Saratoga, and Bakersfield.

The Bakersfield visit was especially memorable. The Bar there has a small-town feeling of people knowing and liking each other, as well as being multi-racial and at least half women. A special pleasure was the introduction of my talk by Patience Milrod, a successful lawyer in Fresno, and a co-author of the contemporary article about Clara that inspired and enabled me at the beginning of my biographical journey.[*]

She told of arriving at U.C.-Davis School of Law in 1974 to find that forty percent of her class was female, while all previous classes had had ten percent women or less. Patience and another woman student, Susan Brandt, were assigned a summer work-study project by the law librarian, Mortimer Schwartz. They first read an account of Clara Foltz and her friend Laura Gordon arguing their right to be law students at Hastings. "We can hardly believe our eyes. The year is 1879—Clara's opponents are the elite of the California Bar, former Supreme Court justices. And Clara is kicking their butt. It is *exhilarating!!*"

Then she told how every day brought "new thrills as we learn about Clara. We cannot believe what we're finding—how come nobody's ever heard of her??" Patience continued: "The summer with Clara was a life-changing experience. . . . she taught me to 'live out loud,' that I can say

---

[*] Mortimer D. Schwartz, Susan L. Brandt, and Patience Milrod, "Clara Shortridge Foltz: Pioneer in the Law," 27 *Hastings Law Journal* 545 (1976).

what I believe, that I can act and live without apology—it's Clara's voice in my ear, whispering, 'Who cares what those staid old grangers think? Do what's right!'"

Patience found Clara to be a companion, as well as model and heroine. I hope the book will accomplish the same for many readers, though of course women lawyers are its most natural audience. From the first, they have been enthusiastic. Dahlia Lithwick, a former student and a senior editor at *Slate*, blurbed on the book cover: "Babcock brings Foltz back to us with great tenderness and subtlety, reclaiming a place in American legal history for a working mother and national thinker who has much to teach us still." I like especially that Dahlia saw the tenderness.

Justice Ruth Ginsburg wrote a positive and thoughtful essay-review, concluding that "*Woman Lawyer* should engage feminists of my era and my children's generation, and history buffs of any age; most of all, the book should amaze and inspire young women and public defenders just embarking on their lives in the law."[*]

Another of my favorite reviews came about six months after the book's publication when I called to congratulate my friend Patsy's mother, Louise Tatspaugh, on turning 100. She said she had read every page and had really enjoyed it—a great accolade from a woman I've known since I was seven.

On my informal book tour, I would give a rousing speech about Clara Foltz, after which it was a pleasure to sign books for people who wanted to read it themselves, and some of whom were buying extra copies for their feminist mothers, their history-loving dads, or their public-defender daughters. Many customers were women lawyers, and many were public defenders, and they often thanked me for writing the book. And I would respond, "I did it for you"—silently adding, "and for her, and for me."

The year of concentrated selling ended dangerously in August 2012 when out of the blue, some cells from the breast cancer of eighteen years earlier reappeared and lodged in my lungs. I had long feared dying before finishing Clara's book, but that did not mean I was ready to go as soon as it was done. It turned out that the cancer was very treatable, as before, and I soon felt fine, and ready to turn to my own recollections.

---

[*] Ruth Bader Ginsburg, Book Review, "*Woman Lawyer: The Trials of Clara Foltz* by Barbara Babcock," 65 *Stanford Law Review* 399 (2013).

Long years ago I thought that I could make my stories part of Clara's, that I would tell them through her, maybe even openly switching to the first person occasionally. But I discovered that my experiences and memories were diversions even when I tried to relate them directly to Clara's.

Nevertheless, the parallels between our lives are striking. At the end of the nineteenth century Clara Foltz lauded the "inventions of an active age"—and mentioned the railroad, the telegraph, the telephone, the street and motor cars, the typewriter, electricity. All of these advances opened the possibility of communication across great distances, which Foltz thought would ultimately bring almost inconceivable improvements in people's lives. At the end of the twentieth century, I had a very similar feeling about the technologies that make global interchange possible, fuel revolutions, open new worlds.

Both activist feminists, Clara and I each took as a major goal improving the lives of women. We both excelled at oratory, especially in closing to juries. Most important, we had the same ideas about defending people accused of crime, and the difficulties of doing it when the accused was poor. Really, the same ideas—only of course she had them a hundred years earlier than I did.

Our diction, both spoken and written, is similar and students sometimes say we even look alike. It is true that as with dogs and their owners, a certain resemblance seems to evolve between biographer and subject. Clara and I have many of the same qualities of temperament—optimistic, energetic, and humorous. Perhaps I am less dramatic, and I know I am less angry, though of course I have had less provocation than she did.

In the years since the Clara book has been out, and even before, especially when I made a speech in Los Angeles or New York, I have met expressions of interest in bringing her to the small or the large screen. The patterns of these interactions are all the same—great enthusiasm at first, demands for more material, and even more after that. Then radio silence . . . no more calls, no returns of my inquiries. This has happened so often that now I'm quite skeptical about shows of media enthusiasm though I hope to live to see Clara Foltz on a screen of some size someday.

Though the Victorian settings and costuming discourages portrayals of Clara's life on stage or screen, I think the main impediment is the lack of an obvious love interest in the story. She seldom spoke of her marriage, and never of her divorce or of any subsequent lovers. Yet from my understanding of her passionate nature and of her inclination to seize the moment, I surmise both that she had some love affairs and that they were helpful to her career.

Certainly she had unusual opportunities. Foltz moved in a heavily masculine legal profession, usually as a divorced woman posing as a widow. She met with men alone in her office and parlor. In courthouses and on political platforms, she mingled with males as equals.

There is also the possibility that her bonds with certain suffragists and with her posse of "female sweethearts" as she called them had physical as well as spiritual love attached. I tell the producers and agents and artists thinking of dramatizing Clara that the lack of certain knowledge gives us the freedom to construct what might well have been.

For many years, I lived alone with Clara Foltz—very few in the law world, and even fewer in the general public, had any idea who she was or what she had done. I tried in the book to convey what I had learned about her character and personality, but it was done in a rather subtle and scholarly fashion. I wasn't sure anyone else, except perhaps my friend Erika Wayne, the librarian and teaching colleague, and my research assistants would come to understand Clara as I did, though making her known was one of my aims in writing the book.

Enter Abigail Rezneck, my student, who had gone on to be a public defender in Alameda County, California. Abby had fallen in love with Clara Foltz, and "got her" in a way even sincere admirers do not always do. Though Abby loved defending, she was finding it hard to combine trial work with raising two small boys.

She had always wanted to be a writer, and proposed to undertake a play based on the life of Clara Foltz. As friend and former student, she asked for my support. I hesitated—thinking that she might end up without a career if the playwriting did not go well. Also I was concerned that to the outside world it would appear egotistical of me to encourage this brilliant Stanford law graduate to dive into the uncertain waters of playwriting, especially when it might redound to my own benefit.

Moreover, Abby's dad, Dan Rezneck, was an old friend and I was almost certain he would disapprove of his highly educated lawyer daughter becoming a Berkeley playwright. Dan had been a prosecutor in D.C. when I was a public defender. At some point we even thought of practicing law together with some other people. (Opening my own office, hanging out a shingle, representing people and causes I cared about, was an ambition I carried for years without coming close to realizing it.)

Though I don't know if withholding my approval would have made any difference, I endorsed the idea of a Clara play. Abby went about playwriting with the thoroughness a good lawyer brings to a task: first, she surveyed the literature on playwriting techniques and examples. Then as a modern young person, she worked the internet for its yields of information and contacts. In the summer of 2014 she won a fellowship for her and me to develop the play at the Ground Floor at the Berkeley Repertory Theater.

For a week, we were one of the projects housed in the theater annex—a warehouse space decorated with posters from past performances, a stuffed alligator, rooms full of props, furniture, costumes—a very funky, non-legal setting. Food was brought in from Gather, a deeply politically correct Berkeley restaurant, which I kept calling "Catch."

Ours was the only historical drama in the works, and we were the only lawyers there. We were assigned eight actors, a director, and a dramaturge. In between readings, and discussions with the actors, Abby and I were nailed to computers in our comfortable office decorated with tapestries from some medieval play set and provided with our own basket of supplies (markers, pencils, pens and post-its).

I have spent most of my adult life among lawyers—and I love our common understandings about the way the world works, or should. But at Berkeley Rep it was fun to be designated an "artist" and consort with theater people, who are not like lawyers, though lawyers can sometimes be theatrical. One of our fellow participants was Adam Sahli, from St. Cloud, Minnesota, where he is the drama teacher at Cathedral High. He asked whether his school could do the play. We said yes, with Abby especially eager because she learns a great deal about the workings of dialog from hearing it performed.

So in March 2015, Abby and I set out for Minnesota, two natives of Washington, D.C. who are now dedicated Californians. St. Cloud is a beautiful little town on the Mississippi, though it was very cold and there were few signs of spring. The students did a wonderful job with the play, not missing a cue or a beat. They were exuberant and wrote feelingly about what they had learned. I was knocked out by their high degree of pro-fessionalism, and will always remember their fresh unlined faces and the sure way they moved on the boards. Whatever the future of our play and whether Clara reaches a big or small screen, the images of these young actors will remain in mind as the first public embodiment of characters once known only to me.

There have been several other post-publication experiences that I especially enjoyed. One was meeting with Emmanuel Garcia, a twelve year old from the central valley, who had entered a statewide history contest, with Clara Foltz's life as his project. He interviewed me with excellent questions, which showed that he had studied and thought a lot. Finally, our admissions director asked me to meet with an applicant, an Asian American man, who had written that Clara Foltz was his heroine. He came to us, though he had offers from Harvard and Yale.

I have written Clara's story and mine at a time when women lawyers have made gains which would have once seemed incredible to most people. Not to Clara Foltz, however, who hoped to find an equal place for herself in 1878 when she joined the bar. Though it did not happen for her or for many generations following her, the moment has finally arrived. Foltz believed that when women were accepted in the profession, they would change it for the better, and she trusted that her own busy career promoting constitutional rights for the criminally accused and civil rights for women would inspire and instruct. I hope the same—for both of us.

AFTERWORD: ABOUT REMEMBERING

Look, what thy memory cannot contain
Commit to these waste blanks, and thou shalt find
Those children nursed, deliver'd from thy brain,
To take a new acquaintance of thy mind.

Shakespeare, Sonnet 77

One early morning in 2003, at age 65, I was puzzling over whether I should take the university's golden handshake: a handsome payment in return for retiring and opening a chaired spot on the faculty. I had never thought about retiring; instead I imagined coming home from teaching a large class on one of those satisfying days when they were with me. I would have a cup of tea, or a glass of wine, and simply keel over for good. It was a scene I had played over mentally many times.

I was at Monterey Dunes where a friend has a house right on the ocean which he has often shared with us. When there, I like to start the day with a hot tub and then have coffee while I read a couple of Shakespeare sonnets and their interpretation by Helen Vendler. As I considered the retirement decision, I opened to Sonnet 77, and found the answer. To me the sonnet meant I should retire and write my recollections (after finishing the Clara Foltz biography).

Though the answer came to me with the force and in the form of revelation, I still had a hard time contemplating retirement, partly because I had been working steadily since I had my first real job at fifteen. In a bank down the street from home, I alphabetized checks and learned to operate a bookkeeping machine. (I wonder what happened to those massive pre-computer record keepers.) Since that summer punching a time clock there had been no significant periods when I did not show up somewhere to work on most days. I could not quite imagine another life.

It turns out, now many years in, that I love retirement—almost as much as teaching a good class or summing up to a jury! Really. Every day I

221

feel blessed, to have my own time; no one is awaiting or needing me. I get my dark strong coffee made by Tom, and head for the computer where I often find that the sleeping brain has resolved the previous day's problems with the text. I start writing, whispering to myself that I deserve this bliss for working so hard, and for being occasionally self-sacrificing, and generally good to others. The sense of exceptional privilege nevertheless almost overwhelms me.

Coming to the close of these recollections, I find that the passage of time has erased or softened some traumas and that other events make more sense than they originally did. Indeed, as with the life of Clara Foltz, one experience seems to lead to another in a way that was neither planned nor visible until it was past. "These children nursed, delivered from [my] brain to take a new acquaintance with [my] mind."

I've remembered how I grew up in the '50s before sex discrimination had a name; how I joined the women's movement in the turbulent '60s; how I loved my work as a criminal lawyer, leader of public defenders, law professor, high government official, and biographer. My career has coincided with the true integration of women into the legal profession. I hope my stories may aid in understanding this revolution and inspire those who will take up its next stage.

Deciding which stories to tell and what to omit is hard. Judy Hope, who wrote of the women in the Harvard law class of 1964 in *Pinstripes and Pearls*, advised showing passages to people who might consider them unflattering, or wrongly remembered, and omitting material if they objected. I've mostly done that. Ed Cohen, my debate partner, wrote that though he did not recall our shared experiences at Penn exactly as I did, "These are your recollections, which have their own truth."

My brothers were somewhat taken aback at my revealing our father's alcoholism, given our rigorous family training in the project of keeping it secret. Partly in deference to their feelings, I have omitted some sad details which do not add to the story. Moreover, my life experience, and maybe the mellowing effects of age, have led me to conclude that succumbing to a crippling addiction is not necessarily the worst possible character flaw.

As for that aspect of my life, I'm passing over any account of my battles against my own addiction. I had my first drink when I worked for Williams, and found it an asset to drink like a man, as well as to think like one. Now in my declining years, I drink only wine, and that in moderation compared to my youth—but would not like to give that up.

I've also omitted most of what I could say about my romantic life in the brief period after birth control became easily accessible and before sexually transmitted diseases were a pervasive threat. Some advisors have said I should tell about the famous and semi-famous males who chased me around the desk, and others I chased in turn. They argue that it would brighten the grim visage of feminism and maybe even sell a few books.

But since a love affair necessarily involves another person for whom one cares, or once did, the secrets are not entirely mine. And virtually all my sexual encounters were also love affairs in my own mind. Though I entered freely into the new sexual mores, I retained my romantic, sentimental nature, which tends to join love and physical intimacy. So, at the risk of being a tease on this subject I will simply say that in my youth and between marriages, I loved some interesting men. They ranged in age, race, and ethnicity but only one was not a lawyer. To me lawyers make the best lovers because they are articulate, often funny, and usually skillful, having read up on the subject.

I have always liked men and had many male friends and allies, as well as lovers—and some who were all three. My favorites have been the male feminists, those masters of empathy. As much as I enjoy men, however, I find few of them as complicated and interesting as many women I have known. I think the relative simplicity of the male nature may be a true sex difference, based on hormones perhaps; I admire and wonder at the straightforward way in which they grasp what they want, in bed and beyond.

At every stage of life I have had the pleasure of close female friendships, some described earlier in these pages, and others as well. As a teacher for over thirty years, I have also had many former students of both sexes who fall into a special category—young friends many of whom I regard almost as my children. It is exciting to see them succeed and grow, and even send children of their own to law school.

As I near eighty, I'm struck by how brief and fast-moving my years have been. I have laughed a lot and tried to live up to my ideals of kindness and patience. While I could perhaps have accomplished more with my gifts and opportunities, I have been blessed by love and friendship—abundantly given and gratefully received.

The author in the early 2010s, photographed for the Clara
Foltz biography cover by Jeanne de Polo, used by permission

Visit us at *www.quidprobooks.com.*

CPSIA information can be obtained
at www.ICGtesting.com
Printed in the USA
LVOW01s2312260317
528557LV00007B/152/P